Philosophy and the Environment

ROYAL INSTITUTE OF PHILOSOPHY SUPPLEMENT: 69

EDITED BY

Anthony O'Hear

CAMBRIDGE
UNIVERSITY PRESS

PUBLISHED BY THE PRESS SYNDICATE OF THE UNIVERSITY OF CAMBRIDGE
The Pitt Building, Trumpington Street, Cambridge, CB2 1RP, United Kingdom

CAMBRIDGE UNIVERSITY PRESS
The Edinburgh Building, Cambridge CB2 8RU, United Kingdom
32 Avenue of the Americas, New York, NY 10013–2473, USA
477 Williamstown Road, Port Melbourne, VIC 3207, Australia
C/Orense, 4, planta 13, 28020 Madrid, Spain
Lower Ground Floor, Nautica Building, The Water Club, Beach Road, Granger Bay, 8005 Cape Town, South Africa

Printed in the United Kingdom at the University Press, Cambridge
Typeset by Techset Composition Ltd, Salisbury, UK

A catalogue record for this book is available from the British Library

ISBN 9781107696075
ISSN 1358-2461

Contents

Contents

List of Contributors

Holmes Rolston III, Colorado State University

Robin Attfield, Cardiff University

Warwick Fox, www.warwickfox.com

Brian Garvey, University of Lancaster

Emily Brady, University of Edinburgh

J. Baird Callicott, University of North Texas

Chukwumerije Okereke, Smith School, Oxford

Allen Carlson, University of Alberta

James Garvey, Royal Institute of Philosophy

David Wiggins, New College, Oxford

Simon Caney, Magdalen College, Oxford

Cameron Hepburn, Smith School, Oxford

Dieter Helm, New College, Oxford

Eric Swyngedouw, University of Manchester

Preface

It hardly needs saying that *the* environmental questions are among the most pressing and hotly debated of our time. The issues are, in an immediate sense, political and scientific, but one's stance on them also reflects basic philosophical and ethical commitments. For its annual lecture series of 2010–2011 the Royal Institute of Philosophy invited a number of distinguished philosophers and environmentalists from a wide range of backgrounds, to reflect on their concerns, and this books is based on their lectures.

I would like to thank all those who contributed to the lecture series and to this book, and also to Adam Ferner for his help with preparing the volume for publication and for the index.

Anthony O'Hear

The Future of Environmental Ethics*

HOLMES ROLSTON, III

Environmental ethics has a future as long as there are moral agents on Earth with values at stake in their environment. Somewhat ironically, just when humans, with their increasing industry and development, seemed further and further from nature, having more power to manage it, just when humans were more and more rebuilding their environments with their super technologies, the natural world emerged as a focus of ethical concern. Environmental alarms started with prophets such as Aldo Leopold, Rachel Carson, John Muir, and David Brower, and have, over recent decades, become daily news.

A massive *Millennium Ecosystem Assessment*, sponsored by the United Nations, involving over 1,300 experts from almost 100 nations, begins: 'At the heart of this assessment is a stark warning. Human activity is putting such strain on the natural functions of Earth that the ability of the planet's ecosystems to sustain future generations can no longer be taken for granted'.[1]

The U.S. President Barack Obama has repeatedly endorsed a greener environmental policy, pushing programs to curb global warming. He went to the Copenhagen Climate Summit in 2009 to urge setting international goals. The once almost-president Al Gore has turned to leading a campaign to wake us up to the threat of global warming, which he considers the biggest issue facing the world today, repeatedly calling it a moral challenge. John Kerry, the former Democratic presidential candidate, together with his wife Teresa Heinz Kerry urge our thinking of *This Moment on Earth: Today's New Environmentalists and Their Vision for the Future.*[2]

Paul Hawken calls environmentalism 'the largest movement in the world', considering the number and force of environmental organizations around the globe.[3] If that seems exaggerated, remember that

* Earlier versions of this paper appeared in *Teaching Ethics*, 2007, Volume 1, and David R. Keller (ed.) *Environmental Ethics: The Big Questions* (Chichester, West Sussex, UK: Wiley-Blackwell, 2010), 561–574 – and it is reprinted with permission from them.

1 Millennium Ecosystem Assessment, 2005a, 5.

2 Kerry and Kerry, 2007.

3 Hawken, 2007

doi:10.1017/S135824611100018X

the United Nations Conference on Environment and Development (UNCED) at Rio de Janeiro in 1992 brought together the largest number of world leaders that have ever assembled to address any one issue. That conference drew 118 heads of state and government, delegations from 178 nations, virtually every nation in the world, 7,000 diplomatic bureaucrats, 30,000 advocates of environmental causes, and 7,000 journalists. The issues that coalesced there have been gathering over the last five hundred years, and they will be with us for another five hundred. *Agenda 21*, produced as UNCED faced the 21st century, is perhaps the most complex and comprehensive international document ever attempted.[4]

All this certainly sounds like the environment is on the world agenda, also on the ethical frontier, for the foreseeable future. Environmental ethics is, at times, about saving things past, still present, such as whooping cranes or sequoia trees. But environmental ethies does not have much future if it is only museum work. Environmental ethics is about once and future nature. Diverse combinations of nature and culture have worked well enough over many millennia, but no more. We face a future without analogy in our past. Our modern cultures threaten the stability, beauty, and integrity of Earth, and thereby of the cultures superposed on Earth. An interhuman ethics must serve to find a satisfactory fit for humans in their communities; and, beyond that, an environmental ethics must find a satisfactory fit for humans in the larger communities of life on Earth.

We worried throughout much of the past century that humans would destroy themselves in interhuman conflict. That fear – at least of global nuclear disaster – has subsided somewhat only to be replaced by a new one. The worry for the next century is that, if our present heading is uncorrected, humans may ruin their planet and themselves with it. American Indians had been on the continent 15,000 years, but with coming of the Europeans in 1492 a disruption was imminent. We are living at another of the ruptures of history, worried whether European-Western civilization is self-destructing and, again, triggering disruptions around the globe.

1. Culture and Nature: Managed Planet? End of Nature?

Possibly with ever-increasing transformation of nature, whatever residual nature remains may cease to be of significance for what it is in itself, with value attached more and more to the artifacted

[4] UNCED, 1992.

characteristics we superimpose on what was once wild nature. There will typically be degrees of modification: the relatively natural, the relatively cultured or agri-cultured, the mostly manufactured. Nature is mixed with human labor or industry. Always in the past, continuing in the present, humans have had to rest their cultures upon a natural life support system. Their technosphere was constructed inside the biosphere.

In the future the technosphere could supercede the biosphere. Evolutionary history has been going on for billions of years, while cultural history is only about a hundred thousand years old. But certainly from here onward, culture increasingly determines what natural history shall continue. In that sense, it is true that Earth is now in a post-evolutionary phase. Culture is the principal determinant of Earth's future, more than nature; we are passing into a century when this will be increasingly obvious. The next millennium, some are even saying, is the epoch of the 'end of nature'. The new geological epoch is the Anthropocene.[5]

That puts us indeed at a hinge point of history. Let's ask whether we ought to open this door. Henri Bergson, writing early in the last century, was prophetic. With the coming of the industrial age, when science joined with technology, we crossed the threshold of a new epoch.

> In thousands of years, when, seen from the distance, only the broad outlines of the present age will still be visible, our wars and our revolutions will count for little, even supposing they are remembered at all; but the steam-engine, and the procession of inventions of every kind that accompanied it, will perhaps be spoken of as we speak of the bronze or of the chipped stone of prehistoric time: it will serve to define an age.[6]

The transition from muscle and blood, whether of humans or of horses, to engines and gears shifts by many orders of magnitude the capacity of humans to transform their world, symbolized by the bulldozer. The pace change is from horse and buggy to jet plane. Even more recently, the capacity to produce has been augmented by the capacity for information transfer. Consider the transition from handwriting to printing, from communication by written mail to radio and television, from information processing in books to information processing by computers. All this has occurred in a few hundred years, much of it in decades that our parents and grandparents can recall.

5 Crutzen, 2006.
6 Bergson, 1911, 146.

In the course of human history, there have been epochal changes of state, such as the transition from hunter/gatherer cultures to agriculture, from oral to written cultures, the discovery of fire, the discovery of iron, the discovery of the New World, of Earth as a planet to circumnavigate, the discovery of motors, gears, electricity, electronics. This new century will indeed launch a new millennium: the super-industrial age. The high-technology age. The postnatural world? In the future we will have increasingly only 'virtual nature'. After Teflon, who wants clay?

'We live at the end of nature, the moment when the essential character of the world … is suddenly changing.' Bill McKibben worries that already 'we live in a postnatural world', in 'a world that is of our own making'. 'There's no such thing as nature anymore'.[7]

Michael Soulé faces this prospect:

> In 2100, entire biotas will have been assembled from (1) remnant and reintroduced natives, (2) partly or completely engineered species, and (3) introduced (exotic) species. The term *natural* will disappear from our working vocabulary. The term is already meaningless in most parts of the world because anthropogenic [activities] have been changing the physical and biological environment for centuries, if not millennia.[8]

'Dominate' remains a disliked word, since it has echoes of the abuse of power. But 'manage' is still quite a positive term. Humans, now and increasingly, want 'ecosystem management', they will say–if ecologists. If religious, they want to be 'good stewards'. Humans want 'sustainable development', they will say, if economists. With so much power and inclination to impose their will on nature, re-making it to their preferences, one does need to ask whether nature will (and ought) increasingly vanish.

Daniel Botkin predicts: 'Nature in the twenty-first century will be a nature that we make.' 'We have the power to mold nature into what we want it to be.' Of course he, like everybody else, urges us 'to manage nature wisely and prudently', and, to that end, ecology can 'instrument the cockpit of the biosphere'. That sounds like high-tech engineering which brings wild nature under our control, re-molding it into an airplane that we fly where we please. So it first seems, although Botkin – the ecologist in him returning – does go on to warn that it is important to recognize that 'the guide to

7 McKibben, 1989, 175, 60, 85, 89.
8 Soulé, 1989, 301.

action is our knowledge of living systems and our willingness to observe them for what they are' and 'to recognize the limits of our actions'.[9]

J. Baird Callicott puts it this way:

> Nature as Other is over. … We are witnessing the shift to a new idea, in which nature is seen as an organic system that includes human beings as one of its components. … A new dynamic and systemic postmodern concept of nature, which includes rather than excludes human beings, is presently taking shape. From the point of view of this new notion of nature, human technologies should be evaluated on their ecological merits.[10]

Spontaneous wild nature dies, and what lives on is not such nature *redivivus*, but a transformed, managed nature, a civilized nature, one also, hopefully, with ecological merits.

Before we ask what *ought* to be in the future, we should take a look at what *is* at present. Certainly, nature now bears the marks of human influence more widely than ever before. In one survey, using three categories, researchers find the proportions of Earth's terrestrial surface altered as follows: 1. Little disturbed by humans, 51.9%. 2. Partially disturbed, 24.2%. 3. Human dominated, 23.9%. Factoring out the ice, rock, and barren land, which supports little human or other life, the percentages become: 1. Little disturbed, 27.0%. 2. Partially disturbed 36.7%. 3. Human dominated 36.3%. Most terrestrial nature is dominated or partially disturbed (73.0%). Still, nature that is little or only partially disturbed remains 63.7% of the habitable Earth.[11]

In another study, researchers found that humans now control 40% of the planet's land-based primary net productivity, that is, the basic plant growth which captures the energy on which everything else depends.[12] That is worrisome, but it does leave 60% still in the spontaneously wild. Also, of course, there is the sea, polluted and overfished, but less affected than the land; and the oceans cover most of the Earth. Lately, scientists have been realizing there is great subsurface biotic diversity.

The conclusion to draw is not that wild nature is impossible on Earth, but that it is threatened. Much remains, some can be restored.

9 Botkin, 1990, 192–193, 200–201.
10 Callicott, 1992, 16.
11 Hannah et al., 1994; compare Ellis, 2008.
12 Vitousek et al., 1986.

Is it the case, for instance, that, owing to human disturbances in the Yellowstone Park ecosystem, we have lost any possibility of having a 'natural' park in the 21st century? In an absolute sense this is true, since there is no square foot of the park in which humans have not disturbed the predation pressures. There is no square foot of the park on which rain falls without detectable pollutants.

But it does not follow that nature has absolutely ended, because it is not absolutely present. Answers come in degrees. Events in Yellowstone can remain 99.44% natural on many a square foot, indeed on hundreds of square miles, in the sense (recalling the language of the U. S. *Wilderness Act*) that they are substantially 'untrammeled by man'. We can put the wolves back and clean up the air, and we have recently done both. Where the system was once disturbed by humans and subsequently restored or left to recover on its own, wildness can return. Perhaps the Colorado River is a 'virtual' river, because it is so managed and controlled that it is no longer wild. But we do not yet have a 'virtual Yellowstone'. Or even a 'virtual Adirondacks'. Bill McKibben, who lives in the Adirondacks, in a subsequent book has *Hope, Human and Wild*.[13] Nature in part has ended, yet there is wild hope.

Environmental philosophy invites the inquiry whether we humans can launch a millennium of culture in harmony with nature. After all, the technosphere remains in the biosphere. We are perhaps in a post-evolutionary phase. Not many new species will evolve by natural selection, not at least by such selection unaltered by human changes. But we are not in a post-ecological phase. The management of the planet must conserve some environmental processes, if only for our survival, and it ought to conserve many more, if we are to be wise.

Environmental ethics ought to seek a complementarity. Think of an ellipse with its twin foci. Some events are generated under the control of one focus, *culture*; such events are in the *political* zone, where 'polis' (town) marks those achievements in arts, industry, technology where the contributions of spontaneous nature are no longer evident in the criteria of evaluation. At the other end of the ellipse, a *wild* region of events is generated under the focus of spontaneous *nature*. These events take place in the absence of humans; they are what they are in themselves – wildflowers, loons calling, or a storm at sea. Although humans come to understand such events through the mediation of their cultures, they are evaluating events generated under the natural focus of the ellipse.

[13] McKibben, 1995.

A domain of *hybrid* or *synthetic* events is generated under the simultaneous control of both foci, a resultant of integrated influences from nature and culture, under the sway variously of more or less nature and culture. 'Symbiosis' is a parallel biological word. In the symbiosis zone, we have both and neither, but we do not forget there remain event-zones in which the principal determinant is culture, and other zones in which the principal determinant remains spontaneous nature. We do not want the ellipse to collapse into a circle, especially not one that is anthropocentric.

Nature as it once was, nature as an end in itself, is no longer the whole story. Nature as contrasted with culture is not the whole story either. An environmental ethic is not just about wildlands, but about humans at home on their landscapes, humans in their culture residing also in nature. This will involve resource use, sustainable development, managed landscapes, the urban and rural environments. Further, environmental ethicists, now and in the future, can and ought sometimes wish nature as an end in itself. That will prove an increasing challenge.

2. Global warming: 'Too hot to handle?'

But wait. There is one human activity that might make everything on Earth unnatural: global warming. Upsetting the climate upsets everything: air, water, soils, forests, fauna and flora, ocean currents, shorelines, agriculture, property values, international relations, because it is a systemic upset to the elemental givens on Earth. The Intergovernmental Panel on Climate Change, sponsored by the United Nations, meeting in Paris in 2007, released a bleak and powerful assessment of the future of the planet, with near certainty that unprecedented warming is human caused.[14]

John T. Houghton is one of the principal figures in the Intergovernmental Panel on Climate Change, also long a professor of atmospheric physics at Oxford. He was once Director General of the UK Meteorological Office (often called the MET). Houghton jarred political leaders with the claim that global warming already threatens British national security more than global terrorists, and that politicians were neglecting this 'one duty above all others … to protect the security of their people'.[15] The heat is first climatological, but secondly economic and political, and in the end moral.

14 Intergovernmental Panel on Climate Change, 2007.
15 Houghton, 2003.

Global warming is a threat of first magnitude and is at the same time 'a perfect moral storm', that is, utter or consummate.[16] The storm is absolute, comprehensive, inclusive, ultimate; there is an unprecedented convergence of complexities, natural and technological uncertainties, global and local interactions, difficult choices scientifically, ethically, politically, socially. There are differing cross-cultural perspectives on a common heritage. There are intergenerational issues, distributional issues, concerns about merit, justice, benevolence, about voluntary and involuntary risk. There is a long lag time, from decades to hundreds of years. Surely but gradually, local *goods* cumulate into global *bads*. There are opportunities for denial, procrastination, self-deception, hypocrisy, free-riding, cheating, and corruption. Individual and national self-interest is at odds with collective global interests. This is Garrett Hardin's 'tragedy of the commons', now taken at the pitch.[17]

Each person's lifestyle – at home, at work, at leisure, shopping, voting – has an ever-enlarging 'ecological footprint', most of all with global warming where effects of our actions are globally dispersed – CO2 in the air moving around the globe. There is fragmented agency; six billion persons differentially contribute to degrading a common resource (the atmosphere), all persons equally depending on climate, but with radically different powers to affect it. Even in the powerful nations, there is a sense of powerlessness. What can only one do? Any sacrifice I make (paying more for wind power) is more likely to benefit some overuser (heating his trophy home), than it is to better the commons. Institutional, corporate, and political structures force frameworks of environmentally disruptive behavior on individuals (such as high use of cars), and yet at the same time individuals support and demand these frameworks as sources of their good life (they love their SUV's).

The global character makes an effective response difficult, especially in a world without international government, where, for other reasons (such as cultural diversity, national heritages, freedom of self-determination), such government may be undesirable. Some global environmental problems can be solved by appeals to national self-interest, where international agreements serve such national interests. But the damage needs to be evident;

16 Gardiner, 2006.

17 A 'tragedy of the commons' occurs when individuals, sharing a resource held in common, each act in self-interest and the collective result progressively degrades the collective resource, illustrated by shepherds placing more and more sheep on land held in common (Hardin, 1968).

the results in immediate prospect (such as with over-fishing agreements, whaling, the Law of the Sea, the Convention on Trade in Endangered Species, or the Montreal Protocol on ozone depleting hydrocarbons). Global warming is too diffuse to get into such focus. Cost-benefit analyses are unreliable in the face of such uncertainties. Who wins, who loses, who can do what, with what result?

Meanwhile we discount the future and shrug our shoulders: we have to look out for ourselves and the future will too. That's the way it has always been. Meanwhile too, the damage is done before we know it and is more or less irreversible.

Generally the developed nations are responsible for global warming, since they emit most of the carbon dioxide. Although global warming affects rich and poor, generally the poorer nations are likely to suffer the most. These nations may have semi-arid landscapes or low shorelines. Their citizen farmers may live more directly tied to their immediate landscapes. Being poor, they are the least able to protect themselves. They are in no position to force the developed nations to make effective response, particularly with effects on future generations on their or any other landscapes.

Tim Flannery, a scientist named 'Australian of the Year' for his work, raises alarm about,[18] fearing a runaway greenhouse effect, where earlier negative feedback processes, tending to keep equilibrium in atmospheric and ocean circulations, have been replaced by positive feedforward processes spinning Earth into dis-equilibrium where humans will be powerless to halt the process. These may also be called non-linear or cascading shifts. We are smarter than ever, so smart that we are faced with overshoot. Our power to make changes exceeds our power to predict the results, exceeds our power to control even those adverse results we may foresee.

Where mitigating action is possible (such as limiting emissions), the present generation may bear costs, the benefits are gained by future generations. Postponing action will push much heavier costs onto those future generations; prevention is nearly always cheaper than cleanup. But the preventers live in a different generation from those who must clean-up. Classically, parents and grandparents do care about what they leave to children and grandchildren. But this intergenerational inheritance is not so local. Americans gain today; who pays the costs when nobody knows. Notice, however, that by 2050, when many of these adverse effects will be taking place, 70% of all persons living on Earth today will still be alive.

[18] Flannery, 2005

Global warming simultaneously affects all life on Earth. Climates have changed in the past. In prehistoric times, with melting ice, species moved north variously from 200 to 1,500 meters per year, as revealed by fossil pollen analysis. Spruce invaded what previously was tundra, at a rate of about 100 meters per year. But plants cannot track climate changes of this order of magnitude. Some natural processes will remain (it still rains on whatever plants are there); but the system is more and more upset.

The plants that can survive tend to be ones that are weedy (kudzu and Japanese honeysuckle). The five hundred wilderness areas will be something like city weedlots, with tatterdemalion scraps of nature that have managed to survive catastrophic upsets. The situation is complex again. Global warming is compounded in effects if there are toxics or pollutants on the landscape, if there are extinctions that upset the ecology, or if there is deforestation and soil loss. These multiple factors combine to drive ecosystems across thresholds beyond which they crash.

Is there any hope, human or wild? Whether we have hope will depend considerably on what we think about human nature and our capacities to face an unprecedented crisis.

3. Human nature: Human uniqueness vs. 'Pleistocene appetites'

Can we be *Homo sapiens*, the wise species, as we have named ourselves? We may have engines and gears, but we still have muscle and blood appetites. The next decades will increasingly see tensions between nature and human nature. One might first think that, since humans presumably evolved as good adapted fits in their environments, human nature will complement wild nature. Biologists may call this 'biophilia', an innate, genetically based disposition to love animals, plants, landscapes with trees, open spaces, running water.[19]

Critics find this a half truth because disconfirming evidence is everywhere. True, people like a house with a view, with a garden, but they do like a house, a big one. People are builders; their construction industry is what is destroying nature. People prefer culturally modified environments. 'Man is the animal for whom it is natural to be artificial'.[20] Neil Evernden says that *Homo sapiens* is 'the natural alien'.[21] The really natural thing for humans to do (our

[19] Wilson, 1984.
[20] Garvin, 1953, 378.
[21] Evernden, 1993.

genetic disposition) is to build a culture differentiating (alienating) ourselves from nature. Human agriculture, business, industry, development consumes most of our lives, and the search for nature is only avocational recreation.

Biophilia might be a positive Pleistocene relic. But other genetic legacies are problematic. Any residual biophilia is weak before our much more powerful desires for the goods of culture. Our evolutionary past did not give us many biological controls on our desires for goods that were in short supply. We love sweets, salt, and fats, of which in Pleistocene times humans could seldom get enough. But now we overeat and grow fat. We love sex; we want children; these urges kept us reproducing in ancient times, when most infants died. Now it pushes overpopulation. Generally, that is a model for the whole overconsumption problem.

There are few biological controls on our desires to amass goods, to secure our families, to consume; for most people it has always been a struggle to get enough (indeed for most it still is). When we can consume, we love it, and over-consume. Consumer capitalism transmutes a once-healthy pattern of desires into avarice. With escalating opportunities for consumption, driven by markets in search of profits, we need more self-discipline than comes naturally. Our self-interested tendencies overshoot; we love ourselves (egoism) and our offspring (genetic self-interest) and find it difficult to know when and how to say enough. A half-dozen graphs will put this graphically (see the following page).

For all of human history, we have been pushing back limits. Humans have more genius at this than any other species. Especially in the West, we have lived with a deep-seated belief that life will get better, that one should hope for abundance, and work toward obtaining it. Economists call such behavior 'rational'; humans will maximize their capacity to exploit their resources. Moral persons will also maximize human satisfactions, at least those that support the good life, which must not just include food, clothing, and shelter, but a better world for our children, increasing abundance, more and more goods and services that people want. Such growth is always desirable.

In the West we have built that into our concept of human rights: a right to self-development, to self-realization. Such an egalitarian ethic scales everybody up and drives an unsustainable world. When everybody seeks their own material goods, there is escalating consumption. When everybody seeks their children's good, there is escalating consumption. When everybody seeks everybody else's good, there is, again, escalating consumption.

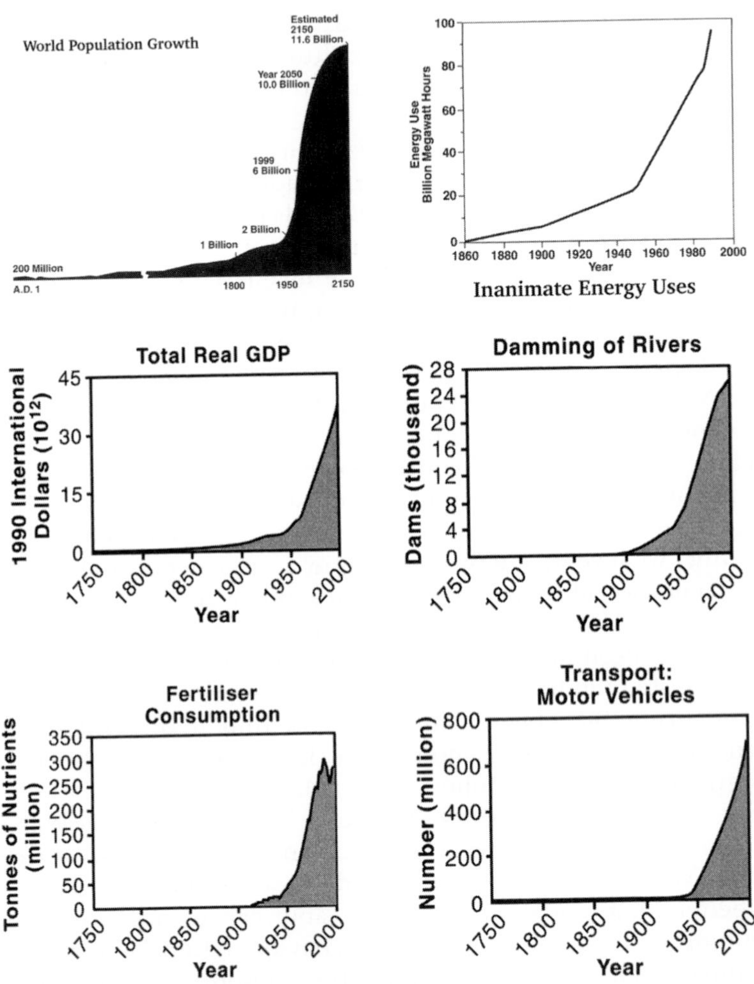

Fig. 1. Escalating Consumption and Population.[22]

[22] Cohen, 1995; Steffen et al., 2004.
The graphs 'World Population Growth' and 'Inanimate Energy Uses' are from J.E. Cohen 'Population Growth and Earth's Human Carrying Capacity', *Science*. The American Association for the Advancement of Science, 1995. Reprinted with permission from AAAS. The graphs 'Total Real GDP', 'Damming of Rivers', 'Fertilizer Consumption', 'Transport: Motor Vehicles' are taken from Will Steffan *et al. Global Change and the Earth System: A Planet Under Pressure*. Berlin: Springer, 2004, and are reproduced with kind permission of Springer Science & Business Media.

Humans are not well equipped to deal with the sorts of global level problems we now face. The classical institutions – family, village, tribe, nation, agriculture, industry, law, medicine, even school and church have shorter horizons. Far-off descendants and distant races do not have much 'biological hold' on us. Across the era of human evolution, little in our behavior affected those remote from us in time or in space, and natural selection shaped only our conduct toward those closer. Global threats require us to act in massive concert of which we are incapable. If so, humans may bear within themselves the seeds of their own destruction. More bluntly, more scientifically put: our genes, once enabling our adaptive fit, will in the next millennium prove mal-adaptive and destroy us.

Both policy and ethics will be required to enlarge the scope of concern. Humans are attracted to appeals to a better life, to quality of life, and if environmental ethics can persuade large numbers of persons that an environment with biodiversity, with wildness is a better world in which to live than one without these, then some progress is possible – using an appeal to still more enlightened self-interest, or perhaps better: to a more inclusive and comprehensive concept of human welfare. That will get us clean air, water, soil conservation, national parks, some wildlife reserves and bird sanctuaries. Environmental ethics cannot succeed without this, nor is this simply pragmatic; it is quite true. This may be the most we can do at global scales, even national scales, with collective human interests.

We may prove able to work out some incentive structures. The European Union has transcended national interests with surprising consensus about environmental issues. Kofi Annan, Secretary General of the United Nations, praised the Montreal Protocol, with its five revisions, widely adopted (191 nations) and implemented as the most successful international agreement yet. All the developed nations, except the United States and Australia, signed the Kyoto Protocol. The Convention on International Trade in Endangered Species of Wild Fauna and Flora (CITES) has been signed by one hundred and twelve nations. There are over one hundred and fifty international agreements (conventions, treaties, protocols, etc.), registered with the United Nations, that deal directly with environmental problems.[23]

Humans have proved capable of advanced skills never dreamed of in our ancient past–flying jet planes, building the internet, decoding

[23] United Nations Environment Programme, 1997; Rummel-Bulska and Osafo, 1991.

their own genome, and designating world biosphere reserves. It would be tragic in the future if we let our left-over Pleistocene appetites become a useful alibi for continuing our excesses. *Homo sapiens* can and ought be wiser than that.

4. Sustainable development vs. sustainable biosphere

The United Nations Conference on Environment and Development entwined its twin concerns into 'sustainable development'. No one wants unsustainable development, so sustainable development is likely to remain the favored model. The duty seems unanimous, plain, and urgent. Only so can this good life continue. Over 150 nations have endorsed sustainable development. The World Business Council on Sustainable Development includes 130 of the world's largest corporations.

Proponents argue that sustainable development is useful just because it is a wide angle lens. The specifics of development are unspecified, giving peoples and nations the freedom and responsibility of self-development. This is an orienting concept that is at once directed and encompassing, a coalition-level policy that sets aspirations, thresholds, and allows pluralist strategies for their accomplishment.

Critics reply that sustainable development is just as likely to prove an umbrella concept that requires little but superficial agreement, bringing a constant illusion of consensus, glossing over deeper problems with a rhetorically engaging word. There are two poles, complements yet opposites. Economy can be prioritized, the usual case, and anything can be done to the environment, so long as the continuing development of the economy is not jeopardized thereby. The environment is kept in orbit with economics at the center. One ought to develop (since that increases social welfare and the abundant life), and the environment will constrain that development if and only if a degrading environment might undermine ongoing development. The underlying conviction is that the trajectory of the industrial, technological, commercial world is generally right – only the developers in their enthusiasm have hitherto failed to recognize environmental constraints.

At the other pole, the environment is prioritized. A 'sustainable biosphere' model demands a baseline quality of environment. The economy must be worked out 'within' such quality of life in a quality environment (clean air, water, stable agricultural soils, attractive residential landscapes, forests, mountains, rivers, rural lands, parks, wildlands, wildlife, renewable resources). Winds blow, rains fall, rivers flow, the sun shines, photosynthesis takes place, carbon recycles all over the landscape. These processes have to be sustained. The economy must be kept within an environmental orbit. One ought to conserve nature, the ground-matrix of life. Development is desired, but even more, society must learn to live within the carrying capacity of its landscapes.

'Sustainable' is an economic but also an environmental term. The Ecological Society of America advocates research and policy that will result in a 'sustainable biosphere'. 'Achieving a sustainable biosphere is the single most important task facing humankind today'.[24] The fundamental flaw in 'sustainable development' is that it sees the Earth as resource only. The underlying conviction in the sustainable biosphere model is that the current trajectory of the industrial, technological, commercial world is generally wrong, because it will inevitably overshoot. The environment is not some undesirable, unavoidable set of constraints. Rather, nature is the matrix of multiple values; many, even most of them are not counted in economic transactions. In a more inclusive accounting of what we wish to sustain, nature provides numerous other values (aesthetic experiences, biodiversity, sense of place and perspective), and these are getting left out. The *Millennium Ecosystem Assessment* explores this in great detail.

A central problem with contemporary global development is that the rich grow richer and the poor poorer. Many fear that this is neither ethical nor sustainable.

> Global inequalities in income increased in the 20th century by orders of magnitude out of proportion to anything experienced before. The distance between the incomes of the richest and poorest country was about 3 to 1 in 1820, 35 to 1 in 1950, 44 to 1 in 1973, and 72 to 1 in 1992.[25]
>
> For most of the world's poorest countries the past decade has continued a disheartening trend: not only have they failed to reduce poverty, but they are falling further behind rich countries.[26]

The assets of the world's top three billionaires exceed the combined gross national product (GNP) of all of the least developed countries. The richest two percent own more than half of global household wealth.[27] The distribution of wealth raises complex issues of merit,

24 Risser, Lubchenco, Levin, 1991.

25 United Nations Development Programme [UNDP], 2000, 6.

26 United Nations Development Programme [UNDP], 2005, 36.

27 United Nations University, World Institute for Development Economics Research, 2006.

luck, justice, charity, natural resources, national boundaries, global commons. But by any standards this seems unjustly disproportionate. The inevitable result stresses people on their landscapes, forcing environmental degradation, more tragedy of the commons, with instability and collapse. The rich and powerful are equally ready to exploit nature and people.

Such issues come under another inclusive term, 'environmental justice'. Now the claim is that social justice is so linked with environmental conservation that a more fair distribution of the world's wealth is required for any sustainable conservation even of rural landscapes, much less of wildlife and wildlands. Environmental ethicists may be faulted for overlooking the poor (often of a different race, class, or sex) in their concern to save the elephants. The livelihood of such poor may be adversely affected by the elephants, who trash their crops. Or it may be adversely affected because the pollution dump is located on their already degraded landscapes – and not in the backyard (or even on the national landscapes) of the rich. They may be poor because they are living on degraded landscapes. They are likely to remain poor, even if developers arrive, because they will be too poorly paid to break out of their poverty.

Ethicists ought to speak the truth to power. They may suffer for it. Joseph E. Stiglitz, Nobel laureate, Chief Economist for the World Bank, became increasingly ethically concerned.

> While I was at the World Bank, I saw firsthand the devastating effect that globalization can have on developing countries, and especially the poor within those countries. … Especially at the International Monetary Fund … decisions were made on the basis of what seemed a curious blend of ideology and bad economics, dogmas that sometimes seemed to be thinly veiling special interests … The IMF's policies, in part based on the outworn presumption that markets, by themselves, lead to efficient outcomes, failed to allow for desirable government interventions in the market, measures which can guide economic growth and make *everyone* better off.[28]

Nor are governments, pushed by such financial interests, always willing so to guide economic growth. Stiglitz wrote in April 2000:

> I was chief economist at the World Bank from 1996 until last November, during the gravest global economic crisis in a half-

[28] Stiglitz, 2002, ix, xiii, xii.

> century. I saw how the IMF, in tandem with the U.S. Treasury Department, responded. And I was appalled.[29]

For such concern he was pressured into resigning and his contract with the World Bank was terminated. Ethicists need now and forever in the future to remember Lord Acton: 'Power tends to corrupt and absolute power corrupts absolutely'.[30] This reconnects us with the worries we had earlier about those Pleistocene appetites driving humans, rich and poor, ever to want more, more, more.

Sustainable development is impossible without a sustainable biosphere. Thirty percent of the *Millennium Ecosystem Assessment* Development Goals depend on access to clean water. A third of the people on the planet lack readily available safe drinking water. Consider the conclusion of some of its principal authors:

> We lack a robust theoretical basis for linking ecological diversity to ecosystem dynamics and, in turn, to ecosystem services underlying human well-being. ... The most catastrophic changes in ecosystem services identified in the MA (*Millennium Assessment*) involved nonlinear or abrupt shifts. We lack the ability to predict thresholds for such changes, whether or not such a change may be reversible, and how individuals and societies will respond. ... Relations between ecosystem services and human well-being are poorly understood. One gap relates to the consequences of changes in ecosystem services for poverty reduction. The poor are most dependent on ecosystem services and vulnerable to their degradation.[31]

People and their Earth have entwined destinies; that past truth continues in the present, and will remain a pivotal concern in the new millennium.

5. Biodiversity: 'Good for me' vs. 'Good of its kind'

'The biospheric membrane that covers the Earth, and you and me, ... is the miracle we have been given'.[32] Earth's biodiversity is in more jeopardy today than previously in the history of life. If we do not shift our present development course, 'at least a fifth of the species of plants would be gone or committed to early extinction by 2030,

29 Stiglitz, 2000, 56.
30 Acton, 1887, 1949, 364.
31 Carpenter et al., 2006.
32 Wilson, 2002, 21.

and half by the end of the century'.[33] The *Millennium Ecosystem Assessment*, reporting a multi-national consensus of hundreds of experts, concluded: 'Over the past few hundred years, humans have increased species extinction rates by as much as 1,000 times background rates that were typical over Earth's history'.[34]

The causes are complex: over-hunting, over-fishing, destruction of habitat, pollution, invasive species, global warming. Measures of loss are multiple: numbers of species, percentages, genetic populations, ecosystems degraded, hotspots lost. Biodiversity (including but more inclusive than 'endangered species') is in subspecies, genetically distinct populations, in diverse habitats and ecosystems. Most species on Earth are yet undescribed; so far only about 10% of fungi, and less for most invertebrates and microorganisms. We hardly know what we are losing. Predictions are difficult. Nevertheless, all the measures find biocide quickening in speed and intensity.

Paleontologists trace an evolutionary natural history with ongoing turnover extinctions and replacements. Anthropogenic extinction (caused by human encroachments) is radically different. One opens doors; the other closes them. In natural extinctions, nature takes away life when it has become unfit in habitat, or when the habitat alters, and supplies other life in its place. Through evolutionary time, nature has provided new species at a higher rate than the extinction rate; hence, the accumulated diversity. Life rebounded even after the six catastrophic extinctions, which often opened up novel opportunities for dramatic respeciation. Artificial extinction shuts down tomorrow because it shuts down speciation. There is no respeciation on Walmart parking lots. Humans dead-end these lines.

But that evolutionary epic is over, critics will say. Most of the species that ever existed in the past are extinct by natural causes, and in the next century more will go extinct by human causes. That may be a pity, but it is inevitable. Nor is it immoral, since humans are worth more than beetles and fungi. We do need to sustain the biosphere, our life support system, as the ecologists were just claiming. So save what is 'good for us', but, beyond that, we have no duties to the living things as 'goods of their kind'. Biodiversity for medical, agricultural, industrial, recreational, scientific uses? Yes, these are instrumental values. But intrinsic value in animals and plants, a 'good of their own' that claims our care? That goes too far.

'Human beings are at the centre of concerns...' So the *Rio Declaration* begins, formulated at the United Nations Conference

[33] Wilson, 2002, 102.
[34] *Millennium Ecosystem Assessment*, 2005b, 3.

on Environment and Development (UNCED), and signed by almost every nation on Earth. This document was once to be called the *Earth Charter*, but the developing nations were more interested in asserting their rights to develop, more ecojustice, more aid from the North to the South, and only secondarily in saving the Earth. The Rio claim is, in many respects, quite true. The humans species is causing all the concern. Environmental problems are people problems, not gorilla or sequoia problems. The problem is to get people into 'a healthy and productive life in harmony with nature'.[35]

Wilfred Beckerman and Joanna Pasek put it this way:

> The most important bequest we can make to posterity is to bequeath a decent society characterized by greater respect for human rights than is the case today. Furthermore, while this by no means excludes a concern for environmental developments – particularly those that many people believe might seriously threaten future living standards – policies to deal with these developments must never be at the expense of the poorest people alive today. One could not be proud of policies that may preserve the environment for future generations if the costs of doing so are borne mainly by the poorest members of the present generation.[36]

That is certainly humane, and no one wishes to argue that the poorest should bear the highest of these costs, while the rich gain the benefits. We are not proud of a conservation ethic that says: the rich should win, the poor lose. That was what appalled Joseph Stiglitz about the World Bank, the IMF, and the U.S. Treasury.

But look at how this plays out with World Health Organization policy:

> Priority given to human health raises an ethical dilemma if 'health for all' conflicts with protecting the environment. ... Priority to ensuring human survival is taken as a first-order principle. Respect for nature and control of environmental degradation is a second-order principle, which must be observed unless it conflicts with the first-order principle of meeting survival needs.[37]

Again, that seems quite humane. But in India this policy certainly means no tigers. In Africa it means no rhinos. Both will only remain in Western zoos. To *preserve*, even to *conserve*, is going to mean to

[35] UNCED, 1992b.
[36] Beckerman and Pasek, 2001, vi.
[37] World Health Organization, Commission on Health and Environment, 1992, 4.

reserve. If there are biodiversity reserves, with humans on site or nearby, humans must limit their activities. Else there will always be some hungry persons who would diminish the reserve. The continued existence in the wild of most of Earth's charismatic endangered species depends on some 600 major reserves for wildlife in some 80 countries.[38] If these are not policed from human intruders, the animals will not be there.

Michael L. Rosenzweig wants a 'win-win ecology' so that 'the Earth's species can survive in the midst of human enterprise'.[39] All these you-can-have-your-cake-and-eat-it-too solutions are welcome, so far as they go. A bumper sticker reads: Re-cycling: Everyone wins. That, some say, is an aphoristic model for the whole human/ nature relationship. If we are in harmony with nature, everyone wins, equally people, rhinos, and tigers.

The conservatives (the skeptics?) will say that win-win is all that is politically, economically, sociologically, biologically feasible, even imaginable. The best you can do is enlighten self-interest. Remember those Pleistocene urges for more and more. This will be especially true in a free-market democracy, which is what most of the world seems to want today. So the best strategy is to argue that persons living abundant lives need to experience the wonderland natural world (those biophilia instincts). Biodiversity was formerly too much devalued, as if it were nothing but consumable resources. Biodiversity in place benefits people. Ecotourists who come to see tigers and rhinos will bring in more money than will cutting the timber and grazing cattle there.

Nevertheless, there is something suspicious about these claims. They seem humane; they also hide an arrogance about human superiority. Let's make a comparison. What if Americans were to say: Always prefer Americans, first order. All other nations are second order. 'We will not do anything that harms our economy', said George W. Bush rather bluntly, 'because first things first are the people who live in America'.[40] Didn't John Houghton, in his warning about global warming, say that the first duty of political leaders is to protect the security of the people within their nations?

But Houghton did not say that the security of the British is first order, that of the Americans second order. Bush did say that the economic health of the American companies takes bedrock priority. And we are suspicious when one group says to another: We will deal with

[38] Riley and Riley, 2005.
[39] Rosenzweig, 2003.
[40] Bush, quoted in Seelye, 2001.

you only in ways that are first beneficial to us. Maybe we begin to see why Joseph Stiglitz, concerned about the world's poor, was 'appalled' by the IMF and U.S. Treasury. None of this bodes well for inter-human justice, much less for inter-specific ethics.

Analogously, what if humans say (as did the World Health Organization): First things first are people. Wildlife, plants, non-humans, second. 'You non-humans can live, only if you are worth more to us alive than dead'. That is the cash value of the policy: Always prefer humans, first order. The other ten million species on the planet come second to us. Brian Child says: 'Wildlife will survive in Africa only where it can compete financially for space'.[41] Likewise and more bluntly: Norman Myers: 'In emergent Africa, you either use wildlife or lose it. If it pays its own way, some of it will survive'.[42]

Ought not really superior humans be willing to sacrifice something for these ten (or more) million other species on Earth? There is something morally naive about living in a reference frame where one species takes itself as absolute and values everything else relative to its utility, even if we phrase it that we are taking ourselves as primary and everything else as secondary. If true to their specific epithet, ought not *Homo sapiens* value this host of life as something with a claim to care in its own right? If we humans continue as we are headed and cause extinctions surpassing anything previously found on Earth, then future generations, rich or poor, are not likely to be proud of our destroying 'the miracle we have been given' either.

Nobody wants to be a loser, so maybe we can put it this way: Humans will win when, and only when, they change their goals. Humans will come to be corrected from a misperception: 'good for us', 'instrumental value' is all that counts. We will win because we get our values right. The loser will be worse off by his lights, but his lights are wrong (nature all and only a resource). If he or she gets things in the right light ('good kinds', 'goods on their own', 'intrinsic values', 'the wonderland Earth'), there is no loss, only gain.

Consider abolishing slavery. Slave-owners lost their slaves as resources. But when the right thing was done, the result was win-win in the long term. Within the next century blacks increasingly prospered and so did the whites. Similarly with the liberation of women or minorities. White males lost some jobs, but the talents and skills of women and blacks, formerly often wasted, now are fully utilized in the work force; family incomes are higher, marriages

41 Child, 1993, 60.
42 Myers, 1981, 36.

are richer, and so on. In environmental ethics, there is a parallel. The person re-forms his or her values and becomes a winner because now living in a richer and more harmonious relationship with nature.

At this point, critics will protest that we insist that humans can win but then redefine winning. We win by moving the goal posts. And that's cheating, like showing a net positive balance in your checkbook by revising the multiplication tables. You will win, by losing at the old game and playing a new game. Some persons did lose, in the sense that losing had when our argument started. They lost timber, or jobs, or opportunities for development, or grazing their cattle.

Yes, you do have to move the goal posts to win. That might be cheating if the game is football. But in environmental ethics, there is a disanalogy. You move the goal posts because you discover that they are in the wrong place. And that is really to win, because getting to the wrong goal is not winning. Moving the goal posts, these 'losers' at the exploitation game will come to live in a community with a new worldview, that of a sustainable relationship with the biodiverse Earth, and that is a new idea of winning. All they really lose is what it is a good thing to lose: an exclusively exploitative attitude toward nature – similar to that once held about slaves. What they gain is a good thing to gain: a land ethic.

'Every form of life is unique, warranting respect regardless of its worth to man.' That is how the UN *World Charter for Nature* begins.[43] This charter is as nonanthropocentric as the *Rio Declaration* is anthropocentric. One hundred and twelve nations endorsed this charter, though the United States vigorously opposed it. This statement was largely aspirational; few took it to require any serious changes in policy. But in a vision for the future, we need aspirations. It is possible, we should notice, for humans to be at the center of concerns and also for every form of life to have its worth regardless of humans. Both can be true.

6. Earth Ethics

We have been traveling into progressively less familiar ethical terrain. We need a logic and an ethic for Earth with its family of life. Ecosystems are ultimately our home, from which the word *ecology* is derived (Greek: *oikos*, house). In the twentieth century, the commons problem became transnational; at the turn of the millennium it has become global. Our citizenship in nations is not well

[43] United Nations General Assembly, 1982.

synchronized with our residence in geographic places, nor with our sense of global dwelling on our home planet.

People are fighting for what is of value in nature but as citizens of nations that have economic policies and political agendas, demanding loyalties in support. Their access to natural resources comes filtered through political and industrial units that are not formed, or continued, with these ecologies in mind. They want resources, but political alignments can often mean suboptimal and unjust solutions to the problems of resource distribution. 'Nationalizing' natural resources can be as much part of the problem as part of the answer, especially when the sovereign independence of nations is asserted without regard for the interdependencies of these nations – both those with each other and those of the global ecosystems. When biological resources are taken to be national possessions in dispute, rather than an Earth commons to be shared, it can become difficult to find a way to share them.

In previous environmental ethics, one might have spoken loosely, perhaps poetically, or romantically of valuing Earth. But that would not have been taken as a serious cognitive claim, no more than was the *World Charter for Nature*. Earth is a mere thing, a big thing, a special thing for those who happen to live on it, but still a thing, and not appropriate as an object of intrinsic or systemic valuation. Thinking this way, we can, if we insist on being anthropocentrists, say that it is all valueless except as our human resource.

But we will not be valuing Earth objectively until we appreciate this marvelous (miraculous?) natural history. This really is a superb planet, the most valuable entity of all, because it is the entity able to produce and sustain all the Earthbound values. At this scale of vision, if we ask what is principally to be valued, the value of life arising as a creative process on Earth seems a better description and a more comprehensive category than to speak of a careful management of planetary natural resources that we humans own. Such a fertile Earth, interestingly, is the original meaning of the word 'nature', that which 'springs forth', 'gives birth', or is 'generated'. This was once explained in the mythology of a 'Mother Earth'; now we have it on scientific authority.

Dealing with an acre or two of real estate, perhaps even with hundreds or thousands of acres, we usually think – and perhaps will continue to do so – that the earth belongs to us, as private property holders. Dealing with a landscape, we think that the earth belongs to us, as citizens of the country geographically located there. So we have our nation states with their territories. But on the global scale, Earth is not something we own. Earth does not belong to us; rather we belong to it. We belong on it. The challenging philosophical question for the new millennium is how we humans belong in this world, not how much of it belongs to us. The question is not of property, but of community. Biospheric Earth is really the relevant survival unit. And with that global vision, we may want to return to our regional landscapes, and think of ourselves as belonging there too, with a deeper sense of place.

In the next millennium, it will not be enough to be a good 'citizen', or a 'humanist', because neither of those terms have enough 'nature', enough 'earthiness' in them. 'Citizen' is only half the truth; the other half is that we are 'residents' on landscapes. Humans are Earthlings. Earth is our dwelling place. From here onward, there is no such thing as civic competence without ecological competence. Many a citizen who is celebrated for his or her humanity is quite insensitive to the boding ecological crisis, or, even were there no crisis, in enjoying the values the natural world carries all around them. Until that happens, no one is well educated for the next century, the century in which many of these problems will have to be solved – if ever they are solved. Somewhat paradoxically, the two new areas in an undergraduate education, differing from the classical education of the past century is that graduates need to be (1) computer literate and (2) environmentally literate.

Our responsibility to Earth might be thought the most remote of our responsibilities; it seems so grandiose and vague beside our concrete responsibilities to our children or next-door neighbors. But not so: the other way round, it is the most fundamental of our responsibilities, and connected with these local ones. Responsibilities increase proportionately to the level and value of the reality in jeopardy. The highest level that we humans have power to affect, Earth, is the most vital phenomenon of all.

Boutros Boutros-Ghalli, speaking as the UN Secretary-General, closed the Earth Summit: 'The Spirit of Rio must create a new mode of civic conduct. It is not enough for man to love his neighbour; he must also learn to love his world'.[44] 'We must now conclude an ethical and political contract with nature, with this Earth to which we owe our very existence and which gives us life'.[45] This does not deny that we must continue to love our neighbors, but it enlarges the vision from a social contract to a natural contract. The challenge is to think of Earth as a precious thing in itself because it is home for us all; Earth is to be loved, as we do a neighbor, for an intrinsic integrity.

[44] Boutros-Ghalli, 1992a, 1.
[45] Boutros-Ghalli, 1992b, vol. IV, 66–69.

Views of Earth from space are the most impressive photographs ever taken, if one judges by their worldwide impact. They are the most widely distributed photographs ever, having been seen by well over half the persons on Earth. Few are not moved to a moment of truth, at least in their pensive moods. The whole Earth is aesthetically stimulating, philosophically challenging, and ethically disturbing. 'Once a photograph of the Earth, taken from *the outside* is available ... a new idea as powerful as any in history will be let loose'.[46] We had to get off the planet to see it whole.

A virtually unanimous experience of the nearly two hundred astronauts, from many countries and cultures, is the awe experienced at the first sight of the whole Earth – its beauty, fertility, smallness in the abyss of space, light and warmth under the sun in surrounding darkness and, above all, its vulnerability. In the words of Edgar Mitchell, Earth is 'a sparkling blue-and-white jewel ... laced with slowly swirling veils of white ... like a small pearl in a thick sea of black mystery'.[47]

'I remember so vividly', said Michael Collins, 'what I saw when I looked back at my fragile home – a glistening, inviting beacon, delicate blue and white, a tiny outpost suspended in the black infinity. Earth is to be treasured and nurtured, something precious that *must* endure'.[48] Earth is a fragile planet, a jewel set in mystery. We humans too belong on the planet; it is our home, as much as for all the others. Humans are certainly a dominant species – what other species takes pictures of Earth from space? But the glistening pearl in space may not be something we want to possess, as much as a biosphere we ought to inhabit with love. Environmental ethics is the elevation to ultimacy of an urgent world vision. We are searching for an ethics adequate to respect life on this Earth, an Earth Ethics. That is the future of environmental ethics.

Colorado State University

References

Acton, Lord (John Emerich Edward Dalberg-Acton), 1949. *Essays on Freedom and Power*, ed. Gertrude Himmelfarb. Glencoe, IL: Free Press.

Beckerman, Wilfred, and Joanna Pasek, 2001. *Justice, Posterity, and the Environment*. New York: Oxford University Press.

[46] Fred Hoyle, quoted in Kelley, 1988, inside front cover.
[47] Quoted in Kelley, 1988, at photographs 42–45.
[48] Collins, 1980, 6.

Bergson, Henri, 1911. *Creative Evolution*, trans. Arthur Mitchell. London: Macmillan and Co.
Botkin, Daniel B. 1990. *Discordant Harmonies: A New Ecology for the Twenty-first Century*. New York: Oxford University Press.
Boutros-Ghalli, Boutros, 1992a. Extracts from closing UNCED statement, in an UNCED summary, *Final Meeting and Round-up of Conference*, June 14. UN Document ENV/DEV/RIO/29, 14 June.
Boutros-Ghalli, Boutros, 1992b. Text of closing UNCED statements, in *Report of the United Nations Conference on Environment and Development, 1992*, vol. **IV**, 66–69. UN Document A/CONF.151.26.
Callicott, J. Baird, 1992. 'La Nature est morte, vive la nature!' *Hastings Center Report* **22** (no. 5, September/October):16–23.
Carpenter, Stephen R. et al., 2006. 'Millennium Ecosystem Assessment: Research Needs', *Science* **314** (13 October): 257–258.
Child, Brian, 1993. 'The Elephant as a Natural Resource', *Wildlife Conservation* **96** (no. 2):60–61.
Cohen, Joel E., 1995. 'Population Growth and Earth's Carrying Capacity', *Science* **269** (1995):341–346.
Collins, Michael, 1980. 'Foreword', in Roy A. Gallant, *Our Universe*. Washington, DC: National Geographic Society.
Crutzen, Paul J., 2006. 'The "Anthropocene"', pages 13–18 in Eckart Ehlers and Thomas Kraft, eds., *Earth System Science in the Anthropocene*. Berlin: Springer, 2006.
Ellis, Erle C. and Navin, Ramankutty, 2008. 'Putting People in the Map: Anthropogenic Biomes of the World', *Frontiers in Ecology and the Environment* **6** (no. 8):439–447.
Evernden, Neil, 1993. *The Natural Alien: Humankind and Environment*. Toronto: University of Toronto Press.
Flannery Tim, 2005. *The Weather Makers: The History and Future Impact of Climate Change*. New York: Atlantic Monthly Press.
Gardiner, Stephen M., 2006. 'A Perfect Moral Storm: Climate Change, Intergenerational Ethics and the Problem of Moral Corruption', *Environmental Values* **15**:397–413.
Garvin, Lucius, 1953. *A Modern Introduction to Ethics*. Cambridge, MA: Houghton Mifflin.
Hannah, Lee, David Lohse, Charles Hutchinson, John L. Carr andAli Lankerani, 1994. 'A Preliminary Inventory of Human Disturbance of World Ecosystems', *Ambio* **23**:246–50.

Hardin, Garrett, 1968. 'The Tragedy of the Commons', *Science* **162** (December 13):1243–1248.

Hawken, Paul, 2007. *Blessed Unrest: How the Largest Movement in the World Came into Being and Why No One Saw It Coming.* New York: Viking.

Houghton, John, 2003. 'Global Warming is Now a Weapon of Mass Destruction', *The Guardian*, 28 July, p. 14.

Intergovernmental Panel on Climate Change, 2007. *Climate Change 2007: The Physical Science Basis.* Online at www.ipcc.ch.

Kelley, Kevin W., ed., 1988. *The Home Planet.* Reading, MA: Addison-Wesley.

Kerry, John, and Teresa Heinz Kerry, 2007. *This Moment on Earth: Today's New Environmentalists and Their Vision for the Future.* New York: Perseus Group, Public Affairs Books.

McKibben, Bill, 1989. *The End of Nature.* New York: Random House.

McKibben, Bill, 1995. *Hope, Human and Wild.* Little, Brown and Company.

Millennium Ecosystem Assessment, 2005a. *Living Beyond our Means: Natural Assets and Human Well-Being: Statement from the Board.* Washington, DC: World Resources Institute.

Millennium Ecosystem Assessment, 2005b. *Ecosystems and Human Well-being: Biodiversity Synthesis.* Washington, DC: World Resources Institute.

Myers, Norman, 1981. 'Farewell to Africa', *International Wildlife* **11**(no. 4):36–47.

Riley, Laura and William Riley, 2005. *Nature's Strongholds: The World's Great Wildlife Reserves.* Princeton, NJ: Princeton University Press.

Risser, Paul G., Jane Lubchenco, and Samuel A. Levin, 1991. 'Biological Research Priorities–A Sustainable Biosphere', *BioScience* **47**:625–627.

Rosenzweig, Michael L., 2003. *Win-Win Ecology: How the Earth's Species Can Survive in the Midst of Human Enterprise.* New York: Oxford University Press.

Rummel-Bulska, Iwona and Seth Osafo, eds., 1991. *Selected Multilateral Treaties in the Field of the Environment, II.* Cambridge: Grotius Publications.

Seelye, Katharine Q., 2001. 'Facing Obstacles on Plan for Drilling for Arctic Oil, Bush Says He'll Look Elsewhere', *The New York Times*, March 30, 2001, p. A13.

Soulé, Michael E., 1989. 'Conservation Biology in the Twenty-first Century: Summary and Outlook', in David Western and

Mary Pearl, eds., *Conservation for the Twenty-first Century*. Oxford: Oxford University Press.

Steffen, Will et al., 2004. *Global Change and the Earth System: A Planet Under Pressure*. Berlin: Springer.

Stiglitz, Joseph E., 2000. 'The Insider: What I Learned at the World Economic Crisis', *The New Republic* **222** (no. 16/17, April 17 and 24):56–60.

Stiglitz, Joseph E., 2002. *Globalization and Its Discontents*. New York: Norton.

United Nations Conference on Environment and Development (UNCED) 1992a. *Agenda 21*. Document No. A/CONF.151/26. http://www.un.org/esa/sustdev/documents/agenda21/index.htm

United Nations Conference on Environment and Development (UNCED), 1992b. *The Rio Declaration*. UNCED Document A/CONF.151/5/Rev. 1, 13 June.

United Nations Development Programme (UNDP), 2000. *Human Development Report 2000*. Oxford, UK: Oxford University Press.

United Nations Development Programme (UNDP), 2005. *Human Development Report 2005*. New York: United Nations Development Programme.

United Nations Environment Programme, 1997. *Register of International Treaties and Other Agreements in the Field of the Environment*. Nairobi: United Nations Environment Programme.

United Nations General Assembly, 1982. *World Charter for Nature*, UN General Assembly Resolution No. 37/7 of 28 October.

United Nations University, World Institute for Development Economics Research, 2006. 'The World Distribution of Household Wealth', online at www.wider.uni.edu.

Vitousek, Peter M., Paul R. Ehrlich, Anne H. Ehrlich, and Pamela A. Matson, 1986. 'Human Appropriation of the Products of Biosynthesis', *BioScience* **36**:368–373.

Wilson, Edward O., 1984. *Biophilia*. Cambridge: MA: Harvard University Press.

Wilson, Edward O., 2002. *The Future of Life*. New York: Alfred A. Knopf.

Wolff, Edward N., 2002. *Top Heavy: The Increasing Inequality of Wealth in America and What Can Be Done About It*. New York: The New Press.

World Health Organization, Commission on Health and Environment, 1992. Geneva: World Health Organization, *Our Planet, Our Health: Report of the WHO Commission on Health and Environment*.

Beyond Anthropocentrism

ROBIN ATTFIELD

After the first wave of writings in environmental philosophy in the early 1970s, which were mostly critical of anthropocentrism, a new trend emerged which sought to humanise this subject, and to revive or vindicate anthropocentric stances. Only in this way, it was held, could environmental values become human values, and ecological movements manage to become social ecology. Later writers have detected tacit anthropocentrism lurking even in Deep Ecology, or have defended 'perspectival anthropocentrism', as the inevitable methodology of any system of environmental ethics devised by and for the guidance of human beings. Human good, broadly enough conceptualised, is held to be the basis of ethics. Besides, it is sometimes added, non-anthropocentric considerations in any case add nothing to anthropocentric ones, when broadly construed.

It is here replied that these revisionary approaches often elide crucial distinctions, and in denying the relevance of nonhuman goods unintentionally narrow the range of human sympathies, and deprive human agents of some of the grounds for environmental concern, as well as of key elements of the basis for preserving ecological systems. Even approaches which allow 'the human scale of values' to range beyond human interests are prone to impose limitations on what humans are capable of valuing that are unduly stringent; we need to be free to preserve possibilities for life beyond human life, and not only forms of life meaningful to humans.

1. The Anthropocentric Reaction

The first generation of environmental philosophers of the early 1970s sought to take ethics and its presuppositions beyond anthropocentrism, and I will be arguing that they were right to do so. Of these founding fathers, Holmes Rolston, whose presentation initiated this series of lectures, has later come to be known as the father of Environmental Philosophy. Others included the late Richard Routley, who changed his name to Sylvan, and who published the

doi:10.1017/S1358246111000191

first paper in the field,[1] and Arne Naess (who died quite recently), one of the founders of Deep Ecology. But I am not endorsing Deep Ecology, or Rolston's ethical holism, or Sylvan's rejection of Western traditions, but rather their shared view that anthoprocentrism is an insufficient and misguided basis for normative ethics.

As for anthropocentrism, what was usually meant, and what I shall mean by the phrase in this essay, is the belief that nothing but human beings has moral standing, or should be taken into account in ethical deliberations; this belief is also sometimes known as 'normative anthropocentrism'. They did not mean the belief that human interests may be ethically central but are not the only ethically relevant considerations (although the term is sometimes used as loosely as this); and nor shall I. And they did not usually have in mind teleological or metaphysical anthropocentrism, the belief that everything exists for the sake of human beings, although this belief was discussed in the first monograph in the field, John Passmore's *Man's Responsibility for Nature*,[2] and is sometimes presented as a ground for adherence to normative anthropocentrism. In urging people to look beyond human interests, this first wave of theorists wanted to stress that not doing so reflected human arrogance, that nature or (more cogently) some segments of nature has or have independent interests that matter, that failure to recognise this can distort and misrepresent our own humanity, and that in any case concern to avert nonhuman suffering cannot consistently be grounded on an anthropocentric basis.

However, the second wave of environmental philosophers often adopted a different approach, and often a more humanistic one. Bryan Norton, for example, argued that there was no need to associate anthropocentrism with shallow rather than deeper environmentalism, concerned with the distant future and with the preservation of other species and their habitats, for human interests are sufficient to underpin the case for preservation, and the interests of the human future call for a long-term approach to nature independently

[1] Richard Routley (later Sylvan), 'Is There a Need for a New, an Environmental, Ethic?', *Proceedings of the World Congress of Philosophy* (Varna, Bulgaria: World Congress of Philosophy, 1973), 205–210. The earliest paper of Holmes Rolston III was his 'Is There an Ecological Ethic', *Ethics*, **85** (1975), 93–109. The earliest relevant paper of Arne Naess was his 'The Shallow and the Deep, Long-range Ecology Movement: A Summary', *Inquiry*, **16** (1973), 95–100.

[2] John Passmore, *Man's Responsibility for Nature* (London: Duckworth, 1974).

of appeal to non-human interests. Certainly if human interests are confined to human preferences, as in what he called 'strong anthropocentrism', not enough preservation will be justified, but this deficiency will be made good (he believes) if instead we adopt 'weak anthropocentrism', and concern ourselves with rational human preferences and thus with human interests much more broadly conceptualised.[3] As we shall see, different versions of this broad approach to human interests have been developed by others, with considerable cogency.

One such philosopher is Janna Thompson, who suggests that natural entities are valuable because they enhance our lives, either through our living in harmony with nature, or through our appreciation of natural processes for what they are.[4] At the same time Thompson berates what she calls 'environmental ethics' for locating intrinsic value in non-sentient creatures, suggesting that those who do so cannot consistently stop short of locating it in machines or in rocks as well; the paper in which she does so is entitled 'A Refutation of Environmental Ethics'. Clearly Thompson does not regard philosophers who are either anthropocentrists or sentientists (people such as Peter Singer and such as herself who restrict moral standing to sentient creatures only) as environmental ethicists at all. But most people have sensibly ignored this implicit terminological suggestion, and have included among environmental ethicists those arguing in environmental contexts for any of the possible range of normative stances concerning moral standing (including that of Thompson herself).

As for Thompson's substantive claim, there is a good reply in Kenneth Goodpaster's point (made in 1978) that it makes no sense to ascribe moral standing to things that lack a good of their own, such as rocks and machines, since they cannot be harmed or benefited (as opposed to merely being damaged or reconstructed), but that it makes much better sense to ascribe it to living organisms, since these really do have a good of their own, can be healthy or unhealthy, and can be harmed or benefited accordingly.[5] So Thompson's

[3] Bryan Norton, 'Environmental Ethics and Weak Anthropocentrism', *Environmental Ethics*, **6** (1984), 131–148; Bryan Norton, 'Why I am Not a Non-Anthropocentrist: Callicott and the Failure of Monistic Inherentism', *Environmental Ethics*, **17** (1995), 341–358.

[4] Janna Thompson, 'A Refutation of Environmental Ethics', *Environmental Ethics*, **12** (1990), 147–160.

[5] Kenneth E. Goodpaster, 'On Being Morally Considerable', *Journal of Philosophy*, **75** (1978), 308–325.

argument for the necessity of stopping short at sentientism miscarries, as would any attempt on the part of anthropocentrists to borrow it to suggest that non-anthropocentrists have no basis for denying moral standing to anything. However, it should be remarked that although she could be construed as criticising the normative stances of the first wave of environmental ethicists, she was not seeking to defend anthropocentrism, as opposed to sentientism. Many others, however, have explicitly espoused anthropocentrism. Thus Peter Carruthers writes: 'For we ought to be able to see clearly that it is only the sufferings of humans that have moral standing',[6] while parallel stances have been taken in the field of animal ethics by R.G. Frey [7] and by Michael Leahy.[8] Besides Norton, other environmental philosophers have adopted recognisable variants of his weak anthropocentrism, including Eugene C. Hargrove [9] and Mark Sagoff.[10]

Before I turn to further forms of anthropocentrism that can be construed as developing Norton's appeal to broad human interests, a moment should be spent on a different basis which some regard as supportive of anthropocentrism, namely the claim that it is human valuations that make valuable whatever has value, and that for that reason ascriptions of value must all be regarded as somehow anthropocentric. For my part, I do not accept the premise of this argument, as I cannot accept that it is human judgements that contribute the value to whatever is valuable, or, come to that, the disvalue of whatever is correspondingly bad. Thus animal pain surely had as much negative value before there were humans to declare it so or make it so as it does now; there again, health would be valuable even if it went unnoticed, or even if all valuers had fallen into a deep sleep and ceased to perform valuations.

But that is not the key point. What we need to avoid here is conflating two separate issues. One of these is the normative issue, of anthropocentrism versus its contraries, concerned with the bearers of moral standing and related questions. Quite a different issue is that of what

[6] Peter Carruthers, *The Animals Issue* (Cambridge: Cambridge University Press, 1992), 169.

[7] R.G. Frey, *Rights, Killing and Suffering: Moral Vegetarianism and Applied Ethics* (Oxford: Basil Blackwell, 1983).

[8] Michael P.T. Leahy, *Against Liberation: Putting Animals in Perspective* (London: Routledge, 1991).

[9] Eugene C. Hargrove, *Foundations of Environmental Ethics* (Englewood Cliffs, NJ: Prentice-Hall, 1989).

[10] Mark Sagoff, *The Economy of the Earth* (Cambridge: Cambridge University Press, 1989).

confers value on its bearers, and whether claims about such value are grounded in human judgements or not. This second issue is a meta-ethical issue, and not at all a normative one. Hence even if someone believes that all value is generated by human judgements, this gives them no reason at all to be anthropocentric, and hold that humans alone have moral standing and that human interests are the only interests that matter. To avoid confusion, another term is needed for the claim that value is generated by human judgements. A suitable term was devised by a philosopher who all but adheres to that view, J. Baird Callicott; such value is, he claims, 'anthropogenic'. (This is of course, the same word as has more recently been used to recognise that global warming is largely humanly generated, a topic to which other speakers in this series are due to return.) As Callicott recognises, an anthropogenic view of value (such as he half-endorses) does not begin to support an anthropocentric stance which (rightly in my view) he opposes. However, since Callicott wants to recognise that other mammals also perform valuations, he ends up preferring the view that values are not strictly anthropogenic but (what he calls) 'vertebragenic'.[11] But this refinement relates to meta-ethics, and need not detain us. The relevant point is rather that no meta-ethical claim (such an the anthropogenic theory of value) supplies grounds for anthropocentrism, and thus that any sympathies we may have for this theory should not incline us to adopt a normative anthropocentric view. (As if to epitomise this, Callicott has persistently opposed Norton's normative anthropocentrism.)

2. Aristotelian Approaches

It is time now to review how Norton's appeal to a broad understanding of human interests has been enlarged upon by other anthropocentric theorists. Such theorists needed a reply to Richard Routley's thought-experiment about the Last Man, the sole survivor of a nuclear catastrophe, who has only hours to live, and who, in setting about a tree with an axe without any possibility of benefitting either himself or anyone else (since everyone else has died) is still usually thought to be acting wrongly. Routley's verdict is effectively that our judgement that the Last Man's act is wrong is best diagnosed as suggesting that we presuppose that the tree matters for itself, or has moral standing, or (as it is sometimes put) that its continued thriving

[11] J. Baird Callicott, 'Rolston on Intrinsic Value: A Deconstruction', *Environmental Ethics*, **14** (1992), 129–143.

has intrinsic value, although I will seek to sidestep the controversies surrounding the notion of intrinsic value for present purposes. John Benson seeks to avoid adopting this diagnosis, and suggests instead that what makes the Last Man's act wrong is that he harms himself.[12] To vindicate this view, he might well need to show that people's well-being depends on the integrity of their character, as many Aristotelians hold. But this view seems heroic, because it effectively denies the possibility that 'the wicked' can 'flourish as the green bay-tree' while remaining wicked; well-being and character seem not to be quite as closely related as Benson requires. Thus Routley's response seemingly remains intact, as long as we stipulate on his behalf that there are no other sentient creatures remaining alive and liable to be benefited by the act of the Last Man.

Another anthropocentric response to Routley's kind of position has been made in the more explicit Aristotelianism of John O'Neill, who makes the flourishing of most living creatures constitutive of human well-being (including, presumably, that of the Last Man). Human good involves the development of characteristic human faculties and capacities, granted the presence of suitable objects and circumstances. Thus 'the flourishing of many other living things ought to be promoted because they are constitutive of our own flourishing', just as, according to Aristotle himself, caring for friends for their own sake is constitutive of the flourishing of the friend who cares about them.[13] (A closely similar position is adopted in the recent monograph of O'Neill, Alan Holland and Andrew Light entitled *Environmental Values*.[14]) The last man's act of vandalism shows him to be living a life below the level that is best for a human being, because he fails to care for, but instead destroys, one of the creatures constitutive of his own good.[15]

These claims about what constitutes a flourishing human life, as O'Neill recognizes, have to be defended. The most promising approach, he suggests, is an appeal to the claim that a good human life requires a breadth of goods, far richer than, for example, egoism could recognize. The connection with care for the natural world turns out to consist in the fact that the recognition and promotion of natural goods as ends in themselves involve just such an

[12] John Benson, *Environmental Ethics: An Introduction with Readings* (London and New York: Routledge, 2000).

[13] John O'Neill, *Ecology, Policy and Politics* (London: Routledge, 1993), 24.

[14] John O'Neill, Alan Holland and Andrew Light, *Environmental Values* (London and New York: Routledge, 2008), 120–121.

[15] O'Neill, *Ecology, Policy and Politics*, 24.

enrichment.[16] Further, when our powers of perception are extended through disinterested study of natural creatures, as in science and art, characteristic human powers are developed thereby,[17] and this is also a component of human well-being.[18]

O'Neill recognizes that this is an anthropocentric ethic, but regards it as not objectionably so, since nonhuman creatures for which people care are not being treated as means or instrumentally. According to this ethic, adults would teach children to care for many (but not all) natural entities for their own sake, but the ultimate object would be not the good of the natural objects of such care but the good of the children. Human good would supply the sole basis for concern for nature, and thus the sole underlying motivation for such care as well.

This account of human good captures some important truths. One is its Aristotelian emphasis on human flourishing involving the development of human capacities, including the capacities for disinterested love, care and friendship. O'Neill would need to supply far more argument to make it seem plausible that all our obligations could actually be derived from our living a flourishing life; but any credible ethic needs a defensible conception of such a life, and O'Neill's account contributes to such a conception, particularly with respect to his claim that a good human life requires a breadth of goods. Having argued elsewhere for a detailed version of an Aristotelian conception of human flourishing, incorporating non-distinctive or generic goods such as physical health as well as distinctive human excellences such as practical wisdom,[19] I welcome O'Neill's general account of human good. Thus it well supplements those of Thompson and of Benson.

There is also good reason to welcome aspects of O'Neill's treatment of the problem of motivation for caring for nature. For the recognition and promotion of natural goods really can comprise an enrichment, as well as contributing a sense of proportion and a heightened sensitivity, and so the argument that caring for nature benefits human beings has substance for at least some cases. But this argument also has its limits, where such caring for nature is in competition with

[16] Ibid., 24–25.

[17] Ibid., 81.

[18] Ibid., 161.

[19] Robin Attfield, *A Theory of Value and Obligation* (London, New York and Sydney: Croom Helm, 1987), chs 3 and 4; *Value, Obligation and Meta-Ethics* (Amsterdam and Atlanta, GA: Éditions Rodopi, 1995), chs 4 and 5.

other sources of benefit, just as there are limits to the argument against ethical egoism that caring for others characteristically produces net benefits for the carer. (For while it characteristically produces benefits, there are also predictable and persistent costs, and so the claim that it characteristically produces net benefits is an exaggeration.) Indeed caring for nature sometimes accompanies alienation from human society. Nevertheless there is merit in O'Neill's argument, which supplies one possible answer to the question 'Why should I care?'

However, the theories holding that care for natural goods is constitutive of a flourishing human life (let us call this 'the constitutiveness theory') and that this is why we should care for and promote these goods (I will call this 'the motivation theory') are open to criticism. Thus while recognition and promotion of natural goods enrich our lives, so too could awareness of quite different ranges of objects of wonder, from mineral gemstones to synthetic gemstones, or again of human performances from sport to ballet. If what is needed for enrichment and a flourishing life is a breadth of goods, cultivation of natural goods is just one of the options, which could be replaced by cultivation of a range of languages or a range of sports or artistic activities, and which could accordingly be discarded as soon as a conflict with clashing human interests arises. Similarly, spiritual fulfilment does not invariably require promotion of natural goods either, as a whole range of other modes and varieties are available. Relatedly, while the development (or 'extension') of our powers of perception normally contributes to human flourishing, this does not require the objects of perception themselves to be flourishing; indeed some branches of science, such as pathology, require the opposite. Even the science of ecology, for which a study of well-functioning systems is central, can develop the powers of its participants in observing declining or disappearing species, or through studying the detrimental effects of climate change.

Besides, human flourishing, as I have argued elsewhere,[20] does not require the development of every one of a person's characteristic human capacities, although it does plausibly require that of most. Although blindness and lameness are liabilities, we would not deny that someone was flourishing or leading a rounded and fulfilling life simply because she was either blind or lame. And even if we are lovers of classical music or of sculpture, we would surely have to allow that people could be flourishing who are unmoved by (or blind to) sculpture, or deaf to the delights of classical music. So

[20] Attfield, *Value, Obligation and Meta-Ethics*, 45–62.

even if the attainment of certain kinds of perception, sensitivity or contemplation relating to nature comprise fulfilments or developments of capacities that would contribute (in conjunction with a range of other fulfilments) to a person's flourishing, it cannot be inferred from their atrophy or their under-development that a person is failing to flourish; for a range of their other powers (of physical prowess, of wit, of musical or artistic performance, or of other kinds of sensitivity such as empathy for friends) might be sufficiently developed as readily to compensate for the apparent deficiency and to undermine this conclusion. But if so, the constitutiveness theory fails, both in itself, and as underpinning for the motivation theory, since neither natural goods nor care for them are, strictly speaking, constitutive of a flourishing human life. To affirm that they are thus constitutive is, I suggest, wishful thinking. Indeed I can think of a philosopher apparently leading a flourishing life who professes no interest whatever in such natural goods.

Similarly, while a reflective awareness of nature's otherness can provide the benefits already mentioned, a comparative unawareness of it (as in failure to reflect on the world of nature at all) need not spell lack of perspective or absence of a sense of proportion. For these benefits could be derived from other sources, such as human conversation, reading novels and biographies, experience of life's vicissitudes, or simply humorous exchanges. Such unawareness certainly need not betoken egoism, from which we may be rescued, for example, through participation in all kinds of inter-human relationships. Hence, while some basic awareness of nature's otherness may be a precondition of human life and thus human well-being, explicit or reflective awareness of this otherness cannot be regarded as constitutive of or essential to human flourishing, even though it can importantly contribute to such a life. Once again, there is certainly no reason why everyone should care or needs to care about natural goods or to seek to promote them; yet this is what environmentally enlightened versions of anthropocentrism ultimately need to show.

The gap between arguments from human flourishing and reasons to care about natural goods becomes apparent in further ways. Let it be granted that some natural goods are somehow constitutive of particular people's flourishing. (This could be because of the contingency that they care about a particular childhood haunt or pet animal, and would become desolate or even fall apart if the haunt were destroyed or the pet were to die.) Even so, not enough natural goods are plausibly constitutive of the flourishing of enough people for this to comprise a sufficiently pervasive reason for their protection or preservation. For even if all so far explored places and all known species were cared about by at least someone, it is fairly certain that unexplored places (such as the ocean depths and the waters beneath the Antarctic icecap) and undiscovered species (including the species in these places, and probably towards some thirty million others located in places such as tropical forests and coral reefs) are not constitutive of anyone's flourishing. Nor, in the many cases where just a few people care about a species, is regard for these people likely to comprise a strong enough ground to outweigh the benefits likely to arise to humanity from building on the habitat or site on which the species depends for its survival. Some of the grounds for preserving species, admittedly, turn on future interests. But the present point remains clear: the particular argument from natural goods being constitutive of the flourishing of current human beings cannot supply grounds for preserving enough nonhuman creatures. O'Neill suggests no more than that it supplies grounds for the preservation of 'a large number';[21] but its scope turns out not remotely to correspond to the range of creatures that environmentalists and environmental ethicists would standardly wish to preserve.

The same gap emerges if we reflect on the future of nonhuman species after the demise of humanity. While the future of humanity may stretch to millions of years, that of nonhuman life could possibly extend to trillions. But the posthuman flourishing of nonhuman creatures is unlikely to be constitutive of the flourishing of many people, present or future, if of any. So the argument from human flourishing (including that of future people) supplies insufficient grounds to facilitate the posthuman survival and flourishing of other creatures through human protection of nonhuman species from extinction in the last few generations of human existence. Human actions could well make a difference to the survival of many kinds of nonhuman life across vast eras of the posthuman future, but arguments from human flourishing would seem to have little or no bearing on such actions.

A related issue arises without any need for a thought-experiment, that of how to account on an anthropocentric basis for the wrongness of cruelty to animals, and neglect of the animals in one's charge. Anthropocentrists have to claim that this is entirely grounded in human welfare, and largely in the difference made either to the flourishing or the character of the human agent concerned. But we do not need to know whether the agent's well-being or character suffers or degenerates to know that such cruelty or neglect is wrong, and this

[21] O'Neill, op. cit., note 13, 24; O'Neill, Holland and Light, op. cit., note 14, 120–121.

would seem to be because the animals' suffering matters in itself, irrespective of effects on the agent. While this is not an objection to sentientism (and thus to Thompson's position), it is a formidable problem for anthropocentrist efforts to make human well-being, however broadly construed, the sole criterion of ethics. O'Neill, Holland, Light and Benson are right to remind us of the breadth of human flourishing and of its far-reaching environmental implications, but environmental ethics (and normative ethics in general) has reason to appeal directly to nonhuman flourishing as well, to account for standard, everyday judgements in these and other areas. These considerations also serve to refute the claim made by Norton that non-anthropocentric considerations are superfluous because they merely uphold the same judgements as anthropocentric ones, and add nothing that is distinctive of their own.[22]

Normative ethics, then, cannot be confined to considerations of human flourishing and related interests; nor, I now want to argue, can human motivation. The motivation theory, it will be recollected, holds that the reason why we should care for and promote natural goods consists in human flourishing (of which these goods are supposedly constitutive), and is often defended on the basis that there can be no other reason for doing this. But this basis should itself be questioned. In one version it suggests that reasons for action always turn on the well-being of the agent herself. But if so, it would make little sense to appeal (as environmentalists regularly do) to the well-being of future generations, and it would be difficult to understand people who devote themselves to the well-being of other people, or of other species, or of causes that transcend their lifetime. It would also be difficult to make sense of genuine friendship, with its concern for the friend for her or his own sake. While, as Aristotle held, such friendship may be constitutive of human well-being, this kind of friendship cannot be entered into or fostered solely for the sake of one's own flourishing. Maybe, as Ernest Partridge has argued, human beings have a need for self-transcendence, for commitment, that is, to concerns and causes that transcend their own interests.[23] But commitments of this kind are not standardly undertaken to gratify this need, and could not in the normal course of events be undertaken on this basis. For if they were undertaken on

[22] Bryan Norton, *Towards Unity among Environmentalists* (New York and Oxford: Oxford University Press, 1991).

[23] Ernest Partridge, 'Why Care about the Future?', in Partridge (ed.), *Responsibilities to Future Generations: Environmental Ethics* (Buffalo: Prometheus, 1981), 203–220.

this basis, this very need could not be gratified. Motivation, then, does not have to appeal to the well-being of the agent. (Much less, as O'Neill shrewdly remarks, does it need to appeal to identification with what the agent cares about; we can be just as concerned about what we regard as other than ourselves as with our own selves, however broadly 'selves' are construed.)[24]

A less implausible version of the claim that human flourishing underlies all motivation holds that reasons for action always turn on the well-being of one or another human being, who need not be the agent in question. This version is less implausible than the egoistic version because (unlike the other) it can explain motivations like friendship, patriotism and loyalty to a good many campaigns and causes. But it fails to account for behaviour motivated by concern for the welfare of animals (except where there are social reasons for such concern, such as the contracts of a veterinarian with her human clients). For example, it fails to account for the motivations of most members of the pressure group Compassion in World Farming. Similarly it fails to account for the disinterested concerns of preservationists, who are not invariably seeking to preserve their own local environment, but often seek to protect spatially distant ones, and not invariably for the sake of any humans that may be affected at that.

As O'Neill recognizes, there is widespread concern for natural creatures for their own sake. While it is true that this does not of itself show that the well-being of these creatures has independent value, the preceding discussion shows that there must be reasons for this concern independent of the well-being of the people who have the concern, and that there can be reasons altogether independent of the well-being of human beings. Further, the analogy with friendship suggests that there can be unconditional concern (which need not be grounded in one's own good) for the good of the other: of the friend, or, in this case, of the creatures concerned. We do humanity a disservice when we pretend that nothing can stir us to action apart from members of our own species and their well-being.

Nor must theories of motivation be confined to the interests of sentient species, or of species with a point of view. Thus the concerns of preservationists are not so restricted; and the Last Man thought-experiment (discussed above) may well be thought to suggest that there is something of intrinsic value, that is, some independent reason for protection, attached to the continued flourishing of a tree.

24 O'Neill, op. cit., note 13, 149–151.

There is also Donald Scherer's thought-experiment. Compare a planet without life (which he names 'Lifeless') with a planet harbouring organisms with capacities for photosynthesis, reproduction and self-maintenance (which he calls 'Flora').[25] Even if neither planet has any potential to benefit sentient beings elsewhere in the universe (not even through aesthetic enjoyment), most people take the view that, while there is no value in Lifeless, there is value in Flora, and understand this as a reason to preserve Flora in the event of human plans to disrupt or destroy it. Flora cannot benefit these same people or other sentient beings, and yet its inhabitants are held to carry intrinsic value in a sense that comprises a reason or ground for action. Perhaps, then, we also do humanity a disservice if we pretend (with sentientists) that nothing can stir us to action apart from the interests of humans and other sentient beings.

It begins to look as if a non-anthropocentric and non-sentientist normative ethic is needed to accommodate the full range of reasons by which human beings are capable of being motivated. Far from being incoherent or vacuous or yielding no clear guidance, theories of normative ethics of these kinds are actually needed if natural goods are to be recognized and treated seriously, and if the pool of human motivation is not to be misrepresented as shallower than it is. We may also conclude, with Thompson, O'Neill and Benson, that human well-being (involving as it does the development of most if not all characteristic human capacities) supplies a broad basis for many kinds of environmental concern, albeit not a comprehensive or all-encompassing one.

3. Other Approaches

However, other philosophical approaches might seem to confer a greater cogency, or even inescapability, on anthropocentrism. Thus one version of anthropocentrism is simply the thesis that we, as human beings, cannot help making all our valuations with human faculties and from a human perspective. Frederick Ferré has named this harmless claim 'perspectival anthropocentrism'.[26] But this harmless and almost tautological stance, which is sometimes regarded

[25] Donald Scherer, 'Anthropocentrism, Atomism and Environmental Ethics', in Donald Scherer and Thomas Attig (eds), *Ethics and the Environment* (Englewood Cliffs, NJ: Prentice-Hall, 1983), 73–81.

[26] Frederick Ferré, 'Personalistic Organicism: Paradox or Paradigm?', in Robin Attfield and Andrew Belsey (eds), *Philosophy and the Natural*

as a vindication of anthropocentrism in general, is far removed from the claim of normative anthropocentrism that only human interests matter, and gives it no shred of support. For human valuers remain free to take nonhuman interests seriously, such as the interests of other primates, despite reasoning within a human perspective. We just need to take care and avoid conflating harmless perspectival anthropocentrism with its normative homonym, just as turns out to be possible when we distinguish anthropocentrism and its non-relation, the anthropogenic theory of value.

Yet others reason inductively to the near-inevitability of adherence to anthropocentrism from its pervasive presence among those who seek to escape it. Thus Eric Katz finds anthropocentrism lurking beneath the surface in the writings of Deep Ecologists, and particularly those who stress the identification of the self and nature, understood as one's greater Self.[27] For example, some Deep Ecologists reason as follows. I have a duty to protect myself. But properly understood, nature and myself are one and the same thing, my greater Self. (Let us for present purposes not question this far-reaching claim.) Therefore I have a duty to protect nature or the biosphere against whatever may be attacking or endangering it. Here Katz is surely right, for the reason given for protecting nature consists in the importance of protecting a human self. Indeed the argument is not only anthropocentric, but is also an appeal to ethical egoism, while at the same time inviting us to suspend our disbelief in there being no boundaries between oneself and the rest of nature. In this and other ways Katz seems to vindicate his claim, where Deep Ecology is concerned.

However, this gives us no reason to conclude that normative anthropocentrism is inevitable. Indeed Katz has also argued, jointly with Lauren Oechsli, that a nonanthropocentric ethic is needed to justify the protection of the rainforest of Brazil, which must be protected not only as a resource, let alone instrumentally, but because of the value of its constituent creatures;[28] human interests, they suggest,

---

Environment (Cambridge, New York and Melbourne: Cambridge University Press, 1994), 59–73, at 72.

[27] Eric Katz, 'Against the Inevitability of Anthropocentrism', in Eric Katz, Andrew Light and David Rothenburg (eds), *Beneath the Surface: Critical Essays in the Philosophy of Deep Ecology* (Cambridge, MA and London: MIT Press, 2000), 17–42.

[28] Eric Katz and Lauren Oechsli, 'Moving Beyond Anthropocentrism: Environmental Ethics, Development and the Amazon', *Environmental Ethics*, **15** (1993), 49–59.

are insufficient alone, even when scientific and aesthetic interests are taken into account. Katz and Oechsli do not put forward a specific value-theory, nor am I defending any such specific theory here, despite holding one. Yet their stance illustrates how a normative theory not grounded solely in human interests is possible and can be taken seriously.

Katz and Oechsli have been well criticised in the recent work mentioned earlier by the trio of O'Neill, Holland and Light, *Environmental Values*. Katz and Oechsli seek to make our direct duties to the rainforest at least tie-breakers to debates between the human interests in preservation on the one hand and development on the other, and effectively trumps which override considerations based on human interests altogether. But, as the trio reply, even if nonanthropocentric values are recognised, the tug between the competing claims of intra-human justice and of human well-being would still be felt. Thus nonanthropocentrism should not be regarded as a new ethical theory that somehow supersedes all our traditional moral perplexities.[29] Katz and Oechsli partially recognise this themselves when, in their concluding remarks, they accept that western countries which expect Brazil to hold back from development to preserve its rainforests are also obliged to compensate Brazil with financial assistance.[30] Yet their critics could continue to ask why the value of the rainforest is taken to resolve the debate about preservation of itself, and to relegate the debate about inter-human equity to a subsequent and subordinate phase of deliberation.

Yet the value of the rainforest and of its constituent creatures should, as Katz and Oechsli affirm, figure in such debates, not only because of the impact of their continuation or extinction on human interests, but for themselves. It is one thing to show that the distinctive elements of nonanthropocentrism cannot be regarded as trumping all other considerations; it is quite another to maintain, as the trio appear to do, that there is no place for those distinctive considerations at all, on the ground that 'the everyday human scale of values', which they interpret as involving anthropocentrism, is sufficient.[31] Human needs, admittedly, sometimes override those of nonhumans; but it by no means follows that nonhuman needs can be ignored. Given, as the trio assert, that there are competing values, issues will not be better resolved by disregarding any of them; and in any case the everyday human values of many human traditions have plausibly included

29 O'Neill, Holland and Light, op. cit., note 14, 179–182.
30 Katz and Oechsli, op. cit., note 28, 58–59.
31 O'Neill, Holland and Light, op. cit., note 14, 179–180.

recognition of the standing and the value of nonhuman creatures all along.[32] It is not anthropocentrism, with its humanity-only approach, that reflects the full range of 'the human scale of values', but non-anthropocentrism. We need a comprehensive ethic, and no ethic will be comprehensive unless it is non-anthropocentric.

Two other prominent British philosophers have recently discussed human values, with contrasting conclusions about environmental values and nonanthropocentrism. The answer given by Bernard Williams to his own question 'Must a Concern for the Environment Be Centred on Human Beings?' (which is also the title of an essay of his) is affirmative; environmental values need not be restricted to human interests, but they must still reflect 'human values', values, that is, which human beings can 'understand themselves as pursuing and respecting'.[33] According to Williams, however, these values probably do not answer to non-human interests, since in his view few such interests have any 'claim' on us, and those that do not are morally irrelevant.

But there is a large implicit assumption here: human beings cannot understand themselves as pursuing or respecting the interests of most non-human creatures. Common experience casts doubt on this suggestion (sufficiently to sustain the credibility of non-anthropocentrism in some of its versions). Instead, Williams considers that our 'Promethean fear' of nature and its sublimity encodes further values concerning the independence of nature as backdrop of human life and as a source of limits to the possibility of controlling it. Perhaps for some this psychological story rings true, but the basis of these further values remains unilluminated. Williams does not explicitly claim that environmental concern rests largely on values grounded in preserving the framework of human culture and agency, as opposed to seeking to discredit theories of a contrary tendency. If, however, someone were to make this claim, it would give humanity-focused theorists an unduly self-preoccupied stance. Perhaps this claim embodies an aspect of the truth; but the implicit suggestion that human beings can only understand themselves as pursuing or respecting either their own interests or the conditions

[32] See Robin Attfield, *The Ethics of Environmental Concern* (Oxford: Blackwell and New York: Columbia University Press, 1983), chs 2 and 3.

[33] Bernard Williams, 'Must a Concern for the Environment Be Centred on Human Beings?' in Bernard Williams, *Making Sense of Humanity and Other Philosophical Papers, 1982–1993* (Cambridge: Cambridge University Press, 1995), 233–240, at 234.

of their own agency has only to be articulated to be exposed for the exaggeration that it is.

While Williams seems close to anthropocentrism, David Wiggins, who is billed as a later contributor to this series, interprets similar ground with wider sympathies. In an address to the Aristotelian Society, Wiggins has developed Williams's themes of human values and nature's sublimity, stressing that 'the human scale of values' extends far enough beyond 'human values' (a phrase used by Wiggins to mean 'values that concern human flourishing')[34], to include disinterested concern for the survival and well-being of wild creatures, and generally 'the great framework for a life on earth in which ... human beings can find meaning'[35], but which has latterly become vulnerable. This is a profound paper, imaginatively supportive of green concerns (far more so than Williams), despite Wiggins' understandable scepticism about some forms of environmental ethics and metaphysics; and in recognising values that transcend human flourishing, Wiggins clearly interprets his own phrase 'the human scale of values' in a non-anthropocentric manner, and thus moves himself decisively beyond anthropocentrism.

Yet Wiggins' paper could be read as implying that human environmental concern (and 'the human scale of values'), apart from its 'disinterested concern for wild creatures' (which might possibly concern sentient creatures only), is confined to this framework alone, that is 'the great framework for a life on earth in which ... human beings can find meaning', as opposed to other frameworks (such as Scherer's planet Flora) related to other worlds, where no human has ever found meaning or perhaps will or ever could find it. But even if no human could ever find meaning there, it is by no means apparent that Flora (with its trees and other plants) has no independent value, and should not be spared destruction if this were ever to become an option for humanity; indeed this point is enough of itself to undermine Norton's claim that exactly the same actions and policies are dictated by anthropocentric as by non-anthropocentric principles. The same applies to the forms of life on our own planet that may well outlive humanity, and thus become a sphere where, because of human extinction, no human could ever live a meaningful life; for it might well become an option for human beings before the demise of our species to preclude the survival of such post-human life, and yet there could be reasons consisting in

[34] David Wiggins, 'Nature, Respect for Nature, and the Human Scale of Values', *Proceedings of the Aristotelian Society*, New Series, **C** (2000), 1–32, at 8.

[35] Ibid., 10; cf. 18.

its independent value not to prevent such life, despite the absence of possibilities for humans of finding meaning there. Making our duties depend on possibilities of meaning for humans (which may, however, be a misreading of Wiggins' intentions) could ensnare us in a covert anthropocentrism all over again. So it is possible for even sophisticated attempts to explore and sift anthropocentrism to fail to distinguish truisms (such as 'all our values are human values'), together with their apparent implications, from traps (such as 'our ethical concerns are confined to what benefits us or makes our lives meaningful'). Where normative principles are at stake, we need to respect not only human beings and their interests, but also forms of life that are other than ourselves, whether they are sentient or not, and whether or not we can identify with them.

None of this suggests that we should give ethical priority to remote species, let alone to distant planets, ahead of humanity. Little that I have said relates to such matters of priorities, although it could be applied so as to do so. What is more to the point is the conclusion that without concern for the living nonhuman beings of the present and the future we unduly narrow our own horizons. It is not just that these creatures matter for themselves, or will matter if allowed to come into being, but that our failure to respect them can distort our own humanity, albeit in the name of humanism, and lead us into too narrow an understanding of what we are capable of, and thus of ourselves.

Cardiff University

Foundations of a General Ethics: Selves, Sentient Beings, and Other Responsively Cohesive Structures

WARWICK FOX

1. A World of Forms of Organization or Structures

Everything we can refer to – physical, biological, psychological, or a human-created entity, institution, activity, or expression of some kind, and whether constituted of brute physical stuff or less tangible complexes of social arrangements, ideas, images, movements, and so on – can be considered in terms of its form of organization or structure. This applies even if what we want to say about these things is that they represent a disorganized or unstructured example of their kind or else that they simply lack any discernible form of internal organization or structure in the sense that their internal structure is undifferentiated or homogenous as opposed to being 'all over the place'. We therefore live in a world in which everything can be characterized, either positively or negatively, in terms of its form of organization or structure. (The terms 'form of organization' and 'structure' can be used interchangeably in the context of this paper, although I will tend to use the term 'structure' in what follows.)

Many structures possess an externally observable form only, whereas others, including ourselves, possess, in addition, an inner, experiential dimension. Moreover, the development of neuroscience allows us to assert that this inner, experiential dimension – however complex or rudimentary it might be in any given instance – is not some kind of fundamentally separate metaphysical 'add-on' that just happens to be bestowed upon or attached to certain structures, but is rather a function of the workings *of* these structures. These structures therefore possess not only an objectively specifiable *form* but also an experiential capacity, which, when not dormant, issues in the occurrent experiential (or, in a broad construal of the term, mental) *content* of that structure.

I am grateful to Isis Brook, Simon Hailwood, and Antony Radford for discussions relating to the theory of responsive cohesion.

doi:10.1017/S1358246111000208

We often find it convenient to refer to structures that possess only a tangible, physical form as (mere) *things* and to structures that possess a tangible, physical form that issues in an inner, experiential dimension as *beings*. As Thomas Nagel has taught us to say, it is 'like' something – it *feels* like something – to be a *being* whereas it is not 'like' anything to be a *thing*.[1] Ethicists mark this distinction in terms of the concept of *sentience*, the capacity to feel: (mere) things are nonsentient whereas beings are sentient. However, we also need to note that there are other kinds of structures in the world besides mere things on the one hand and beings on the other hand. Specifically, there are all the intangible – or at least less tangible – kinds of structures that we routinely refer in to in everyday life, ranging from examples such as the mess on my desk or the kind and degree of order in my thoughts and feelings to the structure of a conversation, theory, drama, or piece of music. We could call these non-thing-like (or at least less-thing-like) and non-being-like structures *complexes*. If we do this, then we can say that the class of structures in general – which is to say everything we can refer to – consists of (intangible) complexes, (tangible) things, and beings. In what follows I will be primarily interested in the distinction between *mere structures* (regardless of whether they assume the tangible form of 'things' or the intangible form of 'complexes') and *beings*.

Within the class of sentient beings themselves, some beings are merely sentient whereas some are conscious *of* their sentient existence or 'inner life'. Beings that are merely sentient experience things in a first-order, moment-to-moment way but do not possess any higher-order consciousness of this fact. Thus, they are not self-aware in any given moment, let alone aware of their own existence in a temporally extended sense. This means that whatever other kinds of implicit memory retention capacities these beings might have, they do not possess what is discussed in the literature as autobiographical memory; they do not constitute autobiographical selves with a personal past, a personal present, a projected personal future, and an awareness that their autobiographical awareness will eventually cease to exist, which is to say an awareness of their own death. In contrast, some sentient beings are aware of their own existence in a temporally extended sense; they possess autobiographical memory and can be characterized as autobiographical selves. It is useful to mark the distinction between these two kinds of beings by

[1] Thomas Nagel's famous 1974 essay 'What Is it Like to Be a Bat?' is reprinted in his collection *Mortal Questions* (Cambridge: Cambridge University Press, Canto ed., 1991), 165–180.

referring to the former as (mere) *sentient beings* and the latter as *selves*.[2]

Epistemologically speaking, there is a crucial difference between sentient beings and selves on the one hand and mere structures on the other hand. As selves we are capable of coming to know – indeed, we can only truly come to know – the nature and value of both sentience and selfhood 'from the inside' whereas we can only come to know the nature and value of structures *per se* (including our own externally observable structure) 'from the outside'. The former perspective has been variously referred to as a first-person, personal, subjective, or internal view or perspective and the latter as a third-person, impersonal, objective, or external view or perspective. Since I want to refer to both selves and other sentient beings in terms of these perspectives, it makes sense to avoid the confusing semantic interference effects that can arise by referring to the inner life of *nonhuman* sentient beings from a 'first-person' or 'personal' perspective, or even from a 'subjective' perspective (since the notion of subjectivity is often associated with the idea of the kind of self-aware subjectivity exhibited by 'persons'). I will therefore simply distinguish these perspectives by referring to them as 'internal' and 'external' perspectives respectively.[3] We can therefore say that although I, a fruit bat (*Megachiroptera*), and a cricket bat can all be viewed from an external perspective, a cricket bat can *only* be viewed from an external perspective whereas we can also

[2] Two points here. First, for an overview of the emerging range of evidence that suggests that beings really do divide into two groups like this, see Warwick Fox, *A Theory of General Ethics: Human Relationships, Nature, and the Built Environment* (Cambridge, MA: The MIT Press, 2006), chs 6–8. See also Derek Penn, Keith Holyoak, and Daniel Povinelli, 'Darwin's Mistake: Explaining the Discontinuity between Human and Nonhuman Minds', *Behavioral and Brain Sciences* **31** (2008): 109–178. Second, ethicists have tended to use the term 'persons' rather than 'selves' in this context. However, although the evidence – more of which I will cite in the concluding section – suggests that people are the only selves we currently know of, there seems to be no reason in principle why there might not be other selves elsewhere in the universe or created by people here on Earth. The term 'persons' – even in the wider sense that some ethicists want to give it (i.e. to cover nonhuman selves) – therefore seems increasingly archaic and parochial, not to mention misleading to ordinary readers, so I prefer to use the term 'selves'.

[3] Thomas Nagel employs this form of the distinction in his influential essay 'Moral Luck', repr. in Nagel, op. cit., 24–38.

sensibly ask what I or a fruit bat is like from an internal perspective, which is to say from the perspective of being me or the fruit bat.

2. Approaching Ethics from the Internal Perspective: the Value of Selves and Sentient Beings

It would seem to be a relatively simple matter to provide a straightforward, naturalistic account of how this epistemological difference between sentient beings and selves on the one hand and mere structures on the other hand has played out in our ethical thinking. In the case of selves, we can say that our own immediate, inner awareness of the value of our own existence and well-being is (in the case of normal, healthy human beings) self-evident and self-validating. (It is self-evident because it is given to us in our immediate experience and it is self-validating because it requires no reference to anyone else to verify the fact of this self-evident matter; indeed, such reference to others would be pointless because others can only directly experience their own experience rather than our experience.) Beyond this, however, other sources of evidence overwhelmingly suggest to us that the same kind of evidence for the value of their existence also applies to everyone else. First, we know this through the explicit verbal – or other symbolically mediated (e.g. sign language) – reports of others. We are compulsive communicators ('mindsharers' in Merlin Donald's telling phrase[4]) who report the same self-evident and self-validating fact to each other in multitudinous ways. Second, we know it because these reports are reinforced by appropriate nonverbal behavior. Third – and this is surely the clincher – it is now undeniable that other people possess the same causal structure (namely, the same kind of central nervous system) that underpins the capacities for selfhood that we value in ourselves. When we put these sources of evidence together with the basic requirement for consistency in our reasoning (without which rational argumentation is not possible), then we are rationally compelled to accept the conclusion that it would be arbitrary to recognize the self-evident and self-validating value of our own existence and well-being but to deny it in the case of others. The mutual acceptance of this conclusion among rational selves in turn drives the development of a variety of implicitly or explicitly codified forms of interhuman ethics. These forms of ethics provide us with a set of reasonable

[4] Merlin Donald, *A Mind So Rare: The Evolution of Human Consciousness* (New York: W. W. Norton, 2001).

expectations to which others can hold us (formally codified as 'obligations') and to which we can hold others (sometimes codified as 'rights'). These expectations are in turn backed up by various kinds of social and legal sanctions whose legitimacy derives from the mutual recognition by rational selves of the value of each other's existence and well-being and whose purpose is to rehabilitate, punish, or deter those who transgress these mutually accepted expectations.

Ethically speaking, something like this position – reached in various historically, culturally, and intellectually influenced ways (all of which applies just as surely to the naturalistic account I have just given) – is how things have stood for a long time: from the time of the Greek philosophers until at least the 1970s, the various dominant versions of philosophical ethics have been overwhelming focused on the flourishing and wellbeing of selves, both individually and collectively, together with concomitant ideas of respect for selves. The upshot is that for most of Western intellectual history, 'ethics' has effectively meant 'human ethics'. This began to change in the 1970s with the difficult, historically late birth of 'environmental ethics', which was generally understood to refer to the study of the ethical relevance, if any, of the beings and entities that constituted the rest of nonhuman nature.

Some of the surest inroads here were made in regard to the moral status of other sentient beings. The fact that these arguments have seemed to many observers to be a on surer footing than a variety of others in environmental ethics is no doubt due to the fact that they have been able to draw on many of the same argumentative resources as those that have informed human ethics – all the more so in the light of the understandings we have been gaining from evolutionary biology, neuroscience, and comparative psychology. Thus, the kind of thinking that informs arguments in animal ethics can be accounted for in roughly similar naturalistic terms to the account I gave for the development of human ethics. First, even if we set aside our own, almost certainly unique, autobiographical sense of self, it remains the case that our own immediate, inner awareness tells us, among other things, that we especially do not like to be subject to pain and suffering. This understanding is again self-evident and self-validating. Second, we can, to a certain degree of refinement, explain both the evolutionary causal development and the existent causal structure of sentience in other animals. This means that we now have overwhelming reasons, based on the relative similarity of evolutionary paths and structure of central nervous systems, to believe that many other animals are sentient and, thus, that they are 'like us' and, conversely, that we are 'like them' to the extent that it would be self-evidently bad to be in their experiential state when they are subjected to any form of pain or suffering. Third, this understanding is reinforced by appropriate nonverbal behavior in nonhuman animals just as surely as it is in other humans.

The main difference in the accounts I have given of the thinking that underpins human ethics and animal ethics is that nonhuman animals cannot also reinforce our appreciation of their sentience in terms of linguistic behavior. (I have therefore referred to nonhuman animals elsewhere as 'iso-experients' – islands of experience – as opposed to 'mindsharers'.[5]) However, this also holds in regard to some categories of humans such as infants, prelingually deaf people who have not been exposed to sign language, wild or feral children who were never exposed to language, and people who have suffered global aphasia after stroke. Yet in none of these cases do we have sufficient reason to think that these people are not sentient; the other sources of evidence are overwhelming as they stand. Thus, coupled with the requirement for consistency in our reasoning, we seem again to be rationally compelled to accept the conclusion that it would be arbitrary to recognize the self-evident and self-validating disvalue of our own pain and suffering but to deny it in the case of other sentient beings. Moreover, the fact that this recognition is not mutual between selves and beings that are merely sentient hardly undermines this conclusion; rather, rational selves can readily appreciate the fact that *they* would not wish to be subjected to unnecessary pain and suffering if they were merely sentient and that *they* would want those who could understand this wish to respect it. In ethical contexts, this point is often referred to by asserting that *moral agents* have moral obligations in respect of not only other moral agents – or healthy, normally developed selves in the foregoing – but also *moral patients*, which, in the context of the discussion to this point, can be taken to include not only sentient nonhuman animals but also certain classes of humans themselves such as infants, those who have never gained language, people with serious dementia, the insane, and people with certain kinds of brain damage.

3. Taking the Internal Perspective too Far: Mere Structures

Beyond this point – or something very like it – environmental ethics is mired in controversy. I think that one reason for this is that a number

[5] Fox, op. cit., *passim*.

of environmental ethicists have tried to continue the tack of arguing along the lines that I have sketched for human ethics and animal ethics in which the internal perspective plays a fundamental role. Thus, those who argue for the value of nonsentient living things have tended to do so on the basis that these things internally embody (albeit in a *nonsentient* way) a 'will to live' (Albert Schweitzer), 'interests' (Kenneth Goodpaster, Robin Attfield), 'needs' (Gary Varner, Attfield), or a 'good of their own' such that 'Things that happen to them can be judged, *from their standpoint*, to be favorable or unfavorable to them' (Paul Taylor, my emphasis).[6] More subtly, Holmes Rolston has argued that a discriminatory ability has been built into living things by natural selection in the form of a 'normative' 'genetic set' that 'distinguishes between what *is* and what *ought to be*' such that the physical state that the organism 'defends' is a 'valued state'.[7] Some environmental ethicists have gone even further and attempted to extend these kinds of nonsentient versions of conativist arguments as far as entities or collectivities such as species, ecosystems, and the ecosphere itself.[8] However, Peter Singer, who insists that the criterion of sentience is 'the only defensible boundary of concern for the interests of others',[9] counters, effectively I think, that ethicists who employ these kinds of arguments

[6] For a general overview and critical introduction to Schweitzer's views, see Mary Anne Warren, *Moral Status: Obligations to Persons and Other Living Things* (New York: Oxford University Press, 2000), ch. 2; Kenneth Goodpaster, 'On Being Morally Considerable', repr. in Michael Zimmerman, gen. ed., *Environmental Philosophy: From Animal Rights to Radical Ecology*, 3rd ed. (Upper Saddle River, NJ: Prentice Hall, 2001), 56–70; Robin Attfield, 'The Good of Trees', repr. in David Schmidtz and Elizabeth Willott, eds, *Environmental Ethics: What Really Matters, What Really Works* (New York: Oxford University Press, 2002), 58–71; Gary Varner, *In Nature's Interests?: Interests, Animal Rights, and Environmental Ethics* (New York: Oxford University Press, 1998); Gary Varner, 'Biocentric Individualism', in Schmidtz and Willott, op. cit., 108–120; Paul Taylor, *Respect for Nature: A Theory of Environmental Ethics* (Princeton, NJ: Princeton University Press, 1986), 'standpoint' quotation, 63.

[7] Holmes Rolston III, 'Value in Nature and the Nature of Value', repr. in Andrew Light and Holmes Rolston III, eds, *Environmental Ethics: An Anthology* (Malden, MA: Blackwell, 2003), 145; Holmes Rolston III, 'Respect for Life: Counting What Singer Finds of no Account', in Dale Jamieson, ed., *Singer and his Critics* (Oxford: Blackwell, 1999), 251.

[8] Rolston, op. cit. (both papers); James Heffernan, 'The Land Ethic: A Critical Reappraisal', *Environmental Ethics* **4** (1982): 235–247.

[9] Peter Singer, Animal Liberation, 2nd ed. (London: Jonathan Cape, 1990), 9.

> ... use language metaphorically and then argue as if what they had said was literally true. We may often talk about plants 'seeking' water or light so that they can survive, and this way of thinking about plants makes it easier to accept talk of their 'will to live', or of them 'pursuing' their own good. But once we stop to reflect on the fact that plants are not conscious and cannot engage in any intentional behaviour, it is clear that all this language is metaphorical; one might just as well say that a river is pursuing its own good and striving to reach the sea, or that the 'good' of a guided missile is to blow itself up along with its target ... [In fact, however,] it is possible to give a purely physical explanation of what is happening; and in the absence of consciousness, there is no good reason why we should have greater respect for the physical processes that govern the growth and decay of living things than we have for those that govern nonliving things.[10]

Singer is, I think rightly, insisting here that all we have in the case of nonsentient natural entities is externally observable structures and, thus, that the attempt to adopt some kind of quasi-internal perspective is misplaced. However, where Singer goes wrong, I think, is in his equally adamant insistence that we have no moral obligations in respect of things that do not have 'interests', which is to say in respect of things that do not have an internal perspective, that are not sentient, that are merely structures. In order to explain this point I need to return to the epistemological difference I referred to earlier between the ways in which we can come to know the nature and value of selves and sentient beings on the one hand and structures on the other hand. Specifically, I noted that just as we can only truly come to know the nature and value of selfhood and sentience from an internal perspective, so we can only come to know the nature and value of mere structures from an external perspective. The upshot is that it is as pointless to look for the value of mere structures 'from the inside' – such as in terms of 'interests' or 'needs' that can be 'benefitted', 'frustrated', or 'harmed' – when they have no 'inside' as it is look for the value of sentient beings and selves 'from the outside' when these features exist only 'on the inside'. Thus, Singer's dismissal of the first-order moral relevance of mere structures strikes me as being as misplaced as a hard-line behaviourist's

[10] Peter Singer, *Practical Ethics*, 2nd ed. (Cambridge: Cambridge University Press, 1993), 279.

dismissal of conscious experience. Both are looking in the wrong place: it make no more sense to dismiss the potential value of mere structures because we have looked in the wrong place to recognize it (i.e. on the 'inside') than it does to dismiss the value of conscious experience because we have looked in the wrong place to recognize it (in this case, on the 'outside'). In order to consider the question properly, we need to look in the right place.[11]

4. Approaching Ethics from the External Perspective: the Value of Responsively Cohesive Structures

This brings us to the question of whether or not some kinds of structures might reasonably be considered to be valuable when considered simply in terms of their externally observable structure. (A closely related possibility is that some kinds of structures might consistently be found to underpin our most informed and considered judgments of value, in which case we could say that value supervenes on these structures.) I want to address this question by arguing, first, that there are three basic or primary kinds of structures and, second, that, other things being equal, we generally have good reasons for thinking that one of these basic structures is far more valuable than the other two – indeed, we often have good reasons for thinking that the other two are disvaluable. I will consider these two points in turn.

(i) Three basic or primary kinds of structures

The single most basic distinction we can make about the structure of anything is simply to note whether (or to what extent) it can be characterized *as* structured in some way or whether (or to what extent) it can't. We trade on this distinction all the time. Of those things that do possess some kind of structure, the next most basic distinction we can make is between those structures whose order can be characterized as generated or maintained by the mutual responsiveness of their elements or salient features and those whose order

[11] Rolston ('Respect for Life', op. cit.) is also quite explicit about the fact that Singer is looking for the value of nonsentient living things – and failing to find any – in what I am calling the 'wrong place'; however, as indicated, Rolston addresses this issue in a quite different way to the way in which I will below.

cannot be characterized in this way. We also trade on this distinction all the time, but we tend to do so in more tacit ways than in the case of structure (or organization) and lack of structure (or disorganization). For example, this distinction underpins the common distinction we make between living and nonliving things. But it is hardly restricted to this distinction; for example, we also trade on this distinction when we refer metaphorically to things that have a 'living' as opposed to a 'lifeless' or 'dead' quality about them, regardless of whether or not they are literally alive.

These considerations give us three basic ways in which things can be structured: they can cohere in a relatively regimented or fixed way; they can cohere by virtue of the mutual responsiveness of their elements or salient features; or they can simply fail to cohere (i.e. be unstructured or disorganized). I therefore refer to these three basic structures or forms of organization as *fixed cohesion*, *responsive cohesion*, and *discohesion*, respectively. If the elements or salient features that constitute examples of fixed cohesion convey a sense of being simply 'stuck together', and if the elements or salient features that constitute examples of discohesion convey a sense of 'failing to stick together', then the elements or salient features that constitute examples of responsive cohesion convey a sense of actively 'sticking together'.[12]

It is important to note that responsive cohesion should not be thought of as constituting some kind of midpoint between fixed cohesion and discohesion. Rather, it is theoretically possible to have an example of something that is a combination – not a genuine mixture, obviously; but a combination – of rigid order and complete disorganization but that contains no aspects of responsive cohesion. It is therefore appropriate to envisage the three logically distinct structures I have outlined as representing the corners or vertices of a triangle that defines an 'organization space' onto which we can plot real world examples. I find it convenient to think of the line between fixed cohesion and discohesion as the base of this notional triangle and responsive cohesion as the apex. (If the appropriateness of this 'superior' location is not already obvious, then it will become so in the next subsection of this discussion.) Exemplary forms of any

[12] The term 'cohere' means to cling, hold, stick, or adhere together; from Latin *cohaerēre*, from *co-* together + *haerēre* to cling, adhere. The term *responsive* derives from the Latin *rēsponsum* answer. Thus, the term *responsive cohesion* can also be thought of as referring to a structure or form of organization that holds by virtue of the mutual 'answering to each other' of its elements or salient features.

one of these structures would then be plotted on or very close to the appropriate corner of this triangle, combinations of any two at an appropriate point along one of the sides of the triangle, and combinations of all three at an appropriate point within the triangle.

The final point I want to make in this section is that the categories I have distinguished – like other terms that apply to notions of order, structure, or organization in everyday use – are readily applicable, and should be understood as intended to apply, in contexts that range across the literal/metaphorical divide, the intentional/functional divide, and the static/dynamic divide. For example, we might say that someone's desk is a 'mess' or that someone's behavior is 'all over the place'. The first sounds literal, the second metaphorical, but we have no day-to-day problem applying or understanding terms relating to the organization of things in ways that might be deemed literal in one context and metaphorical in another. Similarly, the elements or salient features that constitute some item of interest might be intentionally responsive to each other in various ways (e.g. the members of a team, choir, or society) or simply functionally responsive to each other (e.g. the parts of a living organism or the salient features of an artistic work). Finally, the fact that something is (literally) static, like a painting, does not mean that it cannot exhibit a high degree of responsive cohesion since the salient features that constitute it as a painting might be highly (functionally) responsive to each other in the service of the 'whole' painting. By the same token, the fact that something is (literally) dynamic, like an awkward conversation with someone that seems always to repeat the same tired old form ('like a record'), does not mean that it necessarily exhibits any kind of responsive cohesion (indeed, the dynamical conversation I have just referred to is an example of fixed cohesion in the domain of conversation). Thus the notions of 'fixed' and 'responsive' here should not be understood as implying anything about the (literally) static or dynamic dimensions of the structures under discussion, or vice versa.

(ii) The value of responsively cohesive structures

Attempts to describe the structures of responsive cohesion, fixed cohesion, and discohesion in everyday terms inevitably take the form of evaluatively-laden or 'thick' descriptions. For example, depending upon the particular domain of interest in which it is manifested, examples of fixed cohesion will tend to be described in terms such as 'regimented', 'inflexible', 'dogmatic', 'rigid', 'stuck', 'frozen', 'forced', 'mechanical', 'stereotypical', 'formulaic', 'tired', or 'dead'; examples of discohesion in terms such as 'unstructured', 'chaotic', 'anarchic', 'blown apart', 'out of control', 'all over the place', 'exhausted', 'decayed', or 'dead' (lack of structure can be brought about through some kind of violent or explosive form of destruction or through decay or exhaustion; thus, the contrast between some of these terms); and examples of responsive cohesion in terms such as 'flexible', 'flowing', 'fluid', 'adaptive', 'self-organizing', 'creative', 'organic', or 'alive'. Examples of fixed cohesion also tend to be described as 'boring', because they are so predictable; examples of discohesion as either 'anxiety-provoking', because they confront us with a never-ending barrage of incomprehensible change, or again, as 'boring', because they are so *predictably* unpredictable (like random noise compared with good music); and examples of responsive cohesion as 'interesting', 'engaging', or 'absorbing', because they combine a certain degree of predictability with a certain degree of surprise. It should be emphasized here that we do not simply project these reactions onto the structures concerned; rather, these reactions are a function of the intrinsic properties of these structures, for the reasons I have just noted. In this sense, then, these structures are intrinsically boring, anxiety-provoking, or interesting, and any competent, conscious observer will discover them to be so.

It seems obvious from these kinds of evaluatively-laden descriptions that responsively cohesive structures appear, in general, to be far more valuable than fixedly cohesive or discohesive structures – if indeed the latter two have anything other than negative value. I will therefore refer to this claim regarding the value of responsively cohesion structure relative to the other two basic kinds of structure as the 'responsive cohesion thesis'. We could offer a long list of general reasons in support of this thesis. For example, we can, as just noted, offer good reasons for thinking that responsively cohesive structures are intrinsically interesting whereas the other two structures are not; that they offer adaptive and creative possibilities that the other two structures lack; that, depending on the context, they should be judged as having more worth, merit, importance, desirability, beauty, or usefulness than the other two structures, and always for the same reason: because of the way in which their elements or salient features 'work together', 'answer to each other', or 'fit together' to deserve the judgment under discussion; and that, on a more metaphysically inclined level, responsively cohesive structures are 'allied to life' in that they constitute the structure of living things (especially healthy living things) and imbue nonliving things with a sense of life that they would not otherwise have, whereas the other two structures are 'allied to death' in that they constitute the structure of things that have no sense of life about them (in terms of the death metaphor, fixedly cohesive structures speak of rigor mortis and discohesive structures speak of either a violent ending or exhaustion and decay). Valuing those structures that most fly in the face of the universal tendency towards death, decay, and disorder seems to offer as strong a metaphysical basis on which to rest our evaluative judgments as we are likely to find.[13] Even so, we do not necessarily need to move to this particular metaphysical level of discussion in order to secure the value of responsively cohesive structures; the other reasons I have given above are valid too – a point I will return to below.

We could pursue the responsive cohesion thesis much further across a wide range of specific domains of interest in order to show that, other things being equal,[14] the examples that we value most positively turn out, again and again, to be those that most exemplify a responsively cohesive structure. (Here I am necessarily referring to 'open' domains of interest, by which I mean domains of interest that allow for the existence of all three structural possibilities as opposed to domains of interest in which the possibility of responsively cohesive structures has been ruled out either in principle or at a practical level.) The kinds of domains of interest I have in mind here range from theories (whether descriptive or normative), individual psychology, conversations, interpersonal relationships in general, organizational management, politics, and economics to all manner of skills (whether we are referring to trades, crafts, sports, entertainment, and so on), the written, visual, and performing arts, natural environments, gardens, architecture, urban design, and human-constructed objects in general. Thus, to cite just a single example: we generally

[13] Goodpaster, op. cit., 68, has made a similar suggestion.

[14] Other things are not equal – and we modify our judgments of value accordingly – when a particular example of responsive cohesion (e.g. a deadly virus, an assassin, or an invasive species) causes certain kinds of harm to selves or other sentient beings or, especially, works against wider, contextual examples of responsive cohesion. I will briefly discuss these matters – including the kinds of priority rules that apply in these situations – in the final section of this paper. Suffice to say for now, however, that these kinds of examples do not tell against the responsive cohesion thesis but rather speak to its explanatory power when its full implications are developed; when it is advanced, in other words, from being a bare bones 'thesis' to a full-blown 'theory' (on which, see my *A Theory of General Ethics*, op. cit., for the fullest expression of the 'theory of responsive cohesion').

consider ourselves to have good reasons for valuing a well-functioning democracy (the obvious contemporary example of responsive cohesion at the political level) more than a dictatorship (the obvious example of fixed cohesion at the political level) or lawless anarchy (the obvious example of discohesion at the political level). However, given the limits of this paper and the fact that I and others have pursued these kinds of more specifically targeted discussions elsewhere,[15] I must settle for simply noting this point here in order to proceed with the overall argument I want to present in this paper.

The high-level concept of 'value' has multiple meanings, so what do I mean when I claim that responsively cohesive structures are far more 'valuable' than fixedly cohesive or discohesive structures – if indeed the latter two have anything other than negative value? Dictionary definitions of the term 'value' include, most prominently, dimensions such as 'worth', 'merit', 'importance', 'desirability', 'usefulness', and 'interestingness'. I take the responsive cohesion thesis to speak positively to all these meanings and not simply to some more philosophically refined conception of value such as the commonly employed axiological categories of 'instrumental value' or 'intrinsic value' (which, needless to say, come with problems of their own[16]).

[15] Fox, op. cit., see esp. ch. 4; Terry Williamson, Antony Radford, and Helen Bennetts, *Understanding Sustainable Architecture* (London: Spon Press, 2003); Anthony Radford, 'Responsive Cohesion as the Foundational Value in Architecture', *The Journal of Architecture* **14** (2009): 511–532; Anthony Radford, 'Urban Design, Ethics, and Responsive Cohesion', *Building Research and Information* **38** (2010): 379–389; Isis Brook, 'The Virtues of Gardening', in Dan O'Brien, ed., *Gardening – Philosophy for Everyone: Cultivating Wisdom* (London: Wiley, 2010), 13–24. For examinations of the applicability of these ideas to areas such as (environmentally-oriented) aesthetics and political theory, see, respectively: John Brown, 'Responsive Cohesion and the Value of Wild Nature', paper presented to Canadian Society for Aesthetics Annual Meeting, Vancouver, June 2008: http://www.philosophy.umd.edu/Faculty/jhbrown/RCohesion/ Hugh McCullough, 'An Examination of Warwick Fox's Notion of Responsive Cohesion and its Relevance for Environmental Theory', paper presented to the Western Political Science Association Annual Meeting, Vancouver, 18–20 March 2009: http://www.allacademic.com/meta/p_mla_apa_research_citation/3/1/7/4/9/p317491_index.html

[16] For example, Christine Korsgaard ('Two Distinctions in Goodness', *Philosophical Review* **92** [1983): 169–195) argues that the common distinction between instrumental and intrinsic value actually conflates two distinctions that should be kept separate (those between instrumental and final

This is a good thing too, because the fact is that these categories swim together in our most informed and considered real world evaluative judgments, with neither outweighing the other in principle. For example, even in the case of selves – the paradigmatic example of intrinsic value – many informed and considered judges would have little problem concluding that the negative instrumental value of someone like Hitler far outweighed his intrinsic value. Conversely, although functional objects are typically valued primarily for their instrumental value, a particularly well-made example (e.g. a Shaker chair) might be considered by many informed and considered judges to be at least as intrinsically valuable as it is instrumentally valuable. (To mix things up even further here, we might also want to ask if the same sense of intrinsic value is at work in this case as when we refer to selves as being intrinsically valuable.) Thus, it is false to assume either that one kind (or sub-kind) of value automatically trumps the other or to assume that certain kinds of things necessarily exemplify one kind of value more than the other. Given this mixing together of axiological categories (and sub-categories) in real world evaluative judgments, I take it to be a strength of the responsive cohesion thesis that it is held to apply *regardless* of which axiological categories turn out to underpin our most informed and considered evaluative judgments in any given instance.

5. Joining Up the Dots: Grounding a General Ethics in the Value of Selves, Sentience, and Other Responsively Cohesive Structures

What unifies my discussion of the value of selves, mere sentient beings, and mere responsively cohesive structures is the fact that they are all responsively cohesive structures. Or to put it another way, the idea of responsively cohesive structures necessarily frames my discussion of sentient beings and selves because these beings represent a subset of the class of responsively cohesive structures. But how should we conceive or picture the relationship between the value of selves and other sentient beings as revealed from the internal perspective and the value of responsively cohesive structures in

---

value on the one hand and intrinsic and extrinsic value on the other) and is thus an ill-posed distinction in the first place, while John O'Neill draws attention to 'The Varieties of Intrinsic Value' in his paper by that name in *The Monist* **75** (1992): 119–137.

general as revealed from the external perspective? I think it is useful to think of the kind of value revealed by the external perspective in terms of a horizontal value dimension (in which, as I will discuss, responsively cohesive structures can be nested within other responsively cohesive structures) and the kind of value revealed by the internal perspective in terms of a vertical value dimension. The latter seems appropriate because we seem naturally to gravitate to metaphors of height and depth in talking about experiential states; we speak of feeling 'low' or feeling 'high'; of being lost in the 'depths of consciousness' or of experiencing a 'heightened state of awareness'; and psychologists have, of course, drawn on the vertical metaphor for many years in their various approaches to 'depth psychology' and studies of 'peak experiences'.

But how should we connect up and, where necessary, prioritize the value that attaches not only to differently nested levels of responsive cohesion within the horizontal dimension and to beings with different kinds of experiential capacities within the vertical dimension but also to these horizontal and vertical dimensions of value in general? I will briefly consider these questions within the horizontal dimension first, the vertical dimension second, and then the integration of the two.

Reflection on the idea of responsively cohesive structures – or any kind of structure – quickly reveals that every structure exists within a wider context (short of the universe itself, perhaps; although even here, cosmologists now talk openly about our universe itself existing within a 'multiverse'). This means that we can evaluate and distinguish between the degree of both *internal* and *contextual* responsive cohesion that any particular item of interest possesses (note that by 'internal' in this context I am referring to *internal structure* rather than anything to do with an inner, experiential dimension as revealed by the *internal perspective*). It also means that even if an item of interest has an internally responsively cohesive structure (e.g. a well made chair; some compelling bars of music), this does not necessarily mean that it will be responsively cohesive with – that it will 'answer' to – any given responsively cohesive context (e.g. the otherwise responsively cohesive kitchen in which the chair might go; the otherwise responsively cohesive symphony you have nearly finished). Thus, the relationship between a structure that is responsively cohesive when considered in its own right (such as a chair or some bars of music) and its otherwise responsively cohesive possible context can itself be one of discohesion. What to do? Should we privilege an individual example of responsive cohesion over contextual responsive cohesion by, say, tearing apart a kitchen or a symphony and rebuilding or rewriting as required so that these contexts now answer to the new additions, or should we reject or primarily seek to modify the potential new additions in order to fit their pre-established responsively cohesive contexts?

If responsively cohesive structures are valuable, then the answer is obvious, and it corresponds to our common practices: we should in general give priority to contextual forms of responsive cohesion over internal, individual, or subsidiary forms of responsive cohesion. To do otherwise would be to endorse modifying a context's worth of responsive cohesion every time a new responsively cohesive item didn't fit with it. But this would amount to the functional equivalent of discohesion – imagine some builders tearing apart your house and rebuilding it every time something they ordered for it didn't fit; these would truly be the builders from hell. The architect Christopher Day captures the general thrust of this point quite simply when he says: 'To be harmonious, the new needs to be an organic development of what is already there, not an imposed alien'.[17] That said, this priority rule needs to be understood in a responsively cohesive sense; that is, the degree of priority that is accorded to the context vis-à-vis the new item needs to be weighted according to their relative scales: it makes both common and responsive-cohesion-endorsed sense to find a mutual accommodation between potentially equal parts or contributors to something whereas obviously larger or more embracing responsively cohesive contexts should be given appropriately greater weight.

Notwithstanding the tame domestic and musical examples I have employed for the sake of illustration, this priority ordering of contextual responsive cohesion over internal, individual, or subsidiary examples of responsive cohesion has profound implications. Specifically, it means that we should give overall priority to supporting responsively cohesive structure in the largest context in which it can exist. Now for all practical, earthly purposes, this means the healthy functioning of the ecological realm in general – and here I would take not just biodiversity, but indigenous biodiversity (or 'biological integrity') to be a crucial indicator of our success or otherwise.[18] Beyond this, we should seek to support responsively cohesive structures within the human realm, including, most

[17] Christopher Day, *Places of the Soul: Architecture and Environmental Design as a Healing Art* (London: Thorsons/HarperCollins, 1990), 18.

[18] For an enlightening discussion of the principle normative concepts in conservation biology of 'ecosystem health', 'biodiversity', and 'biological integrity', see J. Baird Callicott, Larry Crowder, and Karen Mumford,

obviously, democratic politics that are responsively cohesive with the healthy functioning of the ecological realm. And beyond this, we should create a human-constructed realm, including, most obviously, a built environment, that is responsively cohesive with the ecological realm, the human social realm, and the human-constructed realm *in that order of priority*.

We can see, then, that the concept of responsive cohesion already implies a distinction between contextual responsive cohesion on the one hand and internal, individual, or subsidiary responsive cohesion on the other, and that reflection on the relative priority that should be accorded to these forms of responsive cohesion in turn leads to what we might call a *normative theory of contexts*. This theory of contexts offers a picture of nested responsively cohesive realms in which the ecological realm encompasses the human social realm, and the latter encompasses the human-constructed realm,[19] and it tells us that although we should support (preserve, create, restore) responsively cohesive structures over other kinds of structures in principle, we should do this in ways that give relatively greater priority to contextual responsive cohesion than to internal, individual, or subsidiary forms of responsive cohesion.

Let us now consider where and how the vertical dimension of value relating to selves and sentient beings fits into this picture. In terms of where it fits, the vertical vectors associated with mere sentient beings and selves are located within the ecological and human social realms, respectively. But beyond this we want to know how they fit in; how should we value – in what ways does it even make sense to value – sentient beings and selves? As I have already suggested in my earlier discussion of these beings, the evidence suggests that normally developed humans are the only selves – the only beings with autobiographical self-awareness – that currently exist on earth.[20] I have argued elsewhere that this has significant ethical implications,

'Current Normative Concepts in Conservation', *Conservation Biology* **13** (1999): 22–35.

[19] I offer formal reasons for 'carving nature at its joints' in this way in *A Theory of General Ethics*, op. cit. In the context of that more detailed level of discussion I formally refer to the ecological, human-social, and human-constructed realms as the 'biophysical realm', the 'mindsharing realm', and the 'compound material realm', respectively.

[20] Chris Moore and Karen Lemmon, eds, *The Self in Time: Developmental Processes* (Mahwah, NJ: Lawrence Erlbaum, 2001); Fox, op. cit., chs 6–8; Hans Markowitsch and Harald Welzer, *The Development of Autobiographical Memory* (New York: Psychology Press, 2010).

namely, that whereas both selves and other sentient beings can be harmed by the infliction of unnecessary pain and suffering, only selves can be harmed, in addition, by the infliction of unwanted death *per se*, that is, however painless it might be.[21] This is because only selves can, as it were, be cut off from themselves – from their own awareness of *their* existence; from their memory claims upon *their* past, *their* dreams, plans, and projects for the future, and *their* self-aware location of the present in that autobiographical context – and, thus, only selves can self-reflectively not want this to happen (or, in the case of, say, painful terminal illness, sometimes self-reflectively want this to happen). This means that unwanted death is a harm to autobiographical beings from *their* perspective and is mutually recognized as such by rational selves. In contrast, death *per se* does not cut sentient beings off from 'their' past, present, or future because they are not autobiographical selves; their death simply means that they die in this moment rather than that moment. What concerns them, albeit in a non-self-reflective manner, is simply (but by no means unimportantly) the quality of their moment-to-moment existence in the form of meeting their needs and avoiding pain and suffering.

If we return to the normative theory of contexts picture I suggested above, then I take the implications of these considerations to indicate some additional constraints on the ways in which we should act in those cases in which our actions affect those responsively cohesive structures that we have depicted in terms of a vertical vector, which is to say those responsively cohesive structures that possess an inner, experiential dimension. Specifically, and assuming the standard 'other things beings equal' kinds of clauses, we should seek to avoid inflicting unnecessary pain and suffering on sentient beings in general and we should seek to avoid causing unwanted death to selves in particular.[22]

21 See the extended argument that runs through Fox, op. cit., chs 5–8.

22 As this formulation suggests, the guidance that issues from the full-blown theory of responsive cohesion that informs this paper (for which, see Fox, op. cit.) is couched in agent-relative as opposed to agent-neutral terms. This theory also issues in a range of more nuanced constraints in regard to selves and other sentient beings than these two basic constraints suggest. However, I have been primarily concerned in this paper with offering a different way of approaching the main ideas in this theory to the one I offered in *A Theory of General Ethics* – couched in terms of the contrast between internal and external perspectives – and can otherwise do no more than lay out the bare bones of this theory within the limits imposed by this paper.

The considerations I have discussed here provide us with the foundations – obviously not the fine-grained details in a presentation of this length, but the foundations – of what I refer to as a General Ethics. By this I mean a single, integrated approach to ethics that encompasses the realms of human-focused ethics, the ethics of the nonhuman natural environment (which has been the overwhelming focus of environmental ethicists to date),[23] and the ethics of the human-constructed – or, in a broad sense of the term, built – environment. I submit that this kind of 'joined up' and appropriately prioritized approach to ethics represents the kind of approach that we need to be working – and acting – on at this deeply worrying point[24] in our intimately interwoven ecological and social history.

www.warwickfox.com

[23] I have been arguing for some time that just as the nonhuman world has constituted a major blind spot in theorizing associated with traditional, anthropocentrically focused forms of ethics, so the human-constructed environment has constituted a major blind spot in theorizing associated with the development of environmental ethics to date; see, for example: 'Introduction: Ethics and the Built Environment', in Warwick Fox, ed., *Ethics and the Built Environment* (London: Routledge, 2000), 1–12; *A Theory of General Ethics*, op. cit.; 'Architecture Ethics', in Jan-Kyrre Berg Olsen, Stig Pedersen, and Vincent Hendricks, eds, *A Companion to the Philosophy of Technology* (Oxford: Blackwell, 2009), 387–91; 'Developing a General Ethics (with Particular Reference to the Built, or Human-Constructed, Environment)', in David Keller, ed., *Environmental Ethics: The Big Questions*, (Malden, MA: Wiley-Blackwell, 2010), 213–220.

[24] Graham Turner, 'A Comparison of *The Limits to Growth* with 30 Years of Reality', *Global Environmental Change* **18** (2008): 397–411.

Darwinism and Environmentalism

BRIAN GARVEY

A number of authors have combined a commitment to Darwinian evolution as a major source of insight into human nature with a strong commitment to environmentalist concerns. The most notable of these is perhaps Edward O. Wilson, in a series of books.[1] Yet it may appear that there is a tension between Darwinism as a world-view – or least some major aspects of it – and a concern for non-human entities as worthy of concern in their own right. In the present paper, I want to address some of the reasons for thinking there is such a tension.

Firstly, it might be thought that Darwin has taught us that the relationship between different species is intrinsically antagonistic, and moreover that this antagonism is what drives evolutionary change itself. Thanks to the popular iconography associated with Darwinism, we tend to think of the process of evolution as being primarily natural selection, and of natural selection as a 'struggle' or 'competition' between creatures, where one creature's gain is inevitably another's loss. Moreover, we tend to think of different species, not just individuals of the same species, as in struggle or competition against each other. The popular iconography often portrays this struggle as incessant, so that the day-to-day life of creatures is seen as one of 'kill or be killed', 'eat or be eaten'. This would not in itself show that we should not be concerned about non-human entities, at least not without committing the fallacy of 'is' implies 'ought'. Nor would it even show that it is impossible for us to be so concerned. But it would suggest that, in being so concerned we would be somehow sailing against the wind of evolution, either against the process itself, or against inbuilt tendencies that it has produced in ourselves, or both. Consequently, if we wanted a basis for our environmentalist concerns, we would have to find it somewhere other than in evolution. In this paper, I will attempt to show that this view of evolution is highly misleading, and at best gives us only a very partial picture.

[1] See for example Edward O. Wilson: *The Future of Life* (London: Abacus, 2002); Brian Baxter: *A Darwinian Worldview: Sociobiology, Environmental Ethics and the Work of Edward O. Wilson* (Aldershot: Ashgate, 2007).

doi:10.1017/S135824611100021X

But that, by itself, will not tell us anything about whether, or to what extent, we should care about the non-human environment. As regards this issue, there are two basic positions: (1) *Deep ecology* is the view that non-human entities – such as animals, trees, and even, in more extreme versions, inanimate objects such as hills or islands – have moral standing *in themselves*.[2] That is, they are entitled to certain types of treatment, or we have certain duties towards them, irrespective of any benefits that they confer on us humans. That is not to say that the moral standing of these non-human entities *overrides* that of humans. In deciding what to do, there may, consistently with deep ecology, be a trade-off between benefit to humans and benefit to other things. The key point is that the moral standing of non-human entities is not derived from that of humans: it is not just because they benefit us that they deserve our moral consideration. (2) The opposing view to this is *instrumentalism* as regards the non-human environment: the view that we only have obligations to any non-human entity insofar as it affects us, and that those obligations are entirely dependent upon and derived from our obligations to humans. My aim in this paper is not to defend deep ecology, or indeed to settle the issue between deep ecology and instrumentalism one way or another. Rather, I am attempting to show that what counts as being of instrumental value to humans is rather more than may sometimes be thought. That is, even if we accept the arguments for instrumentalism, we still ought to have a great deal of concern for preserving the environment. The difference between deep ecology and instrumentalism *in practice* may be very little. At the very end of the paper, I will also (tentatively) suggest that a purely instrumental attitude to the environment is not really possible. So I suggest a position somewhere between deep ecology and instrumentalism.

Someone who argues for an instrumentalist position on scientific, and specifically evolutionary, grounds, is Richard Lewontin. According to Lewontin, the idea that we should save the environment, or even that there is an environment independent of us for us to be concerned about, is fundamentally misguided. This is because he thinks there is no such thing as *the* environment: there are only the environments of different types of creatures, which are partially but inextricably constituted by the activities of those creatures and which we, like any other living thing, cannot help but alter to suit ourselves. If this is so, he argues, then the idea that any

[2] See Arne Næss: *Ecology, Community and Lifestyle: Outline of an Ecosophy*. Translated by D. Rothenberg (Cambridge: Cambridge University Press, 1989).

non-human entity has moral standing independent of our interests makes no sense. Thus, Lewontin concludes, any programme of conservation must perforce be subservient to human interests. I wish to address Lewontin's arguments here.

1. The image of evolution as ruthless competition

What implications does Darwinism have for our attitude towards the environment? At first sight, it might look as though Darwinism is not friendly towards environmental concerns. Darwinism is often thought to paint a picture of ruthless competition between, as well as within, species. This, in turn, may be thought to encourage a view of the environment as something to be exploited for self-interested gain. Darwin himself did not use the expression 'survival of the fittest' until the fifth edition of *The Origin of Species*. But he did use the expressions 'preservation of favoured races' (as part of the full title of *The Origin of Species*) and 'struggle for existence' (the title of Chapter 3). What is beyond doubt is that the association between on the one hand the terms 'Darwinism', 'natural selection' and even 'evolution' itself, and on the other the image of ruthless competition between organisms, is powerful and deeply ingrained, in the minds both of the general public and of many scientists. Indeed, the dissemination of Darwin's theory, and of its present-day updated and corrected version (though there is some disagreement as to exactly what that is), often strongly reinforces that association.

I am not about to embark on a lengthy spree of Dawkins-bashing, and I will later argue that some of Dawkins' supposedly more sophisticated opponents are equally guilty of distortions. But it must be admitted that the until-recently Professor for the Public Understanding of Science has been culpable in this regard. In his TV programmes *The Root of All Evil?* and *The Genius of Charles Darwin*, Dawkins introduces the concept of natural selection to the accompaniment of images of a cheetah chasing down and killing an antelope, a spider devouring a fly, and so forth. The voice-over, meanwhile, informs us that natural selection is a process in which the general law is eat or be eaten, kill or be killed:

> As night falls, it's kill or be killed. … During the minute it takes me to say these words, thousands of animals are running for their lives whimpering with fear, feeling teeth sink into their throats, thousands are dying from starvation or disease, or feeling a parasite rasping away from within. There is no central authority, no

> safety net. For most animals the reality of life is struggling, suffering, and death.[3]

Dawkins often describes nature itself as 'ruthless', 'pitiless' and so forth, and he is not alone in this. One thing that might be – and has been – said about this type of language is that it is unduly anthropomorphic. An impersonal natural process cannot be ruthless or pitiless, because it is not the kind of thing that can show mercy (ruth) or pity at all. We might as well say that the process is immoral or has bad taste, as opposed to being something to which the concepts of morality and taste just do not apply. Some people worry about this anthropomorphic language more than I do.[4] We use metaphors all the time, and this does not seem to me to be *in itself* problematic, even in science, as long as we know how to cash the metaphors out in literal terms. And in this instance, the literal meaning of what Dawkins is saying seems clear enough: other metaphors for the same thing include: it is a zero-sum game, one creature's gain is another's loss, etc. Essentially, Dawkins is saying that, as a general rule, when one creature's chances of surviving and reproducing are increased, it is by means of another creature's chances of surviving and reproducing being decreased.

Prior to giving a response, I would like to suggest that there are two different things that Dawkins might be saying. Firstly, he might be talking about the *products* of evolution; that is, he might be saying that what evolution produces, as a general rule, is creatures that are constantly engaged in zero-sum games against each other. Or, secondly, he might be talking about the *process* of evolution; that is, he might be saying that evolutionary change is predominantly produced by the accumulation of zero-sum games. (This is of course assuming that he takes natural selection to be the predominant producer of evolutionary change, but he clearly does, and has said so on many occasions.[5]) At times, it looks as though Dawkins is only making the second claim. In *The Selfish Gene*,[6] he goes to great lengths to explain that natural selection, though in itself 'ruthless' and 'pitiless',

[3] 'The Genius of Charles Darwin', Channel 4, November 2008.

[4] For Example Mary Midgley 'Gene-Juggling' *Philosophy*, vol. **54** (1979) 439–58; Lynn Margulis and Dorion Sagan: *Acquiring Genomes: A Theory of the Origins of Species* (New York: Basic Books, 2002).

[5] For Example Dawkins: 'Universal Darwinism' in D.S. Bendall, ed. *Evolution from Molecules to Man* (Cambridge University Press). Reprinted in Hull and Ruse, ed, *The Philosophy of Biology* (Oxford University Press, 1998).

[6] Second Edition (Oxford University Press, 1989).

can and often does produce behavioural tendencies that are co-operative (reciprocally beneficial) or altruistic (self-sacrificing for the benefit of others). However, the behavioural tendencies of which he speaks are always *between members of the same species*: an individual may co-operate with another individual of the same species for reciprocal benefit; an individual may sacrifice itself for the benefit of another of the same species. So it is not clear whether he thinks co-operation or altruism between members of different species are possible, or at all common, outcomes of evolution. It may be, for all he tells us, that they are only very rare, aberrant, outcomes. The general rule for how creatures fashioned by evolution behave towards each other is: eat or be eaten, kill or be killed.

Now, straight away, and without having to reach for exotic, unfamiliar examples, it can be said that this is *at best* an extremely partial picture of what goes on between organisms of different species in the natural world. Only some animals are carnivores. If he intended to illustrate a perfectly typical product of evolution, Dawkins could have shown us an image of a monkey eating a banana. Not only does the monkey not kill the banana tree by eating the banana; the banana being eaten is in fact the means by which the banana tree produces offspring in the wild. More generally, herbivorous animals very often play this vital role for the plants they feed on – seed distribution. An extremely common pattern is that the seeds are passed out in the faeces of the animal, and the faeces provide a nutrition-rich base from which a new plant can grow. So the animal gets a meal, the plant gets a chance to reproduce – it is reciprocal benefit, not zero-sum. The same is true of bees pollinating plants. It could be added that even carnivorous animals cannot wipe out the animals on which they prey.

But there is a deeper story here, one that has begun to be revealed in the work of Lynn Margulis and others. Margulis became famous for her hypothesis about the origins of the eukaryotic cell, a hypothesis that is now generally accepted, and about which I will say more anon. Margulis argues that mutually beneficial relationships between creatures of different species are in fact all-pervasive, and that what we often think of as a single organism is usually a collection of organisms of different kinds.[7] The most obvious example of this is lichens, which consist of algae and fungi (and often bacteria as well) living in symbiosis. The algal component and the fungal component can in fact live separately, but when they are together, as is the norm,

[7] Lynn Margulis: *Symbiotic Planet: A New Look at Evolution* (New York: Basic Books, 1998).

they share functions rather than duplicating them. But examples of such symbiotic relationships can be found much closer to home, and much more pervasively. Moreover, they are often found to involve much deeper integration than in the lichen case: it is precisely because the two components are not all that deeply integrated that the dual nature of lichens was discovered so relatively early. Cows are renowned for their possession of multiple 'stomachs', and for the process of pre-digestion that one 'stomach' (more properly called the rumen) performs before the cow chews it again and it then food enters the stomach proper. But this process of preparing the cow's food for digestion is carried on in the rumen by a vast array of micro-organisms. The rumen provides a nutrition-rich environment for the micro-organisms, and they in turn play a vital role in enabling the cow to digest. Bacteria in our own intestines perform analogous functions for us, and Margulis estimates that about 10% of our bodies by dry weight consists of such friendly bacteria. A more dramatic example can be found in termites. Up to 30% of their body mass is made up of bacteria which enable to them to digest wood. Within cells themselves, a similar situation can be found. What we might think of as a single cell often contains component parts that have their own separate DNA, thus being in that sense separate organisms. But they are tightly integrated with their hosts in situations of reciprocal benefit. Margulis has argued that the flagella of many bacterial cells may have evolved from separate entities (although this hypothesis is not widely accepted). So, while predation and parasitism do exist – situations in which one creature's gain is another's loss – there is no reason to think it is the norm of what evolution produces.

But what about the *process* of evolution? Recall that Dawkins believes that natural selection is the prime producer of evolutionary change. He is by no means alone in this. Darwin himself wrote that 'I am convinced that Natural Selection has been the main but not exclusive means of modification.'[8] To be fair to Darwin, however, even he makes clear, in the chapter with this title, that the term 'struggle for existence' not only should not be taken as implying any intention on an organism's part, but also should not be taken as entailing that one creature only gains out of another's loss. He says, for example, that a plant on its own at the edge of a desert may be said to be struggling for existence – even though the only things that threaten it are the inanimate physical conditions around it:

[8] Darwin, Charles (1859): *The Origin of Species*. Reprint of the First Edition, W.J. Burrow, ed. (Harmonsworth: Penguin, 1968), 69.

> Two canine animals in a time of dearth, may be truly said to struggle with each other which shall get food and live. But a plant on the edge of a desert is said to struggle against the drought, though more properly it should be said to be dependent on the moisture.[9]

Admittedly, this must be set against his remark about natural selection being the primary driving force, for selection is between creatures and other creatures, not between creatures and their inanimate surroundings. However, our knowledge of evolution has grown since Darwin's time. Think again about the herbivores and the plants they feed off. How did these arrangements come about in the first place? In many cases, the fruit, and the herbivore's ingestive and digestive apparatus are evolved *to fit each other*. The herbivores did not find the fruit ready-made in its current form – they co-evolved. Likewise with bees and flowers. There is an (unintentionally) amusing video, easy to find on YouTube, made by two 'creation scientists', Kirk Cameron and Ray Comfort, entitled 'The Banana – The Atheist's Worst Nightmare'. The presenters point out in great detail how extremely well designed bananas are for being eaten by humans. But there is nothing whatsoever paradoxical about this. If we assume that our ancestors have been eating bananas for a long time – which seems extremely likely, given that both humans and our nearest relatives chimpanzees are very fond of bananas – then we have been co-evolving with bananas for a very long time. *Of course* they are well-designed for being eaten by us! (Given that human hands, mouths, and digestive organs are suited to a very wide variety of different tasks and food-types, it is likely that it was bananas that did most of the adapting to us or our distant ancestors, rather than the other way round. We have also been selectively breeding them for many centuries now, to make them easier for us to eat.)

But once again, such cases of obvious co-evolution are just the tip of a huge iceberg. Margulis has a radical new view on how evolutionary novelties, and in particular new species, arise.[10] Consider again those micro-organisms that live inside the bodies of termites, cows, and us. Note that in every case the micro-organisms perform functions that are useful, and in many instances indispensible, to the hosts. But at some point in the past the ancestors of the micro-organisms must have entered the ancestors of the hosts, and hence before that they must have been able to live separately. So when the

[9] Ibid., 116.
[10] Margulis: *Acquiring Genomes*.

micro-organisms entered the hosts it must have triggered a process of co-evolution, a process by which both parties gained.

The importance of such processes of symbiosis-followed-by-coevolution for bringing about major evolutionary change can be seen most strikingly in the origin of eukaryotic cells. Eukaryotic cells are cells that contain a nucleus containing DNA, and other organelles – e.g. mitochondria, chloroplasts – which contain *their own separate* DNA. The cells of all animals, fungi and plants are eukaryotic. We tend to think of the DNA in the nucleus as 'the' genes of an individual. And it is true that a lot of genetic research has focussed on the DNA that gets recombined in sexual reproduction. We are familiar, for example, with the fact that if your father carries some rare recessive gene (e.g. the cystic fibrosis gene) then the chances that you also carry it are 50%. But that is because your nuclear DNA is inherited from your mother *and* your father. By contrast, the DNA in your mitochondria is inherited *only* from your mother. So if your mother carries some rare mitochondrial-DNA gene, then – barring mutations – the chances of you also carrying it are 100%. Margulis' hypothesis, now generally accepted, was that these organelles carry their own separate DNA because they were once separate organisms.[11] The transition from bacteria to eukaryotic cells involved the coming together into mutual beneficial symbioses of different types of cells, and that relationship became progressively more tightly integrated. The ancestors of (e.g.) our mitochondria entered into a symbiotic relationship with other cells, and have since co-evolved with them. Thus, the great increase of cellular complexity that made possible the existence of all plants, fungi and animals happened because cells of different kinds formed symbiotic relationships – co-operative partnerships, if you will – and then co-evolved to be tightly integrated units functioning as one.

I offer one final, (literally) colourful example: green animals. As you may remember from your high school biology, green plant cells have chloroplasts but animal cells don't, and it is by means of chloroplasts that plants photosynthesise. Chloroplasts, like mitochondria, have their own DNA, and so are almost certainly descended from what were once separate organisms. The simpler varieties of green algae are in fact quite similar to chloroplasts, except that the latter don't perform all their life-sustaining functions for themselves, instead relying on other parts of the cells they are in to do so. So in all likelihood ancestral proto-plants assimilated green algae in some way.

[11] Lynn Margulis: *Symbiosis in Cell Evolution* (San Francisco: W.H. Freeman, 1981).

This implies that green plants did not themselves evolve the ability to photosynthesise: rather, they incorporated organisms that had already evolved it. What is less well known is that there are also some animals that contain chloroplasts, and are in consequence green and able to photosynthesise. For example, green slugs such as *Elysia viridis* can go without food for as long as nine months; instead of eating they bask in the sun in shallow waters. They ingest green algae, but do not digest them; instead they incorporate them into their tissues where they remain alive and active. This, too, must result from co-evolution between the algae and the slugs.

Even if one is sceptical about Margulis' more all-embracing claim about symbiosis being the driving force of evolution, there is no doubt that it has been responsible for some of the most important transitions. So there is no reason to think of the process of evolutionary change as essentially involving zero-sum games, or kill-or-be-killed. It is just as likely to be brought about by the setting up of situations of reciprocal benefit between organisms of different species. Likewise as regards evolution's products: evolution does not invariably produce creatures whose interests are antagonistic to each other. It also produces creatures, very often of different species, who work together for reciprocal benefit. Consequently, there is nothing intrinsically anti-evolutionary in working to help other species. The fact that we have evolved does not imply that we have an inbuilt tendency to be antagonistic towards other living things.

2. Lewontin and the challenge to Deep Ecology

A second challenge to environmentalism from evolutionary theory comes from someone who has been one of Dawkins' severest critics over the last thirty years and more: Richard Lewontin. While Dawkins sees the relationship between different species as intrinsically antagonistic, and such antagonism as essential to evolutionary change, Lewontin claims that the environment does not exist. He says that 'the growing environmentalist movement to prevent alterations in the natural world that will be, at best, unpleasant and, at worst, catastrophic for human existence cannot proceed rationally under the false slogan "Save the Environment". The environment does not exist to be saved.'[12] Rather, he thinks, 'what we can do is

[12] Richard Lewontin: *The Triple Helix: Gene, Organism and Environment* (Cambridge, Massachusetts: Harvard University Press, 2000), 67–8.

try to affect the rate of extinction and direction of environmental change in such a way as to make a decent life for human beings possible.'[13] In other words, we can nurture, preserve, and shape the world in a way that best serves human interests.

Such a view flies in the face of deep ecology – the view that non-human entities have moral standing in themselves. Lewontin's view of our obligations towards the non-human world is an instrumentalist one, as the above quotations make clear.

How does Lewontin argue for this view? The key point he is arguing is that there is no such thing as *the* environment *tout court*. That is, what counts as constituting the environment depends on the type of creature you are, and hence different types of creature, even in the same physical place, will have different environments. We should not think of the world as containing pre-existing niches into which creatures come and adapt themselves. As Lewontin sometimes likes to express it, a world without living things would contain *no* niches, no environments. This breaks down into two points:

(1) *Niche construction:* Any living creature, simply by existing, will physically alter its immediate surroundings.

(2) *Biological Kantianism:* Not everything in the physical surroundings of an organism is relevant to it at all, and the same thing in the same physical surroundings may have different relevance to different organisms.

(1) *Niche construction:* The first point is most obviously true if we consider cases such as the following. Trees create a canopy that changes the temperature, humidity and lighting conditions beneath it in a dramatic way. Termites build vast (nine metres high in some cases) mounds, thus providing for themselves a mini-world whose temperature, humidity and lighting are highly regulated and significantly different from what they are outside. Beavers build dams that alter the flow of rivers. But Lewontin's argument does not depend on the recitation of individual examples. His point is that *any* living creature is constantly taking in matter from its surroundings and giving out matter to its surroundings. It cannot but alter them. Similarly, every living creature gives off or takes in heat, so that the temperature of the zone immediately around its body is something other than it would be were the creature not there. For example, we humans carry around with us an envelope of air that is constantly regulated by the heat of our own bodies: it is the temperature of this air that we are used to. In temperate climates such as Britain's, this means

[13] Ibid.

that our air-envelope is usually warmer than the air would be if we weren't there. This explains why wind makes us feel cold – it momentarily deprives us of our warm envelope. There can, then, be no talk of us, or any other organism, leaving the environment unaffected. Simply by being alive in it, we are altering it.

Moreover, it is this altered environment – altered, that is, by the creature's own presence within it – to which any creature is adapted. It is common to think of the environment as something that exists prior to a given creature living in it, and of the creature as becoming adapted to that environment. It is true that evolution happens because the morphologies of organisms are malleable, and are changed in response changes to the physical surroundings. But what Lewontin wants to emphasise is that the physical surroundings are also malleable, and any living creature perforce changes them just by living in them. Living creatures in general are, as a result of evolution, well-suited to the physical surroundings they live in. But that is not just because they have altered themselves, or been altered, to accommodate to living in those surroundings: it is also because they have themselves altered the surroundings. In some cases (e.g. the termites) they have altered them to produce a niche that suits their needs; in others, they have produced effects as an inevitable consequence of their activities. But in either type of case, the world to which they are suited to live in is not one that existed prior to them. The ambient temperature in which humans feel comfortable is the one produced by our own bodies. And termites doubtless have evolved functions that their ancestors didn't have before they lived in mounds, and lost ones they had. The consequence of all this, then, is that the world we humans live in is a world that we have made. This is true not just of the obvious technology that we have made, but of the grass and the very air that surrounds us. And it is a world to which we are suited. There can be no talk of us making a world that is free of our alterations, and in any event such a world would be impossible for us to live in.

(2) *Biological Kantianism:* But Lewontin's second point is more radical. He argues that not only do creatures inevitably alter their physical surroundings, but that the physical surroundings do not in themselves constitute the creature's environment. To begin with, we can take the environment to mean that to which a creature is adapted, or which poses a problem to which it needs to adapt. If we do so, then two different types of creature (e.g. different species) living in the same physical surroundings – *even taking into account the changes that they both have made to those surroundings* – will, according to Lewontin, be in different environments. The reason

for this is that the entities around them will have different significances for one than for the other. 'Significance' here just means 'the difference something makes'. But the difference something makes to any creature will vary depending on the type of creature it is. For example, a piece of woodland may contain a plant that is a nutritious food for one creature, a deadly poison to another. So, although one and the same plant is in the two creatures' physical surroundings, different things are in their respective environments. Different challenges or opportunities are presented to different creatures by the same plant. Similarly, objects in the physical surroundings may have importance for one creature, but none for another. Lewontin gives the example of a water boatman, a long-legged insect that lives on the surface of ponds. For this creature, the surface tension of water is a significant feature of the environment, something that it is obliged to cope with in a way that we humans are not. Moreover, for a smaller creature that dwells on the surface of water, such as the microscopic *paramecium*, surface tension is a more significant feature of the environment than gravity. Lewontin also mentions the thrushes and phoebes in his garden. Thrushes use small stones to break open snails' shells, but for a phoebe the stones might as well not be there. For one creature, a particular object in its surroundings is of supreme importance. For another, the same object does not exist; it is no part of its environment at all.

A consequence of this view is that a creature can never have direct access to all the things that are in its physical surroundings. It has access to things that are of relevance to it – as dangers, opportunities, obstacles – insofar as they are of relevance to it. Moreover, there is no reason to think that humans are a special case: we are, it is true, exceptionally hungry for information – i.e. we gather information well beyond immediate or even possible utility. But we do so using sense organs and cognitive apparatus that have been shaped through and through by past evolution. There is no reason to think that every bit of our physical surroundings is accessible to or understandable by us, even with all the prosthetics in the world. Ultimately, we can be aware only of what affects us. Affecting us may only mean exciting our curiosity, but our curiosity is a feature of minds shaped by past evolution.[14]

[14] For an elaboration of this consequence of Lewontin's view, see Matthew Ratcliffe: 'An Epistemological Problem for Evolutionary Psychology', *International Studies in the Philosophy of Science* **19** (1) (2005), 47–63.

Hence, on Lewontin's view, we can only be concerned for the environment insofar as it affects humans, which would be bad news for any deeper ecological views. However, Lewontin's point can be turned around: not only is the environment partially constituted by the organism; the organism is partially constituted by its environment. This implies, or so I will argue, that in damaging its environment an organism is damaging itself. In fact, Lewontin's arguments, far from negating this point, actually reinforce it. As some of the examples already mentioned illustrate, creatures shape their surroundings and in turn are shaped by their surroundings. In fact, it is a little misleading to say 'and in turn' since it is an ongoing, cyclical process of reciprocal effects. We make our niches (but, it should be emphasised, not out of nothing) and we ourselves change to fit into those niches. Similarly, if we take Lewontin's biological Kantian point, it too cuts both ways. This is not just because organisms adapt to their environment, but because the development of an organism requires a particular type of environment to go smoothly, or indeed at all. This is part and parcel of the wisdom of developmental biology. It is generally admitted that genes play a key role in shaping the development of any organism, but they do not shape it on their own. Any developing organism depends on resources from its surroundings to develop. If those resources are not there, or are different, the organism will fail to develop normally, or at all. So just as there is no environment without an organism, neither is there any organism without an environment. An organisms' environment – delicate as it is, and partially made and constituted by the organism as it is – is *part* of the organism.

This point can be taken further by drawing on something else that Darwin taught us. All of earthly life is one family. We all, from bacteria and archaea to petunias, platypuses and people, are descended from one common ancestor. In fact, a host of discoveries in different areas of biology have revealed that the kinship goes far deeper than Darwin suspected. The unravelling of the genomes of different creatures has revealed that there is far less genetic variety than we might have thought. For example, the genes involved in building eyes in fruit-flies are the same as those involved in building human eyes. Moreover, recent work in evolutionary developmental biology has revealed previously unsuspected deep structural similarities across a wide spectrum of living things: widely different species can be thought of as combinations of the same basic kit. And the work that Margulis pioneered reveals that the very cells in our bodies, as well as those of other animals, fungi and plants, contain the descendants of what were once separate living creatures, with most of their genotypes still intact. We once thought of evolution as a diverging tree of life, but, because many major evolutionary changes were produced by organisms assimilating other organisms in symbiotic relationships, it might be better to think of it as a web whose strands converge as well as diverge. If we trace our ancestry via our nuclear DNA alone, then we are descended from single-celled organisms called archaea. These archaea were ultimately descended from bacteria. But the bacteria that were the ancestors of our mitochondria diverged from the archaea before they joined up with archaea to form the closely co-operating collectives we call eukaryotic cells. We are clearly descended from archaea, but should we say that we are descended from our mitochondria's free-living predecessors as well? Or should we just say that our mitochondria themselves are? Our mitochondria are part of us in a very strong sense, a stronger sense, for example, than the symbiont micro-organisms that live in our digestive systems. We could stipulate that only our nuclear DNA counts as far as ancestry goes, so we are descended from archaea and not from our mitochondria's free-living ancestors. But the motivation for doing it does not seem very strong. In just what sense are we our cell nuclei but not our mitochondria? Noam Chomsky once remarked that if alien linguists landed on Earth, they might think that all human languages were one language. In a similar vein, I suggest that if alien geneticists landed on Earth, they might be impressed by the genetic similarity between all its living creatures: might they think that we were all one kind?

The overall picture that emerges is of an environment which has shaped, and been shaped by, terrestrial life as a whole. A view of the natural world as in a strong sense 'ours', where this means belonging to life as a whole, makes good sense in the light of evolution. What I suggest is that we should learn to look on the Earth as our home in a very deep sense: it is the home we – all living creatures – have made for ourselves, and to which we have become adapted. Think of armchair into which indentations have been formed by our sitting in it over many years. It has been, entirely unconsciously, shaped by us to suit us. But now imagine that a whole host of things in our surroundings have been so shaped, and that we have in turn been shaped by them, so that they fit us and we fit them. Our 'environment', I want to suggest, is like this. What we think of as the 'natural' environment is in fact a collection of things in our surroundings that we have shaped and to suit us. We can make this point at bigger or smaller magnitudes. It has been suggested that the movement of the Earth's tectonic plates is a result of the action of living organisms at the thermal vents at the bottom of the sea, so that the distribution of the continents is due to living things. And it is not even controversial that all the free oxygen in the Earth's atmosphere is there because of green plants and algae. The blue-green ball with whose appearance from outer space we are all familiar would look very different if living things had not been acting on it for billions of years. If we are willing to think of all of life as 'us', then we should look at that blue-green ball and say: that is our home, which we made. If we are not prepared to go that far, we can focus our attention more narrowly, and think about the world that is our – that is, humans' – home. Our ancestors evolved in African savannah, and the niche that we adapted to and ourselves shaped contains the familiar 'natural' features grass, running water, trees, and so forth. This was the home that we made for ourselves and adapted ourselves to long before we built stone houses. Edward O. Wilson has frequently pointed out that people are happier in a world that has grass, running water etc. We should not think of such a world as 'natural', if natural means in contrast to a human world. It *is* the human world, far more than the world of technological 'conveniences'. We tamper with it at our peril. I will let Wilson speak here:

> It is ... possible for some to dream that people will go on living comfortably in a biologically impoverished world. They suppose that a prosthetic environment is within the power of technology, that human life can still flourish in a completely humanized world, where medicines would all be synthesized from chemicals off the shelf, food grown from a few domestic crop species, the atmosphere and climate regulated by computer-driven fusion energy, and the earth made over until it becomes a literal spaceship rather than a metaphorical one, with people reading displays and touching buttons on the bridge.[15]

But he warns against such a view:

> To disregard the diversity of life is to risk catapulting ourselves into an alien environment. We will have become like the pilot whales that inexplicably beach themselves on New England shores.[16]

Wilson defends this view in part by appealing to the potential obviously instrumental uses to which things in the environment can be put. E.g. by driving species to extinction, we might inadvertently

[15] Edward O. Wilson: *The Diversity of Life*, Second Edition (Harvard: Belknap, 1999), 347.
[16] Ibid., 346.

lose a chance of discovering cures for all kinds of illnesses. But I would like to think that he is saying more than this here: he is saying that a world with significantly reduced species diversity world would be a world in which human life would be greatly impoverished – would be an *inhuman* world. And let us not forget that a world with significantly reduced biological diversity is something that we are currently in serious danger of creating.

I tentatively suggest, then, a position somewhere in between the deep ecology and instrumentalist positions. A purely instrumentalist attitude towards the non-human world, I claim, makes no sense. The environment is part of us, as much as our arms and legs are, and we can no more take a purely instrumentalist attitude towards the environment than we can towards ourselves. But the deep ecology approach presupposes that the non-human environment can have a good that is independent of our good. On an optimistic view, there need be no conflict between an instrumentalist attitude towards the environment and a deep ecology one, once they have both been modified to take into account how evolution actually works, and how organisms, including us, relate to their/our environment.

Lancaster University

The Ugly Truth: Negative Aesthetics and Environment

EMILY BRADY

1. Introduction

In autumn 2009, BBC television ran a natural history series, 'Last Chance to See', with Stephen Fry and wildlife writer and photographer, Mark Carwardine, searching out endangered species. In one episode they retraced the steps Carwardine had taken in the 1980s with Douglas Adams, when they visited Madagascar in search of the aye-aye, a nocturnal lemur. Fry and Carwardine visited an aye-aye in captivity, and upon first setting eyes on the creature they found it rather ugly. After spending an hour or so in its company, Fry said he was completely 'under its spell'. A subsequent encounter with an aye-aye in the wild supported Fry's judgment of ugliness and fascination for the creature: 'The aye-aye is beguiling, certainly bizarre, for some even a little revolting. And I say, long may it continue being so.'[1]

Here, I explore some of the philosophical questions thrown up by this kind of experience. Ugliness has been theorized, not surprisingly, as a category of aesthetic value in opposition to the beautiful. It has been associated with qualities such as incoherence, disorder, disunity, and deformity and is said to cause negative feelings such as uneasiness, distaste, dislike, revulsion, but also fascination. Apart from discussions of tragedy and horror, contemporary aesthetics tends to neglect an exploration of potentially negative forms of aesthetic value. Work on aesthetics of nature and environmental aesthetics has also, on the whole, focused on positive aesthetic value.[2]

[1] Stephen Fry, video clip from 'Last Chance to See', http://www.bbc.co.uk/nature/species/Aye-aye#p004m3h9. Accessed 27/6/10.

[2] An important exception is: Y. Saito, 'The Aesthetics of Unscenic Nature', *Journal of Aesthetics and Art Criticism* **56**:2 (1998), 101–111. Also, Frank Sibley discusses mainly natural objects in his essay: 'Some Notes on Ugliness' in F. Sibley, *Approach to Aesthetics*, ed. J. Benson, J. Roxbee Cox, B. Redfern (Oxford: Clarendon Press, 2000), 191–206. Umberto Eco has edited a fascinating book relating to ugliness and the arts: *On Ugliness*, trans. A. McEwen (London: Harvill Secker, 2007).

doi:10.1017/S1358246111000221

While positive aesthetic value is important to human life and significant in motivating action to protect and restore environments, we can learn a great deal from looking at negative aesthetic value in nature too. I will examine negative aesthetic value in the form of ugliness, and the place of ugliness in our aesthetic experience of environment.[3] In opposition to a thesis popular in environmental aesthetics, 'positive aesthetics', I will argue that ugliness in nature is real, and that ugliness is a type of negative aesthetic value. I then make moves toward answering a question that lies at the intersection of aesthetics and ethics: what reasons might we have for thinking that there is some kind of value, if not aesthetic value, in our experiences of ugliness?

2. Positive Aesthetics

I object to a common approach which argues that ugliness is only apparent, and that what might seem to be ugly is in fact beautiful. This view holds that ugliness is really just a variety of beauty, and there is no negative aesthetic value in the world. This view has had a number of followers, including Augustine and, more recently, Stephen Pepper, John Dewey, and George Santayana.[4] In environmental aesthetics, this view takes the form of 'positive aesthetics', which has been developed by a number of philosophers, most notably, Allen Carlson.[5] As he puts it: 'the natural environment, insofar as it is untouched by man, has mainly positive aesthetic qualities; it is, for example, graceful, delicate, intense, unified, and orderly, rather than bland, dull, insipid, incoherent, and chaotic.'[6] Positive aesthetics can be analyzed into a set of stronger and weaker theses. The stronger theses include Carlson's claim, above, and the views that: (1) All of the natural world is beautiful; and (2) All of virgin

[3] I will deal exclusively with cases of ugliness in natural environments, rather than ugliness in cultural landscapes, the built environment, or human impacts on environments, e.g. clear-cutting.

[4] For some discussion of these views see R. Moore, 'Ugliness', in M. Kelly, ed. *Encyclopedia of Aesthetics* (New York: Oxford, 1998), 417–421.

[5] A. Carlson, 'Nature and Positive Aesthetics', *Environmental Ethics*, **6** (1984), 5–34. Other adherents include E. Hargrove, *Foundations of Environmental Ethics* (Englewood Cliffs: Prentice Hall, 1984); H. Rolston III, *Environmental Ethics* (Philadelphia: Temple University Press, 1988), 239ff. The position probably also has some roots in pre-Enlightenment theological views which held that one could not find ugliness as such in nature, since only beauty exists in God's creations.

[6] Carlson, 1984, 5.

nature is essentially good. Two weaker theses are: (3) Being natural is connected, in an essential way, to positive aesthetic qualities; and (4) Nature which is not affected by humans has more aesthetic value than nature which is.[7]

Several objections can be raised against these different theses. What is wild nature and does such a conception have any real meaning today given widespread anthropogenic effects on the environment? The position appears to favour wild over cultivated nature, but this seems wrong-headed. What justifies this? There may well be cases of cultivated nature that are beautiful. More worryingly, while some comparative aesthetic judgments of wild nature are possible, these will lie on a scale of the more or less beautiful, with apparently no negative aesthetic value in wild nature.[8] I will focus on this problem in the position, arguing against it that ugliness in the natural world is, in fact, real. Let me clarify from the start what I mean by ugliness being 'real'. I will not be arguing for a strong form of aesthetic realism. I take aesthetic properties to be relational and response-dependent. My use of the term 'real' is intended to support the idea that our judgments of negative aesthetic value are justifiable and ugliness cannot be explained away or replaced by some other property in the ways various writers have attempted. As I see it, the negative aesthetic value we call 'ugliness' is anchored in some ways in the object's non-aesthetic perceptual properties, such as colours, textures, forms, arrangements of elements, sounds and smells.

Now, how exactly does positive aesthetics hold that all wild nature is beautiful? The central claim is that something which appears to be ugly is in fact judged to be beautiful when we adjust aesthetic appreciation through a more holistic scientific story. Holmes Rolston, for example, argues that the apparently repulsive experience of a

[7] Based on a discussion by J. A. Fisher, 'Environmental Aesthetics' in D. Jamieson, ed. *Companion to Environmental Philosophy* (Malden, MA: Blackwell, 1998).

[8] For various discussions of positive aesthetics and its problems, see Saito, 1998; M. Budd, *Aesthetic Appreciation of Nature* (Oxford: Oxford University Press, 2002); S. Godlovitch, 'Offending Against Nature', *Environmental Values*, **7** (1998), 131–150; N. Hettinger, 'Animal Beauty, Ethics, and Environmental Preservation', *Environmental Ethics*, **32** (2010); G. Parsons, 'Nature Appreciation, Science and Positive Aesthetics', *British Journal of Aesthetics*, **42**:3 (2002), 279–295. Budd points out the problems too in establishing the most 'ambitious' form of the position, which would appear to demand that everything in wild nature has roughly equal (positive) aesthetic value (Budd, 2002, 127).

rotting elk carcass teeming with maggots has positive aesthetic value when we grasp that this natural occurrence is a key part of the successful, healthy functioning of an ecosystem. He says: 'the ugly parts do not subtract from but rather enrich the whole. The ugliness is contained, overcome, and integrates into positive, complex beauty.'[9] So, ugliness becomes part of a complex holistic beauty when we take on board the bigger ecological picture.

There are a number of problems with this type of explanation. First, it begs the question. How do the qualities of decaying flesh and the deformity of the carcass become beautiful? What is identified now as beautiful is not the qualities of the carcass itself, but the healthy functioning of an ecosystem that we find in some greater narrative. For comparison, consider a scab on human skin. The scab is ugly, evidence of a wound, and although part of a healing process with positive value, this doesn't convert the scab itself into something beautiful. This sort of reply denies the existence of ugliness by reframing the aesthetic object into a whole and avoids the point in question, which is particular perceptual qualities rather than broader, holistic knowledge of some natural event or system. Saito also raises this objection, pointing out that it is no longer clear what constitutes the aesthetic object: 'Is it the entire ecosystem or an individual object (like the carcass)?'[10] And even if one were to agree with the holistic beauty of the carcass within an ecosystem, 'it does not follow that the beauty of the whole implies the beauty of its parts'.[11] Ugliness cannot be explained away by a holistic story unless that story can show how the relevant aesthetic qualities themselves are beautiful. In arguing against this reframing, I do not intend to set up a dichotomy between aesthetic experience and knowledge. Knowledge of all kinds will inform and potentially enrich aesthetic experience, however, I maintain a distinction between aesthetic and scientific appreciation. In light of this, we can see how the positive aesthetics claim represents some sort of slide from the aesthetic to the scientific.

Leading from this issue, Rolston's explanation is undermined by a second problem, one which also arises for the 'conversion theory', a theory offered in answer to the problem referred to as the paradox of tragedy.[12] The paradox of tragedy rests in what is seen to be the

[9] See Rolston, 1988, 241.

[10] Saito, 1998, 104.

[11] Saito, 1998, 104.

[12] According to Moore, the paradox of tragedy is the 'generic parent' of the paradox of ugliness (1998, 420). There's been a long debate, reaching as far back as Aristotle, about how to resolve the paradox of tragedy. Also, there

paradox of feeling pleasure in response to painful, tragic subject matter in artworks. As David Hume once put it, 'It seems an unaccountable pleasure, which the spectators of a well-written tragedy receive from sorrow, terror, anxiety, and other passions, that are in themselves disagreeable and uneasy? The more they are touched and affected, the more they are delighted with the spectacle…'.[13] The conversion theory – which some say Hume held – argues that our displeasure in response to painful content is converted into something pleasurable through pleasure taken in the representational or depictive aspects of the artwork.

We can put the elk carcass problem in terms of a paradox of ugliness: how is it that something seemingly ugly and repulsive turns out to be something that has positive aesthetic value for us; something we can admire? Rolston and others argue that scientific knowledge frames and supports appropriate aesthetic judgments of nature, and such knowledge, it appears, is responsible for converting apparent ugliness into something beautiful. Yet, we are given no explanation about how such a conversion or transformation takes place.

A possible explanation might be found in discussions of ugliness and the arts. The aesthetic theories of Aristotle, Kant and many others have argued that ugliness and repulsiveness can be rendered beautiful through artistic representation. Kant writes, 'Beautiful art displays its excellence precisely by describing beautifully things

---

are a range of experiences and associated aesthetic qualities which fall into the category of what we might call 'difficult' or 'challenging' aesthetic experience or appreciation. In respect of both art and nature, and environments falling in between, several forms of appreciation can be included here, but perhaps most commonly: the sublime, tragedy and ugliness. In aesthetics, especially in the eighteenth century when these topics reached a pinnacle in philosophical debates, experiences falling into these categories were seen as difficult because they involve, commonly, a mixed response of negative and positive feelings, or just negative feeling, to qualities that are challenging or unattractive. The response to the sublime mixes liking, pleasure or delight with uneasiness, anxiety, fear, terror, and a feeling of being overwhelmed or overpowered (for example in accounts by Burke and Kant). Tragedy (as tragic drama) has been argued to involve a mix of negative and positive emotions, with negative or painful emotions such as fear or horror at the tragic events portrayed, and positive emotions in response to the artful representation of these events.

[13] D. Hume, 'Of Tragedy', in *Four Dissertations* (1757), reprinted in A. Neill and A. Ridley, ed., *Arguing About Art*, (New York: McGraw-Hill, 1995), 198.

that in nature would be ugly and displeasing. The furies, diseases, devastations of war, and the like can, as harmful things, be very beautifully described, indeed even represented in painting.'[14] So the argument would go that analogous to the way the representational and creative aspects of artworks are supposed to render unpleasant subject matter attractive, even beautiful, the 'content' of the aesthetic experience of the rotting elk carcass, that is, the putrefying flesh and feasting maggots, coupled with a rotting stench, are rendered beautiful and somehow pleasant through an ecological story. But it is difficult to grasp how such a transformation can take place through a scientific story rather than the imaginative, artistic one provided through a painterly representation, poem or fictional description. Instead of a second artistic object we have, rather, a live squirming phenomenon framed through an ecological context. It may be that we come to recognize how the rotting carcass represents the incredible life and death at work before our eyes, yet the sensuous qualities remain ugly.

My point here has also been made in relation to the conversion explanation in tragedy. The subject matter remains bleak and cannot be readily explained away, and the negative feelings evoked by tragedy are not converted at all, they remain negative. Of course, there may also be some pleasure, perhaps from the representational qualities of the artwork, but this does not obliterate the negative strand in our experience. Likewise, in the case of ugly nature, it remains ugly, even if our response is mixed, involving dislike but also curiosity, wonder or fascination rooted in the new knowledge we take on board. One of the main reasons such a conversion cannot take place is that to a great extent the concepts and knowledge of an ecological story just cannot penetrate the perceptual, sensuous experience of ugliness.

A further objection which supports real ugliness has been raised by Malcolm Budd. Essentially, he argues that all the scientific knowledge in the world cannot alter our judgments of negative aesthetic qualities in malformed nature: 'grossly malformed living things will remain grotesque no matter how comprehensible science renders their malformation.'[15] For example, learning that a bulbous growth on a tree or loss of hair on some animal is due to disease

[14] See I. Kant, *Critique of the Power of Judgment*, P. Guyer and E. Matthews, trans. (Cambridge: Cambridge University Press, [1790] 2000), §48, Ak. 312, 190. See also Aristotle, *Poetics* (1448b); Eco, 2007, 19.

[15] M. Budd, 'The Aesthetics of Nature' *Proceedings of the Aristotelian Society*, **100** (2000), 149.

may not render it less ugly. So, while knowledge acquired and fed into aesthetic appreciation can enrich our experience and enable us to see some qualities in a new light, it does not follow that knowledge will transform the ugly into the beautiful. Of course, it is also possible that the more knowledge we have the more ugly something becomes.

The aye-aye presents another type of case where knowledge does not shift perceptual qualities. Fry describes the lemur as looking 'as if someone has tried to turn a bat into a cat... and then stuck a few extra gadgets on it for good measure'.[16] The aye-aye is all out of proportion: small eyes, huge ears, a baldish body with a scrappy, shaggy coat and sharp razor-like incisor teeth. We learn that it gets much of its food through 'percussive foraging', tapping tree trunks and then scooping out grubs from inside the tree, using its teeth and a long, narrow, creepy middle finger. The aye-aye's calls have been described as 'grunts, screams and whimpers, as well as eerie sounds that can only be described as "fuffs" and "hai-hais"'.[17] It is native only to Madagascar and endangered as a result of habitat destruction. According to local folklore the aye-aye is a harbinger of evil, and apparently so-named because it is what people cry out when they see one. The more knowledge one has, perhaps the more one reacts with mild revulsion. In Fry's response, which is supported by both formal scientific knowledge and local knowledge, there is curiosity and wonder, but this does not discount or outweigh his negative reaction connected to the ugly mix of features.

To take another example, predation is a natural occurrence which enables mammals to exist and prosper. When we observe acts of predation they display positive aesthetic qualities such as the remarkable, graceful action of a cheetah chasing a gazelle. But the activity witnessed is also violent and bloody, leading to the death of another animal.[18] Explaining such activity only in positive aesthetic terms verges on a kind of aestheticization of nature (I have more to say about this below).

Some philosophers have taken a slightly different route to trying to explain ugliness in the world. Samuel Alexander has argued that 'Ugliness...is an ingredient in aesthetic beauty, as the discords in music or the horrors of tragedy. When it becomes ugly as a kind of

[16] Reported by Mark Carwardine in, 'Last Chance to see the aye-aye?' BBC Earth News, 18/9/09 http://news.bbc.co.uk/earth/hi/earth_news/newsid_8258000/8258569.stm. Accessed 2/11/09.

[17] M. Cawardine, 'The aye-aye', http://www.bbc.co.uk/lastchancetosee/sites/animals/?set=ayeaye. Accessed 27/6/10.

[18] See Hettinger, 2010.

beauty it has been transmuted. Such ugliness is difficult beauty.'[19] Although some forms of ugliness border on difficult beauty or overlap with terrible and horrible qualities in the sublime, I maintain that ugliness exists independently of other kinds of aesthetic value and disvalue. This needs teasing out.

First, the cheetah-gazelle chase and kill presents a case of something that has both beautiful and ugly elements: the grace of the chase and the bloody attack of the kill. But the beauty does not negate the ugliness that is found there. On my approach, it is judged as a beautiful chase with an ending causing revulsion, rather than something holistically beautiful, where beauty overcomes any other elements. This is of course from the human point of view – but that is my concern here: aesthetic judgments by humans of the rest of nature.

This suggests a similar type of case, where an unattractive thing, perhaps a tree or animal ravaged by disease, has beautiful aspects. Also, we often talk of the 'inner beauty' of things. What's going on in these cases, I believe, is not a rejection or explaining away of the perceptual qualities of ugliness, but a recognition of *other* features that are appealing, perhaps beautiful actions of some kind. So, as Ron Moore points out: 'an ugly thing may have its appealing, even beautiful aspects without thereby becoming "negatively beautiful" or "beautifully ugly"'.[20]

To conclude this section, two further, brief points provide additional support for my argument. Against views that attempt to explain away ugliness, we want to know what constitutes proper cases of negative value. Just as we want to understand what makes something beautiful, we want to understand what makes something ugly. It does not reflect our experiences of the world to identify only instances of terrible beauty, without recognizing that there are instances of true ugliness. Also, it is notable that Marcia Eaton, a philosopher who supports a cognitive approach to aesthetic appreciation of nature similar to views put forward by Carlson and Rolston, disagrees with the positive aesthetics thesis. While she believes that knowledge can enable shifts in perception, she also holds that cases of genuine ugliness remain. Eaton uses the example of an ugly

[19] S. Alexander, *Beauty and Other Forms of Value* (New York, 1968), as quoted in Moore, 1998, 418. Carolyn Korsmeyer argues for this kind of position in 'Terrible Beauties', in M. Kieran, ed. *Contemporary Debates in Aesthetics and Philosophy of Art* (Blackwell, 2005), 47–63.

[20] Moore, 1998, 418.

shell, the pen shell, described in shell guidebooks as unattractive and avoided by collectors.[21]

3. What is ugliness in nature?

If ugliness in nature cannot be explained away as some variety of beauty, then we need some kind of explanation of what ugliness is. What kind of substantive account can be given about ugliness in nature? To explore this issue, I begin with a few distinctions. Many theories of ugliness, importantly, distinguish it from the non-aesthetic reaction of *strong* repulsion or disgust.[22] Repulsion or disgust of a strong kind may be so overwhelming that attention to the object either never gets a foothold in the first place or is cut short. Because, as many would argue, the aesthetic response necessarily involves some kind of sustained perceptual attention, disgust must be classed as a more visceral sensory reaction. This is not to say that ugliness in a person or an animal, say, could not include repulsive qualities or that the aesthetic response might have elements of disgust in a weaker sense. My point refers to what lies at an extreme and at what point the response becomes non-aesthetic.

Another important point relates to how beauty and ugliness are related. We can view them as lying on a scale of positive and negative values. On the positive side of the scale are varieties of beauty, while varieties of ugliness lie on the negative side. The scale is intended to show that ugliness is something associated with objective qualities; that it can exist in greater or lesser degrees; and that the concept of ugliness is not simply an empty notion understood as the absence of beauty.[23] Some have argued that a zero point lies in the middle, suggesting a kind of aesthetic indifference, where one does not care one way or the other about the object. It could be that this represents some sort of aesthetic neutrality. Frank Sibley suggests that this neutrality is given content in terms of our use of certain aesthetic

[21] M. Eaton, 'Beauty and Ugliness In and Out of Context' in M. Kieran, ed. *Contemporary Debates in Aesthetics and Philosophy of Art* (Oxford: Blackwell, 2005), 48.

[22] On disgust, see D. Pole, 'Disgust and Other Forms of Aversion' in G. Roberts, ed., *Aesthetics, Form and Emotion* (London: Duckworth, 1983); C. Korsmeyer, 'The Delightful, Delicious and Disgusting', *Journal of Aesthetics and Art Criticism*, **60**:3 (2002), 217–225; W. Miller, *The Anatomy of Disgust* (Cambridge, MA: Harvard University Press, 1997).

[23] Moore, 1998, 419.

concepts like 'plain', 'ordinary', or 'undistinguished'.[24] These expressions are used in aesthetic judgments of things that are unremarkable. I think Sibley's got it wrong here. Such judgments are not really neutral at all, but rather belong to aesthetic disvalue. To call a person plain-looking or ordinary is surely to make a negative judgment. The person does not exhibit any positive qualities, that is, there is an absence of attractive features. It makes more sense to describe unremarkable things as lying on the side of negative aesthetic value, although not synonymous with ugliness. Ugly things can be new and remarkable in our experience, invoking curiosity, as in the case of the aye-aye.

How might we unpack that negative side of the scale in relation to nature? Ugliness, like beauty, varies with objects, environments, etc., being more or less ugly. It is associated, certainly, with qualities like deformity, decay, disease, disfigurement, disorder, messiness, distortion, odd proportions, mutilation, grating sounds, being defiled, spoiled, defaced, brutal, wounded, dirty, muddy, slimy, greasy, foul, putrid, and so on.[25] This is not to suggest a universal view of what ugliness consists in. Ugliness may be real but it is not reducible to one property or another, and we could not know that something is ugly without experiencing it firsthand for ourselves. Also, as noted earlier, qualities we associate with ugliness may exist alongside attractive ones, just as negative and positive aesthetic values can be associated with the same thing, for example an attractive bird with an ugly, grating call.

In thinking through ugliness, we ought to embrace a broad understanding as indicated by some of the terms just listed. Because beauty has been historically associated with order and harmony, many philosophers have identified ugliness with disorder and disharmony.[26] For example, Rudolf Arnheim describes ugliness as 'a clash of uncoordinated orders…when each of its parts has an order of its own, but these orders do not fit together, and thus the whole is fractured.'[27] This captures the ugliness identified in the aye-aye's odd features, but this view is both too formal and too narrow because it does not capture the more disgusting-type features of ugly things such as slimy textures, rotting stenches or horrible sounds.

24 Sibley, 2001, 192.

25 See Sibley, 2001, and also Eco's (2007) list, 16.

26 See R. Lorand, 'Beauty and Its Opposites', *Journal of Aesthetics and Art Criticism*, **52**:4 (1994), 399–406.

27 Lorand, 1994, 402.

Some philosophers have argued that ugliness in nature is essentially connected to deformity or malformation, where this counts as an aesthetic defect in some natural form or kind, usually of the organic variety.[28] Sibley rightly points out that only things capable of being deformed can be understood as such and thus ugly in this way. For example, while it might make sense to judge a tree to be ugly due to its deformity, he says it would be odd to describe a stone as deformed.[29] However, and in any case, ugliness is not always tied to deformity, and we need to understand ugliness more broadly as connected to a variety of qualities, like those mentioned above. A wolf fish may be judged as ugly in virtue of its odd features – bulgy eyes, widely spaced teeth, outsize mouth and dull grey colour – without being a case of a deformed fish. The aye-aye is ugly in virtue of having a discordant mix of features, especially, but not solely, when compared to the features of human beings.

So far I have been referring mainly to ugly qualities or properties. But judgments of ugliness are, in my view, importantly made by valuers ascribing negative value to things and having particular reactions such as shock, repugnance, aversion, and so on. In this respect, ugliness relates to both properties in objects and to the cognitive stock, imaginative associations, emotions and biases of individual valuers across communities and cultures. Ugliness, like other aesthetic properties, is response-dependent, depending upon a valuer valuing something. Undoubtedly, while we will find agreement on ugliness across cultures, ugliness will also vary culturally and historically, as Umberto Eco has shown so well in his recent anthology, *On Ugliness*.[30]

Let me take this analysis a step further by classifying ugliness, rather tentatively, into three types.[31] This will help to flesh out

[28] See Sibley, 2001; Glenn Parsons makes the claim that deformity only applies to organic nature, a point which he uses to support positive aesthetics in relation to inorganic nature. See: 'Natural Functions and the Aesthetic Appreciation of Inorganic Nature', *British Journal of Aesthetics*, **44**:1 (2004), 44–56; Cf. Budd, 2002.

[29] I'm not convinced that Sibley's second example is apt – a geologist tells me that we can understand deformity in rocks (particularly crystals) in terms of irregularities through malformation.

[30] Eco, 2007.

[31] For some other ways of classifying ugliness, see J. Stolnitz, 'On Ugliness in Art', *Philosophy and Phenomenological Research*, **11**:1 (1950), 1–24; P. Carmichael, 'The Sense of Ugliness', *Journal of Aesthetics and Art Criticism*, **30**:4 (1972), 495–498.

some of the complexities that arise with ugliness as an aesthetic category.

(i) *Relative ugliness* is ugliness relative to some norm. Probably most cases of ugliness are of this type. For example, humans may find the faces of some other humans ugly because they are being compared to some ideal of human beauty. Or, a human may find a toad's face ugly relative to some norm of human facial beauty. It's not uncommon for humans – and possibly other species – to judge ugliness relative to norms set by their own species. Comparisons to such norms also explain differences between cultural norms and why some things may be judged as ugly in some cultures while not in others.

(ii) *Inherent ugliness* identifies something which is ugly in itself and not in relation to any norm. There may be fewer instances of this, but it is certainly the case that some things are just ugly. Some candidates frequently mentioned are eels, spiders, ticks, mosquitoes, mudflats, muddy rivers and burnt forests. The objection could be made here that these sorts of things aren't really ugly at all, rather there is some deep-seated or not so deep-seated bias operating on our judgment which makes them so. (I deal with this sort of problem below.)

(iii) *Apparent ugliness* identifies cases where things are considered in themselves, wholly apart from any comparisons to other things, and wholly apart from any knowledge or unfavourable associations; a purely formal appreciation, if you will. Considering toads in themselves or even a wound or bruise, we might in fact see these things as beautiful, whereas if we were to compare them to some ideal norm, for example, healthy, glowing skin, they would be ugly. We might have to sever a bruise from its extra-aesthetic context, say, the causes and pain related to the bruise to see it as beautiful. As Frances Hutcheson points out: 'there is no form which seems necessarily disagreeable of itself when we…compare it with nothing better of a kind…swine, serpents of all kinds, and some insects [are] really beautiful enough'.[32]

The category of apparent ugliness suggests another form of the argument which attempts to explain away ugliness if we take a certain kind of approach. In this case it is not the role played by knowledge, but rather, the role played by keen attention alone, and importantly, setting aside or backgrounding biases, cultural norms, comparisons, context, etc. In some cases it will be true that setting aside cultural or personal biases will enable us to appreciate the beauty of something. Snakes are a possible case in point. Yet, it does not necessarily follow

[32] Quoted in Sibley, 2001, 205.

that things appreciated apart from negative associations and so on will be judged to be, after all, beautiful. This raises a similar problem for apparent ugliness, which I call the 'familiarity effect'. There will be cases where the more familiar we become with something, the less ugly it will seem to us; the initial shock will have worn off. Perhaps the more time we spend with a toad, the greater aesthetic interest of a positive kind we might find. Yet, it will still be possible that it just remains ugly, and in fact, we may come to grasp better why we find its features so ugly. It does not follow from keen perceptual attention or repeated viewings that an aesthetic object gains in aesthetic value (or indeed, the other way around: a beautiful thing does not necessarily lose value after repeated experiences of it).

Some headway has been made in arguing for and substantiating the reality of ugliness in nature. Given the categories of ugliness set out above, I have suggested that most cases of ugliness will be relative to some norm, but there are also cases of inherent ugliness. I have challenged the ideas underlying the category of apparent ugliness, that is, keen and exclusive perceptual attention deal with all cases of apparent ugliness, and so ugliness is not always apparent. There is much that I have not been able to address here. Further work is needed, for example, in thinking through more finely grained distinctions between kinds of natural ugliness (e.g. grotesque, disgusting, disordered).

I have also set aside cultural issues and a discussion of moral issues involved in aesthetic appreciation of ugliness, for example, where ugliness is used to identify evil character, a view taken by the ancient philosopher, Plotinus, and others.[33] Another key issue in discussions of moral ugliness is the nature of our reactions to ugly things and how that reflects on our moral character, e.g. the problem of taking delight in the misfortune of deformed, mutilated, etc., nature, or treating ugliness as some sort of spectacle. These topics take us into the realm of moral philosophy, and I am not able to pursue those tricky issues here.

4. Why care about ugliness?

In working toward a conclusion, I would like to suggest some ways that natural ugliness has significance in human lives. Given that ugliness is unpleasant and unattractive, if not entirely repulsive, why

[33] See Moore, 1998; Stolnitz's (1950) discussion of Stephen Pepper's position, 8ff; and K. Rosenkrantz's study, *The Aesthetic of Ugliness* (1853).

might it matter? In other words, what value, if not aesthetic value, does it have? To ask this question is not to explain ugliness away and assert its positive aesthetic value, but rather to ask what sort of place negative aesthetic value holds. The answer to my question is also significant in conservation terms. Natural beauty and its aesthetic value can provide one reason among others for conserving environments and species, but in the case of negative aesthetic value there is no obvious *aesthetic* reason to motivate conservation of ugly environments or species.

When ugliness is mixed with fascination and curiosity, this explains why we might be engaged by ugly things – as mentioned above, ugliness is not synonymous with being boring, dull or insignificant. There is no doubt that ugly things can capture our imagination in some ways, at least because of their novelty. Now, while this answer helps in understanding the significance of some forms of ugliness, it does not really address the difficult or challenging nature of ugliness, and it is this that especially interests me. In thinking through the place of ugliness in human lives, I want to avoid a strategy which relies exclusively upon a hedonic theory of value, that is, an approach where aesthetic experience is understood in terms of pleasurable responses, rather than also valuing the more nuanced responses or effects that arise from such experience. As we have seen, a common move is to try to explain away ugliness, to show that it is in fact a variety of beauty where the pleasant things in life, nature and so on, are always the case. In opposition to this, in response to why we engage with tragic art, Stephen Davies argues that we engage all the time in activities that are difficult, painful, challenging, and we come back for more. That's the kind of creatures we are.[34] Challenging experiences contribute to the worthwhile life; and they have value in ways unconnected to pleasure. I believe this is also the case with ugliness in nature.

In an effort to explain the paradox of ugliness, some approaches try to show 'how our experience of ugliness can be edifying, no matter how negative its inherent character.'[35] This connects to a long tradition in aesthetics which argues that negative emotions can be edifying in various ways.[36] Experiencing the full range of emotions can deepen our experience of other humans, other forms of life, and things unlike ourselves. These negative feelings in aesthetic

[34] S. Davies, *Musical Meaning and Expression* (Ithaca: Cornell University Press, 1994), 316–320.

[35] Moore, 1998, 420.

[36] See note 12; Korsmeyer, 2005.

experience can acquaint us with a range of feelings not available with easy beauty. This kind of exploration is also a feature of the sublime and the tragic, where we confront things that terrify or disturb us, though at some safe distance.

It is also a kind of exploration evident in various forms of avant-garde art and some forms of land and environmental art which challenge norms of beauty, art as beauty and the scenic. I have in mind, in particular, Robert Smithson's 'esthetics of disappointment', as he called it, his own artistic exploration of how both human and non-human forces of entropy and decay permeate our experience.[37] Aesthetic engagement of this kind can have the effect of discovering a capacity to apprehend ugliness beyond, or indeed, because of, ourselves and our own actions. Sheila Lintott, Jason Boaz Simus and Thom Heyd have argued that some environmental artworks remind us of the destructive forces wreaked by humans upon nature, functioning to raise environmental awareness.[38] In this vein, we might think of Smithson's *Asphalt Rundown* or *Partially Buried Woodshed* – certainly not beautiful works – as evoking a sense of destruction and accompanying feelings of unease. In the non-artistic context, the contemplation of ugliness in nature caused by humans – aesthetic offences against nature as some philosophers have described them (graffiti in national parks; strip-mining, clear-cutting) – may also be explored, with these kinds of cases having the effect of an enhanced understanding of environmental harm.[39]

Proponents of positive aesthetics might object that connecting ugliness in nature with these edifying effects smacks of humanizing nature and failing to take it on its own terms, that is, bringing value somehow back to ourselves. The account of ugliness I have given here does not attempt to sidestep the cultural context we bring to our judgments of ugly nature. Positive aesthetics and scientific cognitivism together argue for the importance of taking nature on its own terms and getting past what might be seen as a shallow form of aesthetic valuing which ignores the deeper ecological story. What

[37] See various essays by and interviews with Smithson in, J. Flam (ed), *Robert Smithson: The Collected Writings* (Berkeley: University of California Press, 1996).

[38] S. Lintott, 'Ethically Evaluating Environmental Art: Is It Worth It', *Ethics, Place and Environment*, **10**:3 (2007), 263–277; J. Boaz Simus, 'Environmental Art and Ecological Citizenship', *Environmental Ethics*, **30**:1 (2008); T. Heyd 'Reflections on Reclamation Through Art', *Ethics, Place and Environment*, **10**:3 (2007), 339–345.

[39] See Godlovitch, 1998; A. Carlson, *Aesthetics and the Environment* (New York and London: Routledge, 2000).

responses can be given to this type of concern? First, it can be argued that science is itself shaped by culture, and its categories are not necessarily the best ones through which to aesthetically value nature. Second, while positive aesthetics would appear to value nature in itself, on its 'own terms', it may be in danger of aestheticizing nature, that is, not fully grasping or taking on board negative aesthetic value and how this kind of value operates in human-nature relations.[40] While the environmental education implicit in positive aesthetics is laudable, especially in how it functions to move beyond personal and potentially distorting biases, fears, narrow norms or standards and in turn reassess previous negative aesthetic judgments, it would be naïve and idealistic to assume that this approach will always eliminate negative aesthetic value. Positive aesthetics is liable to present an incomplete theory of environmental aesthetics, risking an attitude which ignores the true diversity of characteristics possessed by a range of environments and animals. Ignoring ugliness potentially impoverishes this dimension of our experience of environments and creatures of all kinds that fall beyond the realm of comfortable aesthetics.[41] We might also find that experiences of ugliness fulfill some function in human and non-human lives, where disgust and revulsion play some key role in enabling survival.[42]

Ugliness expands our emotional range and widens our experience of challenging things, leading to a richer awareness of environments both familiar and strange. We might say that it increases our 'aesthetic intelligence' through developing engaged attention to the great diversity of aesthetic qualities. Through exploration of the negative side of aesthetic value, a more uneasy and distanced kind of relationship with nature emerges. Depending on the mix of reactions, curiosity and the charm of fascination can decrease the distance, but with no aesthetic attraction as such, the relationship is more strained. Our interactions with ugliness are potentially more complex than easy beauty, as the

[40] Parsons (2002) argues that although there can be a variety of aesthetic categories through which we can aesthetically appreciate nature, we ought to choose those as most appropriate via a beauty-making criterion, which gives us the best aesthetic value.

[41] See also Korsmeyer, 2005; and S. Lintott, 'Eco-Friendly Aesthetics' *Environmental Ethics*, **28** (2006), 56–76.

[42] In so far as there could be some biological advantage to negative values in nature, disgust, fear, aversion, and alienation from nature, for example, have been seen as functioning in ways that provide security, protection, and safety. See S. Kellert *Values of Life* (Washington, DC: Island Press, 1996).

peculiarities of nature become foregrounded in our experience. The edifying effects arising out of this aesthetic relationship can feed into attitudes of care and concern, and with additional values such as biodiversity and existence values, lead to the protection of the bizarre aye-aye or ugly toads. Life just wouldn't be the same without them.

University of Edinburgh

The Temporal and Spatial Scales of Global Climate Change and the Limits of Individualistic and Rationalistic Ethics

J. BAIRD CALLICOTT

Here I argue that the hyper-individualistic and rationalistic ethical paradigms – originating in the late eighteenth century and dominating moral philosophy, in various permutations, ever since – cannot capture the moral concerns evoked by the prospect of global climate change. Those paradigms are undone by the temporal and spatial scales of climate change. To press my argument, I deploy two famous philosophical tropes – John Rawls's notion of the original position and Derek Parfit's paradox – and another that promises to become famous: Dale Jamieson's six little ditties about Jack and Jill. I then go on to argue that the spatial and especially the temporal scales of global climate change demand a shift in moral philosophy from a hyper-individualistic ontology to a thoroughly holistic ontology. It also demands a shift from a reason-based to a sentiment-based moral psychology. Holism in environmental ethics is usually coupled with non-anthropocentrism in theories constructed to provide moral considerability for transorganismic entities – such as species, biotic communities, and ecosystems. The spatial and temporal scales of climate, however, render non-anthropocentric environmental ethics otiose, as I more fully explain. Thus the environmental ethic here proposed to meet the moral challenge of global climate change is holistic but anthropocentric. I start with Jamieson's six little ditties about Jack and Jill.[1]

[1] These 'ditties' (as I call them) were first published in Dale Jamieson, 'The Moral and Political Challenges of Climate Change', in S. Moser and L. Dilling, eds., *Creating a Climate for Change: Communicating Climate Change and Facilitating Social Change* (Cambridge: Cambridge University Press, 2007): 475–484. They have been variously presented in subsequent work by Jamieson as 'examples' or 'cases'. I take responsibility for calling them 'ditties' (in homage to the song 'Jack 'n Diane' by John Mellencamp) and I have also taken the liberty of editing them for a bit more elegance and clarity of phrasing.

doi:10.1017/S1358246111000233

> Ditty 1.
>
> Jack intentionally steals Jill's bicycle. One *individual* acting intentionally has harmed another *individual*; the *individuals* and the harm are clearly identifiable; and they are closely related in time and space.

This is as clear a case as one could want of the classic parameters of modern moral philosophy. An identifiable individual human agent acts reprehensibly on an identifiable individual human patient. Whether we account for the reprehensibility of Jack's action in terms of Jill's lost utility or in terms of the violation of Jill's dignity and associated rights is beside my point here.

As Jamieson goes on to say, 'If we vary the case on any of these dimensions, we may still see the resulting cases as posing a moral problem, but their claims to be … paradigm moral problems will be weaker…'[2]

> Ditty 2.
>
> Jack is part of an unacquainted group of strangers, each of whom, acting independently, takes one part of Jill's bike, resulting in the bike's disappearance.

In this case, the reprehensibility of bicycle theft is distributed over a set of agents, Jack among them, and thus the personal reprehensibility of Jack's action is proportionately attenuated.

> Ditty 3.
>
> Jack takes one part from each of a large number of bikes, one of which belongs to Jill.

This case is the obverse of the previous one. The harm Jack inflicts is distributed over a set of patients, and the harm Jill suffers is proportionately attenuated. Jill still has a bicycle, but she has to replace, say, the saddle. And Jack presumably assembles a bicycle from the parts he steals – a saddle from Jill, a sprocket from Jane, a wheel from Joan, and so on.

[2] Dale Jamieson, 'The Post-Kyoto Climate: A Gloomy Forecast', *Georgetown International Environmental Law Review* **20** (2009): 537–551, 545.

Ditty 4.

Jack and Jill live on different continents, and the loss of Jill's bike is the consequence of a causal chain that begins with Jack ordering a used bike at a shop.

In this case, the spatial dimension is varied. Jack does not act in proximity to Jill. Further, Jack does not intend to harm Jill. Jack innocently buys a bicycle in Jamaica, let us say, which was stolen by Joe from Jill in Japan.

Ditty 5.

Jack lives many centuries before Jill, and consumes materials that are essential to bike manufacturing; as a result, it will not be possible for Jill to have a bicycle.

In this case, the temporal dimension is varied. Here too Jack does not act in proximity to Jill, nor too does he intend to harm Jill. Indeed, as I shall show with Parfit's help, had Jack and his cohort been more frugal, Jill would not exist and Jane would have her bicycle.

Ditty 6.

Acting independently, Jack and a large number of unacquainted people set in motion a chain of events that causes a large number of future people who will live in another part of the world, from ever having bikes.

In this case all the dimensions of the original paradigmatic (un)ethical exchange vary at once: multiple agents adversely, but unintentionally, affect multiple patients who are distant in both time and space.

Jamieson's Ditty 6 is an allegory about climate change. Acting independently, we in the industrialized world have unintentionally set in motion a chain of events – burned fossil fuels and in consequence increased atmospheric carbon and other green house gases – that will cause a large number of future people to suffer the potentially catastrophic effects of climate change. Clearly, this a moral problem; indeed a moral problem of colossal proportions. But by the classical eighteenth-century ethical über-paradigm (inclusive of both its consequentialist and deontological variants), we can intelligibly assign responsibility for this problem only to individual agents – Jack_1, Jack_2, Jack_3 ... Jack_n – for the harm they inflict on innocent individual patients – Jill_1, Jill_2, Jill_3 ... Jill_n. If so constrained in our moral ontology, then individual responsibility for causing global climate change and for mitigating it or for aiding individual patients in adapting to it is so distributed (over literally billions of individual agents) that each contemporary denizen of the industrial world can be assigned only a negligible share. Those conscientious enough to install solar-energy panels on their rooftops, drive hybrid vehicles, and undertake other life-style changes to reduce their carbon footprints also negligibly contribute to mitigating global climate change. Such an ethic of personal virtue is spiritually ennobling, but relieves the human suffering or the violation of human rights attendant on global climate change – presently, soon, or in the distant future – not one iota.

If we hold the temporal dimension constant and consider only the present generation and foreseeable future generations, the classic individualistic moral ontology can be made to serve, at least in theory. Those who are presently and will soon suffer the greatest harm from global climate change are the least responsible for causing it and the least able to cope with it. Thus philosophers wed to the classic individualistic moral ontology approach the problem as one of international justice.[3] In theory, the individual industrialized Jacks of the world could be compelled to compensate the individual non-industrialized Jills. Attempting to match up an individual Jack with an individual Jill to effect such compensation is as incoherent as it is impractical – because, as Jamieson's allegory clearly shows, the causal chain of events that link individual agent and individual patient are indirect (and indeed nonlinear). Industrial governments might tax their citizens and pay into a global escrow fund in proportion to the aggregated carbon footprints of their citizens and the fund might be distributed to governments of the countries most vulnerable to global climate change, with the presumption that the recipient governments spend the restitution payments for adaptation projects, such as sea walls. In addition, the governments of the industrialized Jacks might impose a carbon tax on their citizens or adopt

[3] Notable among such philosophers are Stephen M. Gardiner, 'Ethics and Global Climate Change', *Ethics* **114** (2004): 555–600; James Garvey, *The Ethics of Climate Change: Right and Wrong in a Warming World* (London: Continuum, 2008); Dale Jamieson, 'Climate Change and Global Environmental Justice', in P. Edwards and C. Miller, ed., *Changing the Atmosphere* (Cambridge, Mass.: MIT Press, 2001): 287–308; Henry Shue, 'Climate' in D. Jamieson, ed., *A Companion to Environmental Philosophy* (Oxford: Blackwell, 2001): 449–459; and Peter Singer, [Chapter] 2. 'One Atmosphere' in *One World: The Ethics of Globalization*, Second Edition (New Haven, Conn.: Yale Nota Bene, 2004): 14–50.

cap and trade measures to reduce green house gas emissions and thus mitigate more drastic global climate change.

Of course, there are huge practical impediments to the success of such an international climate-justice regime – the political intransigence of the governments of industrialized nation states and rampant corruption in the governments of non-industrialized nation states being, perhaps, the most salient. But, this is philosophy and we are here concerned only with the conceptual cogency of essentially Enlightenment moral philosophy confronted by the biggest moral problem of the new millennium. And an actually implemented government-to-government international climate justice regime – however improbable it may be to effectively implement – would penalize individual Jacks and compensate individual Jills for harms indirectly and unintentionally inflicted on the latter by the former.

So far, so good: Enlightenment moral philosophy meets the challenge by (1) collectivizing moral agents and patients via state-to-state exchanges and (2) then distributing monetized penalties to individual perpetrators and damages to individual victims. The prevailing individualistic ethical ontology is strained by the planetary *spatial scale* and causal indirection and diffusion of the moral problem of global climate change. But, as we see, it holds up under the strain, at least in theory. The centennial and millennial *temporal scale* of global climate change, however, swamps that ontology and challenges environmental philosophers to think in new and fresh ways about ethics.

For those of us of a certain age – my age – future generations exist right along side us. Let us stipulate that the span of a generation is twenty-five years. I am about seventy years old. My son is about forty-five years old and his son, my grandson, is about 15 years old. Suppose I live to see my grandson's son or daughter – my great grandson or great granddaughter – born five or ten years hence. Someone born in the year 2015 or 2020 has an excellent chance to live into the twenty-second century. I can thus be concerned personally about individuals who now exist or fairly soon will exist about a century out. And I badly want the world they will inherit to be habitable and a world worth living in. But beyond a century into the future it is logically impossible to be concerned about future generations *individually* – because of a permutation of the Parfit Paradox.

Derek Parfit considers two cases of pregnancy.[4] Parfit's own imagined case of a fourteen-year-old girl who decides to become pregnant

[4] Derek Parfit, *Reasons and Persons* (New York: Oxford University Press, 1984).

and thus give her son or daughter an ill-defined 'bad start in life' is problematic for obvious reasons.[5] So let's construct a clearer permutation: A woman discovers that she is both pregnant and ill with a disease that, if untreated, will cause her child to be born with a serious disability. Surely classic individualistic ethics, whether utilitarian or deontological, would mandate that the woman treat her disease and spare her child living a life burdened by a serious disability. Another woman is not now pregnant, but she has been trying to become pregnant, whereupon she discovers that she is ill with a different disease that would cause a child she might conceive to be born with a serious disability. Her disease, however, cannot be treated, but she will get over it and return to health in a few months. Should she postpone her pregnancy? The two cases seem to be morally identical except for the temporal dimension, but the temporal dimension sharply divides them. If, in the second case, the woman postpones her pregnancy a different individual will be born because a different egg, with a different set of genes, will be fertilized by a different sperm. One individual who might have existed did not exist because the woman postponed her pregnancy. Is it better to exist and to be burdened by a deformity or to have been deprived of existence altogether?

Peter Singer infamously endorsed infanticide because, in his utilitarian opinion, it would indeed be better not to exist at all than to exist with a serious disability that caused or occasioned much suffering.[6] The storm of outraged protest by disabled persons that subsequently greeted Singer – he was shouted down, during the summer of 1989, and prevented to speak in Germany, Switzerland, and Austria – suggests that his answer to that question is by no means definitive.[7] Indeed, those who have the greatest stake in how that question is answered – those who would not have existed if Singer had been able to influence reproductive policy – answered that question oppositely to him.

One may wonder if such speculation about the preferences of nonexistent individuals is so much philosophical nonsense. John Rawls is one of the most highly acclaimed and persuasive moral philosophers of the twentieth century. His theory of justice as fairness rests on the conceptual plausibility of imagining a purely hypothetical 'original

[5] Ibid. 358.

[6] Peter Singer, *Unsanctifying Human Life: Essays on Ethics*, Helen Kuhse, ed. (Oxford: Blackwell, 2002).

[7] Peter Singer, 'On Being Silenced in Germany', *New York Review of Books* (August 15, 1991).

position' behind a 'veil of ignorance'.[8] Rawls asks us to imagine a cohort of free and rational individuals about to enter into a social contract who do not know with what the accidents of birth will endow them. They do not know their eventual gender, race, physical and mental endowments, tastes, values, and so on. Free from all such potential biases, Rawls inquires into what basic principles of justice persons in the original position would settle on and what policies and laws, flowing from those principles, they would write into a social contract that all would be willing to sign? Surely they would prohibit discrimination based on race or gender, for example, not knowing what race or gender they might turn out to be. We might parfit, as it were, Rawls's original position and imagine that some of their policy choices would expose them to the risk, not that they would suffer from discrimination, but that they would not exist at all. Quite apart from speculation about what policies those in this parfited original position would be inclined to enact, my point is simply that, thanks to Rawls, we have become quite complacent about considering the preferences of non-existing but potentially existing individuals.

Still, one may wonder what has all this to do with intergenerational ethics and the temporal scale of global climate change. Just this. As Parfit goes on to note, if now we make radical changes in environmental policy and law (in an effort to mitigate global climate change) that will entail radical changes in such aspects of our lives as transportation, lighting, heating, diet, and so on. Those changes will lead to changes in the way men and women chance to meet, to fall in love, when they will copulate, and thus what individuals will be given birth to. So, return now to Rawls's original position, as parfited. Those in it would have us make no change whatsoever in environmental policy and law because those changes would entail that other individuals would exist instead of them. Or, to make another permutation of the Rawls-Parfit paradox, those individuals destined to compose future generations if we do nothing to mitigate climate change, would, if given the choice, have to choose between living in a world of ever more violent weather, ever more impoverished biodiversity, ever more virulent disease, ever more extreme heat and drought – or not living at all.

It might be objected that I am taking Rawls too literally and not appreciating the force of the hypotheticality of his original-position/veil-of-ignorance philosophical trope. But my point can be made by

[8] John Rawls, *A Theory of Justice* (Cambridge, Mass.: Harvard University Press, 1971).

reference to the actual past as well as to the imagined future. The Great Depression of the 1930s caused great suffering. It might have been foreseen, by economic policy makers in the 1920s, and thus averted with the implementation of more conservative fiscal and monetary policies. But if it had been averted I would not exist. My parents postponed marriage and child bearing because they were jobless and poor during the Depression. Thus, I find it hard to regret the occurrence of the Great Depression of the 1930s, even with all the suffering it caused. Lest you think I am being unconscionably selfish – condoning pandemic economic suffering just so I can exist – probably half my generational cohort would not exist had the Great Depression not unfolded as it actually did. Nor would any of our children, grandchildren, or great grandchildren – those for whom we so dearly care and those for whom we are willing to take pains now so that their world will remain habitable.

An enormous philosophical literature has been generated by the Parfit paradox, much of it devoted to avoiding the 'repugnant conclusion' to which Parfit himself was led by it. An equally enormous philosophical literature has been generated by Rawls's notion of the 'original position'. I do not pretend to contribute to those literatures by fusing these two famous philosophical tropes. Rather the Rawls-Parfit paradox, as I have here sketched it, exposes the bizarre quandaries to which we moral philosophers are led by cleaving to a hyper-individualistic moral ontology. It does not demonstrate that which is introspectively false: that we cannot or should not be concerned about distant future generations or that we cannot and should not imagine that we have moral obligations to distant future generations. What it demonstrates, as it seems to me, is that we are concerned about future generations in general, collectively, not the particular persons who will compose future generations severally and individually.

Now, let us consider the full temporal scale of global climate change. Currently (June, 2011), carbon dioxide constitutes 389 parts per million of the molecules composing Earth's atmosphere and is increasing by 2 parts per million every year.[9] In fifteen years CO_2 concentrations will rise to 400–410 parts per million. No one knows if after that emissions will continue to rise, stabilize, or fall, but the 2007 Intergovernmental Panel on Climate Change (IPCC) report predicts that average global temperature will rise at century's

9 'Trends in Atmospheric Carbon Dioxide', US Department of Commerce/National Oceanographic and Atmospheric Administration http://www.esrl.noaa.gov/gmd/ccgg/trends/

end by 1.5–6.5 degrees Celsius and sea levels will rise from a quarter to half a meter.[10] Four years later, the IPCC report seems quaint because polar ice has since been observed to be melting faster than anyone then thought possible.[11] If we make no radical changes in energy policy, Earth's sea level and climate may be radically altered by the end of the twenty-first century. Positive feedback loops may result in even more carbon dioxide and methane, an even stronger greenhouse gas, released from melting arctic tundra.[12] Ever soaring levels of greenhouse gases, decade after decade, century after century, in Earth's atmosphere could result in a total meltdown of continental ice sheets and thus ever greater elevation of the ocean, swamping oceanic islands and shrinking the continents. Further, the oceans may so acidify with dissolved carbon that the formation of the silica frustules of the diatoms at the base of the marine food chain is inhibited by carbonic acid, resulting in a total collapse of marine ecosystems.[13]

At the millennial temporal scale the rationalism of the classical moral paradigm becomes problematic. A pillar of the classical paradigm is the axiom that equal interests should be treated equally. The principle of equality is based on the rational law of self-consistency or non-contradiction. To treat equal interests unequally is inconsistent and therefore irrational.[14]

As before indicated, the individualistic moral ontology of the prevailing moral philosophy can be made to undergird global climate justice, in theory, by the collectivization of the world's Jacks and Jills through government-to-government transfers of wealth followed by its just distribution of penalties and damages payouts. But the Jamieson Ditty 4 spatial variation of the Jamieson Ditty 1 paradigm case of an ethically reprehensible action of agent Jack on patient Jill stretches the credulity of the rational principle of equality. A

[10] 'IPCC, 2007: Summary for Policymakers', in S.D. Solomon, D. Qin, M. Manning, Z. Chen, M. Marquis, K.B. Avery, M. Tignor, and H.L. Miller, eds., *Climate Change 2007: The Physical Science Basis. Contribution of Working Group I to the Fourth Assessment Report of the Intergovernmental Panel on Climate Change* (Cambridge: Cambridge University Press, 2007).

[11] For a recent and sober assessment see Bill McKibben, *Eaarth: Making a Life on a Tough New Planet* (New York: Henry Holt, 2010).

[12] 'IPCC, 2007'; McKibben, *Eaarth*.

[13] K. Caldeira and M. E. Wickett, 'Anthropogenic Carbon and Ocean pH', *Nature* **425** (2003): 365–365.

[14] Garvey, *Ethics of Climate Change*, nicely brings out the centrality of consistency in the classical moral paradigm.

person who actually treated equally the equal interests of a total stranger on another continent with the equal interests of a proximate relative or friend would, by the tribunal of moral common sense, be judged to be daft. My son had an interest in a college education. Was I ethically remiss to pay for his college education rather than that of a young man, randomly selected from a pool of young men equally interested in a college education, living in Delhi or Bangkok? Notoriously, Peter Singer violated the consistency axiom of his own utilitarianism by lavishing expensive medical care on his mother in her latter stages of Alzheimer's.[15] Despite recklessly philosophizing that such non-persons, in a vegetative state incapable of suffering, should be euthanized – apparently so long as they were someone else's kith and kin – he acted as he should have done, by the tribunal of moral common sense, when the chips were down. Did Singer fail in his duty to be consistently impartial? Hardly; for there really is no such duty. Rather, he exposed the pernicious silliness of the classical moral paradigm.

The rationalism of the prevailing paradigms in moral philosophy – utilitarianism and deontology, originating, respectively, with Jeremy Bentham and Immanuel Kant in the late eighteenth century – is closely connected to the individualistic ontology of those paradigms. If we conceive of persons as externally related social atoms then of course the equal interests of each individual social atom appear to every other social atom to be of equal weight and thus to demand equal consideration and equal treatment. But human beings are not externally related social atoms. We are rather internally related to one another in many ways. We are mothers and fathers, sons and daughters, brothers and sisters, lovers, friends, colleagues, fellow citizens. These relationships engender different duties and obligations. It seems inhuman to suppose that, in the name of ethics, I should consider the equal interests a stranger half a world away to demand equal regard with those of my son, my grandson, my partner, my friends, and my colleagues. Only if we believe that we are externally related social atoms, not internally related social beings, could we also believe that it is only consistent, only rational, to treat equal interests equally irrespective of the particularity – and partiality – of relationships.

[15] Ronald Bailey, 'The Pursuit of Happiness: Peter Singer Interviewed by Ronald Bailey', *Reason* (December 2000) http://reason.com/archives/2000/12/01/the-pursuit-of-happiness-peter; Anonymous, 'Peter Singer: A Slippery Mind' http://notdeadyetnewscommentary.blogspot.com/2008/03/peter-singer-slippery-mind.html

Certainly, the rational principle of equality – the principle that one treat equal interests equally on pain of inconsistency – seems to be utterly preposterous when we vary the temporal dimension and go from Jamieson Ditty 4 to Jamieson Ditty 6, the allegory of global climate change. The rational principle of equality would require us to regard the interests of people living everywhere on Earth hundreds of years in the future as equal to our own and to those of our proximate contemporaries. As we try to expand our thoughts to embrace the billions of individuals that now exist on Earth and the billions more that will exist over the next several thousand years – but whose identities and thus whose interests are presently indeterminate – how we might begin even coherently to apply the principle of equality is literally mind boggling, literally unthinkable. In the face of the colossal moral problem posed by global climate change, the classic ethical paradigm, exemplified by Jamieson Ditty 1, is bankrupt. The colossal moral problem posed by global climate change mandates a fundamental paradigm shift in ethics.

Homo ethicus and *Homo economicus* are two sides of the same individualistic and rationalistic coin. *Homo economicus* is rational only when he deploys his resources to serve his and only his own interests. *Homo ethicus* is rational only when he deploys his resources to serve the equal interests of all persons equally including his own. *Homo economicus* has been roundly criticized as an inhuman invention of the dismal science. I suggest it is time we commit *Homo ethicus* to the dustbin of the noble, but equally inhuman, Enlightenment science of moral philosophy.

In my opinion, David Hume correctly identified the wellspring of ethics not in reason and its most fundamental law of non-contradiction or self-consistency but in the other-oriented moral sentiments. And the other-oriented moral sentiments are many, nuanced, and selective in their proper objects. Love is strongly felt and powerfully motivating, but a moral sentiment that is narrowly bestowed. I paid for my son's college education motivated principally by love not a coldly rational duty. Sympathy is a less strongly felt and moderately motivating moral sentiment that may be widely bestowed, even to sentient animals, but seems to require the proximity of its proper objects to be fully engaged. To arouse sympathy for distant persons or animals it seems that they must be drawn near and made present through images of their suffering. Benevolence, as a general affective posture toward the world, seems to be broad in scope, but a weak motivator for specific actions on behalf of its beneficiaries. A benevolent person may be universally well wishing, but largely unmoved to do much of anything to actually benefit others.

Some of the moral sentiments seem to be stimulated by and are directed toward collective, not individual social entities. Patriotism is often a strongly felt and powerfully motivating moral sentiment stimulated by and directed toward a nation state. Lack of patriotism is counted a moral defect and *unpatriotic* is a condemnatory epithet. Worse, the betrayal of patriotism is strongly condemned with such expressions as *turncoat* and *traitor*, and sometimes severely punished by imprisonment or even death. Loyalty seems only a little less strongly felt and powerfully motivating and is stimulated by and directed toward other social wholes or collectives. Rather trivially, many people feel intense loyalty to a football team, such as Manchester United or the Dallas Cowboys. *Fair weather fan* is a phrase reeking of moral censure, however inconsequential. We often experience loyalty to institutions, such as universities, as well as to persons functioning in such institutions.

A diehard reductionist might contend that patriotism and loyalty can be reduced to moral sentiments directed to the individuals composing such collectives. Love of a particular country would, accordingly, be just fraternal love of the individual citizens of that country. In the case of American patriots, at least, that is manifestly not the case. The most ardent patriots in the US often have strongly antipathetic feelings toward the great majority of their fellow Americans if you aggregate African Americans, Mexican Americans, and gay and lesbian, politically liberal, and hippie Americans of all ethnicities. As to loyalty, sports fans remain loyal to their favorite team even as the players shuffle in and out; and should a star player join a rival team, once adored, he or she is immediately loathed – loathed indeed as the sporting equivalent of a traitor by the same fans.

What then is the fitting object and what is the fitting moral sentiment toward that object commensurate with the spatial and temporal scales of global climate change? Life on Earth is in no danger. In its 3.5 billion year biography, life has endured through many cataclysms, including devastating meteor strikes, near total glaciation, periodic fluctuations in Earth's orbit and axis of rotation. Some of these cataclysmic events have entrained mass extinctions, only for life on Earth to speciate more prolifically. *Homo sapiens*, the species, is probably not at risk of total extinction. If post-apocalyptic fiction is at all prescient, humans will survive a climate apocalypse no less than a nuclear apocalypse – but likely in a barbaric state of existence. Hobbes wonders if the state of nature ever actually existed universally in the past; we may wonder if it lies not in the past but in the future. What does seem to be at risk, then, is not the human species, but human civilization. And the moral sentiment that the fair prospect of human civilization stimulates is pride and a kind of fiduciary sense of care.

Aldo Leopold's 'The Land Ethic' begins with these oft-quoted words: 'When god-like Odysseus returned from the wars in Troy… '[16] Leopold deliberately takes his reader back in imagination to the earliest extant literature in Western civilization, and thus to the dawn of that civilization, and specifies its temporal scale: 'During the three thousand years which have since elapsed …'[17] If Western civilization has endured for three thousand years, surely it does not stretch credulity to think that it might well endure for another three thousand years. Leopold may not have intended to distract his audience with feelings of wonder and pride over the magnitude and duration of that cultural enterprise – traceable back to Homer, if not to Odysseus himself. But surely such feelings of wonder and pride must well up in us as we contemplate the achievements of Western civilization – in every domain of culture, high and low: in the graphic and plastic arts, in music, theater, literature, philosophy, science, architecture, engineering.

If Western civilization goes back three thousand years, other of the world's civilizations go back even farther in time. The Greeks of Plato's day acknowledged the Egyptian civilization, which began some five thousand years ago, as more venerable than their own. Contemporary Indians can trace the origins of their civilization almost as far back in time to cities in the Indus Valley. Contemporary Chinese and Mexicans can trace the origins of their civilizations back some four thousand years – to the Xia and Maya, respectively. Iranians have perhaps inherited the current cultural legacy of the oldest extant civilization in the world, going back some six thousand years. Thanks to globalization these various streams of regional civilizations have merged to form a single mighty river of a global human civilization. We are the current custodians of that civilization. If it is difficult to muster up concern for the indeterminate interests of the indeterminate billions of human individuals who will exist over the next five thousand years, it seems equally difficult to avoid feeling concern about the very real prospect of the imminent collapse of human civilization.

The temporal scale of this proposed moral ontology – moral considerability for human civilization *per se* – is proportionate to the spatial and temporal scales of global climate change. Global human civilization thus appears to be the appropriate moral patient for global-

[16] Aldo Leopold, *A Sand County Almanac and Sketches Here and There* (New York: Oxford University Press, 1949), 201.
[17] Ibid. 202.

climate-change ethics. What about the appropriate moral agent? Global climate change moralists often end their sermons with a list of things that each Jack and Jill of us can individually and voluntarily do to shrink our individual carbon footprints: replace halogen with compact fluorescent light bulbs, drive less, bike more, insulate, turn down the thermostat in winter and turn it up in summer … The Jack-and-Jill ethical paradigm is so ingrained in our thinking that we seem to suppose that duty-driven voluntary change in individual behavior is all that global-climate-change ethics is about. If so, catastrophic global climate change and the likely demise of human civilization is all but inevitable, due to the familiar free-rider problem. If there is a chance at averting climate catastrophe it lies in scaling up the moral agent as well as the moral patient.

The identity of that moral agent is no mystery: the world's several governments acting in concert to create policy and law that will effectively drive changes in individual behavior. The manufacture of halogen light bulbs might be discontinued through international agreement. A steep excise tax on gas-guzzling SUVs might be globally imposed. A transnational carbon tax might be imposed or an international cap-and-trade market might be instituted. Research on alternative fuels might be lavishly subsidized. And so on and so forth. My purpose here is not to provide an inventory of actions that governments can take, but to identify the effective moral agent for an ethics of global climate change.

Nor do I mean to reject altogether out of hand the efficacy of voluntary individual effort to stem the tide of global climate change. When one see others undertake lifestyle changes, especially if such changes, as they often do, entrain other personal benefits – such as better fitness attendant upon biking, better nutrition attendant upon the consumption of local foods, the economic savings of lower domestic energy consumption – there is a contagious effect. That, in turn, leads to self-organizing communities to promote such things as car pools, urban gardens, and reforestation projects, not to mention organizing for greener policies and laws. After all, in a democracy, change in policy and law must have some degree of support by individual citizens in order to be enacted. And once enacted into law, the ethical status of the newly mandated behavioral changes is reinforced. Now that it is against the law, submitting others to second-hand smoke or endangering infants by not restraining them in rear-facing car seats, is considered to be quite wrong and irresponsible as well as illegal.

Unfortunately, there is a limit to this contagious effect. Environmentalism has created a backlash among certain segments of society who feel that their lifestyles are threatened – the mechanized recreationalist, for example. Even more unfortunately, environmentalism has become entangled in partisan politics, associated in the US with 'liberal' as opposed to 'conservative' political allegiance. Thus in the end, whether we would wish it or not, achieving the changes in human behavior and lifestyle necessary to meet the challenge of global climate change will require changes in policy and law, because a significant sector of society is likely to resist such changes as one dimension of a complex political struggle sometimes characterized as 'the culture war'.

I now conclude. This essay has not been about practical ethics, but about ethical theory. Or to say the same thing in different words, it has been about moral philosophy, not normative morality. We most certainly have moral obligations to distant future generations. However, we cannot – for the reasons I have given here – conceive of those obligations as obligations to future individuals particularly and severally. Rather, we must conceive of those obligations as obligations to future generations collectively. In short, the hyper-individualism that has characterized the ethical theory dominating Jack-and-Jill moral philosophy for more than two centuries now becomes incoherent when we contemplate our obligations to future generations on the temporal scale – calibrated in centuries and millennia, not years and decades – of global climate change. Implied by the abandonment of an individualistic ontology for an ethics of global climate change is the abandonment of ethical rationalism. Both Kantian deontology and utilitarianism derive our moral obligations from the most fundamental law of logic, the law of non-contradiction or self-consistency. Both the spatial and temporal scales of global climate change and the billions of individuals, who have intrinsic value and/or equal interests with our own, swamp our capacity to treat all individual persons, living now and in the future, as ends in themselves, and/or our capacity to give equal weight to their equal interests. More deeply, shifting from an individualistic to a holistic moral ontology, persons are not conceived as externally related social atoms. Our internal relationships – the relationships that make us the persons that we are – are multiple and various, each kind of which plays differently on our finely tuned moral sentiments. Thus we may be passionately concerned for the global climate of the near future because our loved ones, for whom we passionately care, will have to live in it. We may be passionately concerned about the global climate of the far-flung future because the now contingent and thus indeterminate individual members of distant future generations will be heirs and custodians of human civilization, for which we passionately care. Moreover, we cannot effectively act, as individual moral agents, in such a way as to significantly benefit or harm near-term future generations or to conserve human civilization in the long term. The colossal moral problem presented by the prospect of global climate change demands a shift from ethical individualism to ethical holism in regard to moral agency as well as to patiency. The only moral agents commensurate with the spatial and temporal scales of global climate change are national governments and for them to be effective in mitigating global climate change, they must act in concert.

University of North Texas

Moral Foundations for Global Environmental and Climate Justice

CHUKWUMERIJE OKEREKE

Aspirations for global justice have, in the last two decades, found their most radical expressions in the context of global environmental governance and climate change. From Rio de Janeiro through Kyoto to Copenhagen, demands for international distributional justice, and especially North–South equity, have become a prominent aspect of international environmental negotiation. However, claims for international environmental and climate justice have generally been deployed in the form of instinctive gut reaction than as a closely argued concept. In this paper, I outline the ways in which issues of international justice intertwine with notions of global environmental sustainability and the basic premises on which claims for North–South equity are entrenched.

1. The link between environmental and social justice

Environmental issues have provided space for the 'loudest' and most radical demands for global distributional justice over the last two decades. Contrary to traditional approaches in which the notion of environmental sustainability was firmly linked with species' conservation, market efficiency or technological innovation, it is now widely acknowledged that some of the main controversies surrounding the paradigm of sustainable development and global climate governance revolve around questions of justice.[1]

The 'unavoidability of justice'[2] in the pursuit of environmental sustainability resides in the fact that environmental issues are *not* distinguishable but rather interwoven, into the fabric of racial, social and economic (in) justice. One of the clear ways in which this

[1] World Commission on the Environment and Development (WCED), *Our Common Future* (Oxford: Oxford University Press, 1987).

[2] H. Shue, 'The Unavoidability of Justice', in A. Hurrell and B. Kingsbury (eds), *International Politics of the Environment: Actors Interests and Institutions* (Oxford: Clarendon Press), 373.

doi:10.1017/S1358246111000245

manifests, is 'that the effects of environmental degradation are not necessarily experienced as costs by the people who cause – and most benefit – from them'.[3] In other words, environmental costs and benefits are often distributed such that those who already suffer other socio-economic disadvantages tend to bear the greatest burden. Thus understood, environmental degradation and ecological crisis for a wide majority of people, become, as Lorraine Elliot puts it, 'symptomatic of a broader structural oppression and silencing'.[4]

In international fora, questions of distributive justice arise manly in the context of North–South equity and mostly involve 'the justice of the international allocation of the costs of dealing with global environmental problems'.[5] That is, the ways in which the costs and benefits of any policy should be shared out between the rich and the poor countries. The political South generally emphasizes the need for solutions that recognise and reflect differentials in contribution, vulnerability and capabilities. The political North, on their own part, tend to emphasize corruption and population growth in the South and on this basis question the fairness of suggestions that they should bear a disproportionate burden of global environmental co-operation. Some of the debates also relate to, and draw from, broader issues of structure and patterns of international economic and social relations.

However, claims for justice in global environmental institutions for the most part have been subject to little definitional and philosophical precision. In general, the notion of environmental justice has been 'deployed more as an instinctive gut reaction than as a closely argued concept'.[6] There are of course some extensive and rigorous treatments but generally the impulse has been 'to call for environmental justice as a response to perceived injustice judged through observations of unreasonable inequality in outcomes'[7] and apparent lack of fair treatment of countries that are already considered marginalized and disadvantaged. The overall situation remains one in which the rhetorical inflation in claims for North–South distributional

[3] T. Hayward and J. O'Neill, (eds), Justice, *Property and the Environment: Social and Legal Perspectives* (Aldershot, Brookfield: Ashgate), 1.

[4] L. Elliott, *The Global Politics of the Environment* (London: Macmillan Press, 1997), 147.

[5] Op. cit., note 2, 373.

[6] G. Walker H. Bulkeley, 'Geographies of Environmental Justice', *Geoforum*, **37** (2006), 656.

[7] Ibid., 656.

justice in international environmental regimes have not produced corresponding self-conscious conceptual treatments of the assumptions upon which these claims are entrenched. Given that there are some shared commonsense understandings of justice it might be argued that there is no need for further deliberation and clarification and that the focus should be in designing a fairer system. However, as questions of justice become more acute in the international negotiation circles, and given mounting evidence that the proliferation of justice claims has not necessarily translated into significant equity policies, there would seem to be an increasing need for more robust conceptual treatments.

My aim in this article is to facilitate a more structured debate on the core themes and grounds for international environmental justice. I attempt to do this by outlining the basic premises for claims of North–South distributional justice in the context of global environmental sustainability. These include the: (i) factuality of natural resource limits; (ii) negative social and ecological externalities of economic globalisation; and (iii) need for greater democracy and participation in international environmental decision-making. Furthermore, drawing mainly from the problem of climate change, I suggest that the central obstacle to global environmental co-operation has to do with the failure of relevant governance regimes to attend seriously to questions of North–South distributional justice.

2. Biophysical Limits and Ecological Space

The notion of natural limits occupies a central position in the paradigm of sustainable development. Whether one's concern is climate change, the hole in the Ozone layer, biodiversity loss or the degradation of world's fisheries, the key underlying notion is that there is a limit to which the earth system can be pushed without altering it beyond a state that is conducive for life. The basic tenet of the notion of limits is, that the planet is a materially finite and non-growing system. There are of course huge debates over where these limit lie; the possibility of finding out and the degree of uncertainty that can or should be tolerated. And by the way, these debates are not purely scientific but inherently moral and ethical questions.[8] At any

[8] See M. Charlesworth and C. Okereke, 'Policy responses to rapid Climate change: An epistemological critique of dominant approaches', *Global Environmental Change*, 20(2010), 121–129.

rate, only a few would reject, at least on a thought level, the idea that limits exist.

The concept of ecological limits is foundational in the discourse of global environmental justice because questions about rights over resources and the fairness of appropriation, use and distribution within communities and nation states have always been predicated upon conditions of critical natural capital. Interestingly, one of the first notable works to explicitly link the idea of distributional justice with the concept of natural limits was John Locke's *Two Treatise of Government*.[9] In this work, Locke was among other things concerned with the conditions under which the appropriation of natural resources by members of a given political community may be considered just and defensible. After affirming that 'the vast resources of the earth and all the "inferior creatures" [there in] belong commonly to all men',[10] he argued that the appropriation which is justified is one that leaves 'as much and as good'[11] for other men to appropriate. In other words, Locke's position was that it is unjust to take from nature quantities of resources that deprive other men of equal chances to appropriate. He was clear about the need for prudence and fairness in appropriation, observing that '...what portion a man carved to himself, was easily seen; and it was useless, as well as dishonest to carve to himself too much, or take more than is needed'.[12] Hence, although Locke is generally regarded as the *locus classicus* on property rights, a dispassionate reading would indicate that his idea of property rights and accumulation has strong moral and ethical boundaries. Quite clearly, for Locke, justice in appropriation is determined by the level of abundance of the particular resource under consideration.

The problem, of course, with Locke was that he assumes limitless natural resources, suggesting that 'there would always be more than the yet un-provided for could use'.[13] However, the failure to pre-empt resource limits does not vitiate the importance of Locke's argument linking environmental sustainability with distributional justice.

In a different but equally striking fashion, Garrett Hardin[14] also demonstrates the centrality of natural limits to questions of resource

9 J. Locke, *Two Treaties of Government* (London; Dent [1690], 1924), 130.

10 Ibid., 130.

11 Ibid., 130.

12 Ibid., 130.

13 Ibid., 140.

14 G. Hardin, 'The Tragedy of the Commons', Science, **162** (1968), 38–58.

rights and justice of appropriation. Setting aside the point about whether or not enclosure is the best way of avoiding the 'tragedy of the commons,' it is clear that the original problem of distribution and survival – both of the common and those dependent on it – arose primarily because of critical natural limits.

In short the relationship between resource limits and distributional justice at community and national levels is well appreciated and bears no argument. What is less entrenched is the idea that the boundedness and limits of the earth system implicate questions of global distributional justice in no less serious fashion than is the case for communities and countries. In other words, there is little or no difference conceptually, in the relationship between distributional justice and limits at community level and the global sphere. Indeed, given what is now know about global ecological and economical independence it is fair to suggest that, in the final analysis, the only system that really matters is the planetary or global. If it is accepted that the human race, regardless peoples' geographic and political locale, ultimately depend on this bounded planetary system for their survival, then it would seem that there is no *a priori* reason why questions of domestic justice should take priority or precedence over questions of global resource justice.

Many environmental problems such as climate change amply demonstrate the physical unity of, and our mutual dependence on, a single natural system. They remind us of the boundedness of the earth system and the inevitability of holistic approaches to questions of natural resource use and distribution. For example, scientists calculate that one trillion tonnes of carbon is the maximum limit our planet can take without warming beyond the safe level of 2°C.[15] Now, industrial activity since the mid-18th Century up till the 1990s means that 500 billion tonnes of carbon – half of the 1-trillion-tonne budget have already been emitted. Critically, scientists calculate that at the current rate, the remaining half a trillion tonnes of carbon will be emitted by 2040.[16] This means that the entire global community have 500 billion tonnes of carbon to share between them. Based on this perspective, one sees the utter futility of any attempt to manage the challenge of climate change exclusively in lesser political boundaries such as countries and regions. At the same time, given that developed countries are clearly responsible for vast amount (about 80%) of

[15] M.R. Allen, D.J. Frame, C. Hutingford, et al., 'Warming caused by cumulative carbon emissions towards the trillionth tonne', *Nature*, **458**: 7242 (2009), 1163–1166.

[16] Ibid.

historical carbon emissions, it would seem incontrovertible that they should take full responsibility and lead in the global management of climate change even if this requires a large amount of North–South financial and technology transfers.

A similar scenario obtains with regards to global oceans, fisheries and forests, where developed countries in each case are clearly responsible for a vast proportion of historical and current use and for driving these ecosystems towards their natural limits. The UNDP Human Development Report of 2004 makes this point eloquently. Here, it is indicated that industrial countries with 15% of the world population account for 76% of the global consumption expenditure; consuming 70% of the world energy, 78% of its metals and 85% of its timber. Yet, 154 million hectares (about three times the size of France) of the total global forest lost in the last ten years have been in the developing countries. Carley and Spapens were therefore absolutely right when they asserted that the 'entire world has served as resource base for the development of the 25 or so industrialised countries which have between them just 20 percent of the world's population'.[17] Further research has shown that extrapolating current industrial consumption and production patterns in the developed countries to the entire world would require about nine times the existing resources, that is, equivalent of nine additional planets.

Where does this leave international co-operation for global environmental governance? A reasonable answer, surely, is that the search for environmental sustainability among nations demands an absolute reduction in the throughput of natural resources but also an urgent move towards globally equitable redistribution of resources. Specifically, it requires that the rich countries, acting through relevant international institutions are obliged to make significant transfers to alleviate ecological poverty in the South. The notion of sustainable development certainly demands the recognition of universal values that goes beyond the context of traditional nation states and gives attention to interdependencies and the survival of the entire human race. This is more so essential in the current context of economic globalisation with its pertinent transboundary movement of environmental harm and risk – at theme to which I should now turn.

17 M. Carley and P. Spapens, Sharing the World: Sustainable Living and Global Equity in the 21st Century (London: Earthscan, 1998), 41.

3. Globalization, Risk and the Imposition of Harm

The second argument for North–South environmental distributive justice relates to economic globalization and its effects on the environment and welfare opportunities of the South. The intensification of economic globalisation has now resulted in a 'full word economy'[18] with resources and wastes moving freely across different ends of the globe. However, it is often so easy to forget that the globalization of economic activity is taking place under a set of trading rules and broader structural inequity that severely disadvantages and harms the South.

The process is complex and has many strands. Primarily, though, current international trading and accounting practises tend to discount the social and environmental costs of production. Developing countries, as a result, are virtually forced to degrade their environmental resources and natural capital in the bid to stay competitive in the international market. At the same time, the dependence of a multitude of developing countries on the same range of primary goods – cocoa, coffee, tea, maize, sugar and tropical timber – results in a situation where the real prices of these commodities still fall far below the basic cost of production even after externalising the environmental costs of products. The consequence is that despite the liquidation their natural capital; many developing countries are still unable to generate sufficient income for sustenance let alone achieve economic prosperity and independence.

This state of economic subservience and natural resource degradation is further exacerbated by a range of trade-distorting subsidies in developed countries which drive commodity prices so down that developing countries are unable to service their debts or trade their way out of poverty no matter how much they keep degrading their already stressed resources. As commodities prices decline, poor countries are encouraged to borrow more to increase exports. Yet, increased export when pursed simultaneously by all the developing countries result in further fall in prices due to over production. This leads to the so-called vicious cycle: more debt, more stress on the environment, fall in prices and again more debt.

Consider, for example, that the United States currently pays around $20 billion per year to farmers in direct subsidies as 'farm income stabilization'. Similarly, in 2010, the EU spent €57 billion on agricultural development, of which €39 billion was spent on

[18] H. Daly, Beyond *Growth: The Economics of Sustainable Development* (Boston: Becon Press, 1996).

direct subsidies with agricultural and fisheries subsidies forming over 40% of the EU budget. Furthermore, analysis indicates that since the Doha talks were launched in 2001, over $30 billion of trade distorting subsidies have been provided to cotton farmers in the US and Europe, reducing the opportunity for West African countries, where cotton accounts for as much as 60% of export earnings to earn decent prices for their products. There is little wonder then why coffee farmers in Mexico and cocoa farmers in Africa continue to live in a state of abject poverty and stressed environmental conditions despite the ever increasing expansion of coffee shops in almost every high street in America and Western Europe. It is very instructive that in real terms, the price of coffee, and therefore the income coffee farmers have to provide for their families, has actually fallen by more than two thirds in the last 40 years.

Now, apart from the harm caused indirectly by prevailing conditions of international trade, developing countries also suffer a lot of direct harm as a consequence of economic globalisation. These range from the pollution of local water bodies; loss of income and livelihood due to deforestation, waste dumping by resident and non-resident multinational companies; dispossession or violent removal from ancestral lands; and deaths due to droughts, famine and climate change induced extreme weather events.

Across Africa, it is suggested that more than 10 million people have been forced to migrate over the last two decades due to desertification or environmental degradation. Currently there are well over 25 million environmental cross-border refugees around the globe with a Red Cross research indicating that more people are now displaced by environmental disasters than by war.[19] Looking forward, the Intergovernmental Panel on Climate Change (IPCC) has estimated that climate change will increase the number of environmental refugees over the next fifty years to about 150 million. Meanwhile, available reports suggest that climate change already causes about 345,000 deaths every year, mostly in Africa. These reports further calculate that without any efforts to minimize the pace of climate change or prevent harm to public health, nearly 5 million people, a vast majority of which will be from the developing countries, may die because of drastic climate change in the next 10 years.[20] Yet, these countries and their people are the ones least responsible for the cause of climate change.

[19] S. Castles, 'The International Politics of Forced Migration', *Development*, **46**: 3 (2003), 11–20.

[20] DARA Climate Vulnerable Forum, Climate Vulnerability Monitor 2010: A State of the Climate Crisis (Spain, 2010).

Overall, it is clear that many global ecological problems faced today are largely the result of historic and current economic processes which have benefited the Northern developed countries and exposed the poor South to incalculable human and environmental risks and harm. It would appear that for the most part, economic globalisation now suffices as a new way of meeting a need that has been historically tackled by the North through the means of colonialism, slavery and forced labour.[21] Put simply, The liberalisation of trade and investment has provided a veneer for developed countries and their corporate agents to swamp southern markets, exploit their labour and natural resources at next to nothing cost; and dump their toxic wastes on the poor while producing prosperity for a people and shareholders that are far removed from, and oblivious of the consequences of the wealth they enjoy.

Industrialised countries are, of course, very aware of the negative consequences of economic globalisation on the environment and people of the South. The inescapable moral impact of this awareness largely accounts for the many positive noises by developed countries on development assistance, aid and the notion of global social justice. However, after nearly five decades of North–South environmental cooperation, starting from the United National Conference on the Human Environment (UNCHE) in 1971, it is fair to say that developed countries have shown themselves prone to cheap talk and heart-hearted gestures but lacking in serious commitment to change the *status quo*. Time and again, observers of global environmental co-operation have seen developed country governments which profess a desire to global social justice oppose proposals for albeit modicum reforms in institutions of global economic and environmental governance. The anger of many in developing countries against this recurring Western hypocrisy is reflected in the following extracts from the speech of the Malaysian Prime Minster, Dr. Mahathir Mohamad, during the 1992 Earth's Summit in Rio:

> Obviously the North wants to have a direct say in the management of forests in the Poor South at next to nothing cost to themselves. The pittance they offer is much less than the loss of earning by poor countries and yet it is made out as a generous concession [...] The Poor are not asking for charity [but] for the need for us to co-operate on an equitable basis. Now the rich claim a right to regulate the development of the poor

[21] Op cit. note, 14, 38.

countries. And yet any suggestion that the rich compensate the poor adequately is regarded as outrageous.

Ever since the UNCHE in 1971, developing countries have consistently highlighted the connection between the environment, international trade and economic development. They had been clear that a basic precondition for addressing global environmental injustice is the revision of the subsisting international economic infrastructure, the rules of trade, and the cancellation of the strangulating debt under which many countries in the South currently labour. These inequitable and undemocratic structures, which in the words of Vanadan Shiva, are based on "monopolies and monocultures"[22] would need to 'give way to an earth democracy supported by decentralization and diversity'.[23] As Shiva puts it, 'the rights of all species and the rights of all peoples must come before the rights of corporations to make limitless profits through limitless destruction.'[24] And it is to this democratic deficit in global environmental decision making that I now turn.

4. Participation and Democracy in Global Environmental Institutions

The preceding discussion has made clear that environmental problems and the policies designed to combat them do not affect people equally. This is true for both within and cross-border environmental challenges. Within a country, decisions on what type of environmental policies to pursue depend very much on who holds the power and what their interests are. For example, it is as much a political decision as an environmental one where a waste plant, landfill or a hydro dam should be cited.

In the same vein, decisions about environmental standards, targets, policies and instruments of governance at the international level are by no means based on purely 'objective' sciences. Rather, they reflect preferences and power equations across societies. High power politics is involved in deciding fishing boundaries, allowable catches of fishes in the ocean, how the total available quota might be shared. Likewise, interest-based politics have crucial influence in the decision about the pollutants that should be included in the

[22] V. Shiva, Biopiracy, *The Plunder of Knowledge and Nature* (Cambridge, MA: South End Press).

[23] Ibid.

[24] Ibid.

basket of regulated gases, the base year against which emission reduction should be set; methodologies for counting, countries that should be designated as most vulnerable to ecological change; and so on.

Philosophers have long recognised the close connection between fairness of an outcome and the legitimacy of the process by which such an outcome is determined. Aristotle distinguished between substantive and procedural justice and noted that a significant aspect of justice has to do with the fairness of the bargaining process. Similarly, Rawls' theory of 'justice as fairness' is firmly based on a stylised condition of bargaining designed to eliminate the effect of power asymmetry amongst co-operating agents. The point is that if the distribution of the costs and benefits of global environmental co-operation is to be fair, it must proceed from a democratic process where parties have equal say in deciding policy objectives, instruments and the architecture of governance institutions. Specifically, those who are affected by key decisions would need to have some say in how relevant decisions are made.

The importance of stakeholder involvement in environmental decision making within Western democracies is well recognised. However, this basic condition of justice is not nearly appreciated or satisfied with respect to environmental decision making at the international level where the North commands massive political, economic and scientific advantage over the South. Consequently, the countries and people of the South who are most adversely affected by international environmental problems are in many instances, permitted little or no say in the political and decision-making processes designed to tackle these challenges. The result is that global environmental institutions and policies, for the most time, do not reflect the aspirations of the majority of the people that actually bear the brunt of the problems. And in some cases the North has actually engaged in callous opportunism seeking to transform institutions for global environmental governance into instruments for further exploitation and domination.

One clear case that illustrates this point is the Clean Development Mechanism (CDM) established under the United Nations Convention on Climate Change (UNFCCC). In theory the CDM was conceived as a means of promoting clean, low carbon technologies and accelerating foreign direct investment (FDI) into developing countries by creating conditions that reward investors for emission reduction projects in these countries. In 1997, the CDM was hailed as the ultimate equity policy of the UNFCCC and an innovative alternative to traditional official development Assistant

(ODA). However, several years after the establishment of this mechanism, many of the poor countries that are supposed to be the main beneficiaries of the this equity policy are yet to understand even the basics of how the mechanism works let alone benefit from it. In a real sense, though, this is hardly surprising because the poor countries never really participated actively in the negotiation and decision of the rules of the CDM. The effect has been that while the CDM may have served the interest of the highly industrialised countries like China and India (which negotiated the rules), it has been of no practical value to the poor countries in Africa. Indeed some have argued that in many cases, the CDM served as instruments for impoverishing local communities, and for reinforcing prevailing patters of hierarchies and patters of domination and power dynamics between the poor South and the rich North.[25]

There are, indeed, many interesting accounts illustrating the frustrations and limitations suffered by developing countries as they seek to participate in international environmental negotiations and how they ultimately become overwhelmed and excluded from these destiny deciding processes.

Firstly, due to high costs of travel and hotels, many developing countries are unable to attend many of these important conferences which most often take place in North America and Western European countries. For example while the US, Canada, Australia, UK and other rich countries in the West sponsor scores of delegates to the UN climate change conventions; many African countries in contrast are often only able to send one or two delegates per time. Second, and related, the poor countries are heavily under represented or completely absent in many committees, negotiating groups and breakout sessions where crucial texts are negotiated. Consequently, they are unable to make contributions let alone influence policy. Thirdly, many present day environmental negotiations involve and require the mastery of complex scientific and technical details. The complexity and technicality of these negotiations mean that even when developing country delegates are in the room; chances are such delegates might not have the requisite technical knowledge required to engage and shape debates. At the same time, the requirement for negotiating environmental agreements goes beyond technical knowledge and includes other specialized skills such as legal, economic and diplomatic expertise. Because developing countries are

[25] H. Bachram, 'Climate Fraud and carbon colonialism: the new trade in Greenhouse gases', *Capitalism Nature and Socialism* 2005, **15** (2005), 5–20.

mostly unable to afford the services of these professionals in high numbers; the few that attend are stretched beyond limit with practically no time to digest the relevant volumes and weigh the pros and cons of important proposals. Roberts and Parks[26] capture this well:

> It is also not uncommon for developing country delegates to be "buried" with paper, brought to the point of extreme fatigue, and then presented with a *fait accompli* in the eleventh hour of negotiations and asked to accept or reject the proposal in an unrealistically short period of time.

Another angle to the 'negotiation by exhaustion' often adopted by developed countries in global environmental negotiations is that sometimes, documents on existing treaties in the North, with which developed country politicians are very familiar are taken and slightly adapted to a new issue. Then developing country delegates are expected to read and digest these documents within minutes. A good example can be found in the negotiation process of the Basel Convention in which negotiators basically used the existing text on OECD documents on the issue as the basis of negotiation and expected developing country negotiators to digest and form their opinion on this document in matter of hours.[27] These practices reveal something of the real goal of participation as conceived by the more powerful actors. Often the aim is not to have a meaningful and mature dialogue with the developing countries but simply to get them to sign an agreement defined and shaped in the terms to which the powerful actors are happy. The implicit assumption, in this practice, is that developing country parties lack intellectual aptitude and necessary information and would thus likely come to an 'informed' conclusion if they were sufficiently educated with respect to the issues at stake.

In addition to above points, there is also the huge problem of language and cultural differences which can easily intimidate and impede the ability of otherwise clever professionals from the South from pulling their weight in negotiations. After all, real participation in huge international negotiations is not simply about attending plenary meetings and making occasional interventions. It also involves a lot of back room politics – using formal and informal contacts to shape the agenda and process; drafting and circulating informal

[26] J. T. Roberts and B. Parks, *A* Climate of Injustice, (Cambridge, MA: MIT Press, 2006).

[27] Kummer, International *Management of hazardous Wastes: The Basel Convention and Related Legal Rules* (Oxford: Claderon Press, 1995).

texts; sounding out the positions of others informally, doing deals and a bit of horse trading.

Indeed, one of the curiosities of the modern political order is that the international system has somehow managed to remain somewhat insulated from the wave of democratization that has swept national political institutions even in the context of pervasive interdependence and a much-vaunted weakening of states' power due to socio-economic globalization. Despite the ever increasing number in the NGOs and non state actors that attend global environmental conferences, the decision making process has continued to remain in the hands of powerful states and few elites who manipulate the process to achieve their narrowly defined self interest. However, as Henry Shue argues, a commitment to justice requires 'willingness to choose to accept less good terms than one could have achieved' under egoistic bargaining. It means, he says, 'granting what the other party is in no position to insist upon'. On such a basis, developed country would not seek to exploit the weak bargaining power of poor countries to their advantage but invest in working towards a just and equitable international agreement. A just climate agreement is a reward of its own since supposedly such an agreement would enjoy broad acceptance and stability.

5. Compound Injustice and the future of North–South Climate Equity

The three factors discussed above are all in themselves very significant sources of North South environmental injustice. However, in practice they often work in combination to produce even more devastating conditions of inequity and reinforce patterns of domination – situation Shue describes as condition of 'compound injustice'.[28]

The problem of climate change exemplifies the nature of this interaction and compound injustice. First, the North through the process of industrialisation has drastically reduced the available global carbon space, reaping significant economic, political and technical benefits in the process. Second, the industrialization process has caused, and continues to cause devastating negative effects and deaths in the developing countries. These negative consequences decrease the opportunity and chance of developing countries to dig themselves out of poverty. Furthermore, through economic globalization,

[28] Op. cit. note, note 2, 390.

developed countries are continually increasing the climate vulnerability and poverty of the poor countries through deforestation, unfair terms of trade and the environmentally destructive activities of their multinational company proxies. Moreover the bargaining power of the South is severely weakened through historical relationship broader structural injustice. Yet, in climate negotiation circles, the industrialised countries have no qualms in exploiting their political, economic and technical superiority to establish self serving rules and muscle out any opposition from the poor South. Authors of the Bruntland Report[29] has precisely this kind of compound injustice in mind when they wrote:

> ....developing countries must operate in a world in which the recourses gap between most developing nations and industrialised nations is widening, in which the industrialised world dominates in the rule–making of some key international bodies, and in which the industrial world has already used much of the planet's ecological capital. This inequality is the planets main environmental problem, It is also it main "development" problem.

Consider that in 1992 when the UNFCCC was negotiated, it was widely thought that climate change provided an opportunity to rebalance issues of injustice and inequity in the global economic system. The prevailing thinking among scholars was that the international regime will sanction large scale North–South transfers as to help developing countries adapt to climate change and adopt low carbon development trajectories. Following this sentiment, a number of scholars provided calculations and estimates of the amounts that might be needed to secure and maintain international climate cooperation with figures ranging from US$100 annually[30] to US$529 billion,[31] payable by an annuity of about US$34 billion over a 30-year period. However, after over 20 years of the existence of the UNFCCC no North–South financial transfer of any worth has yet taken place. Developed countries have not only managed to evade all the equity responsibilities penned down in the climate

[29] Op. cit, note 1, 5–6.

[30] M. Grubb, J. Sebenius, A. Magalhaes, Who Bears the Burden? Equity and Allocation in Greenhouse Gas Emissions Abatement. Paper for SEI project for UNCED, June, 1991.

[31] P. Hayes, 'North–South Transfer', in P. Hayes and K. Smith (eds), *The Global Greenhouse Regime: Who Pays?* (London: EarthScan, 1993).

regime, they have also failed to take significant action to cut their domestic emissions.

At present, negotiations are focused upon what will happen when the first commitment period of the Kyoto Protocol ends in 2012. It is unlikely that developed nations will sign up to a second commitment period of emissions reductions without the involvement of developing countries. Russia and Japan have categorically stated that they will not be signing up to a second commitment phase of the Kyoto Protocol. The United States have continued to play the blame game deciding to castigate China for pursuing economic development rather than take any action and the European Union, which had previous shown strong moral ship has now capitulated to the strong lobby of high carbon emitting companies. At COP15 in Copenhagen in 2009 an Accord bearing its name was produced. On the basis of this Accord, a total of 76 emission targets were submitted by both developed and developing countries. This submissions which were given a formal status under the UNFCCC process at COP 16 in Cancun mark the first occasion that the developing countries have put forward mitigation actions and have accepted any type of internationalisation of their climate change policies. Interestingly, while these Agreements included targets from both developed and developing nations they still maintain the language of equity and justice. The new emphasis appears to be that the emissions reductions signed up to by developing countries are voluntary. Regardless, the very fact that the larger developing countries in particular have taken on emission reduction targets reflects the fact that developed countries have now all but succeeded in getting developing countries to take on emission reduction targets that are subject to international monitoring, verification and valuation while avoiding any serious emission reduction and financial commitments.

6. Rebuttals

The sort of arguments assembled in the sections above could, and do in fact provoke some responses from developed country governments and their academic ideologues. Before concluding I would like to briefly discuss these and examine their merits. The first response from those that oppose the idea of global (environmental) justice is to say that the presence of natural resource limits does not necessarily commit the international community to the ethic of need and redistribution. Proponents of some form of libertarianism often assert that even in the face of established ecological limits, peoples and nations ought still be free to order their lives in accordance with their chosen value system and preferences. Since heterogeneity in the conceptions of the Good Life is the starting point for this thesis, adherents insist that reordering international policies to meet needs would impinge on the liberty of many others who in the process might be forced to part with their market-allocated entitlements. William Nordhaus[32] does in fact defend a strand of this view. His argument embodies the suggestion that since it would cost the US far less to respond to the threats of Climate Change than to adapt to preventive strategies, that a business-as-usual approach (not minding the fate of other countries who would be severely affected) should inform energy policies in the United Sates.[33]

The second line of argument is the sort advanced by scholars such as Bhagwati[34] and Anderson and Leal.[35] These ones argue that free trade boosts the economy and in so doing generates the growth that both increases the demand for high environmental standards as well as the resources necessary to provide for it. They accept the importance of recognising ecological limits and that of meeting needs but then claim that the present institutions and capitalist economies are the best suited to respond to such demands of justice while simultaneously rewarding enterprise in line with notions of justice as merit. When pressed, they admit that unrestrained growth may widen the gap between the rich and the poor, but insist the poor are still made better off in absolute term by the success of the rich.

The third line of defence comes from those that tend to deny, despite the seeming evidence that there are in fact no limits. Here, the basic claim is that human ingenuity and the possibilities of technological inventions offer humanity boundless opportunities for growth. The claim also is that notions of sustainability which stress the preservation of natural capital at all cost, is misguided since man-made capital and natural capital are largely substitutable.

But in the end, these arguments run into serious difficulties. The first line of rebuttal for example completely fails on the ground that nations, as the preceding sections have demonstrated, are by no

32 W. Nordhaus, 'To slow or not to slow: The Economics of the greenhouse effect', The *Economic Journal* **101** (1991), 920–937.

33 There are some who believe that the nonchalant attitude of the US towards to Kyoto protocol is actually underpinned by this reasoning.

34 J. Bhagwati, 'The Case for Free Trade', *Scientific American* November (1993), 42–49.

35 T. L. Anderson and D. R. Leal, *Free Market Environmentalism* (Oxford/San Francisco: Westview Press, 1991).

means self-sufficient entities. Neither do environmental problems respect artificially constructed political boundaries. Hence, even where a nation chooses to value optimum consumption per time over conservation, it has no moral right to pursue such a hedonistic value by destroying other nations' resources or to transferring the pollution arising from such life styles to neighbouring countries. The Congo, Mali, and Bangladesh may not have the right to impose conservation values over the US, but the US reserves no right to annihilate Bangladesh through climate change induced flooding or sustain its profligacy through the resources that come from the Congo and Mali.

The second line of rebuttal which defends injustice on the basis of the 'trickle down' argument is also inherently faulty because, in the end, it does not address the question of ecological limits. Nor does it engage with the problem of underlying structural inequality and the hideous terms of trade under which developing countries labour. Finally even if there were no limits, it is not simply the case that natural and man-made resources are perfectly substitutable. Guiseppe Munda makes this point well when he argues that 'since resources are required to manufacture capital goods, the success of any attempt to substitute capital for resources will be limited by the extent to which the increase in capital requires an input in resources'.[36] Besides, he points out that natural capital has the feature of providing multiple value and functions (including life support functions) in ways that man-made capital cannot such that both then could be marginal but definitely not perfect substitutes.

The developed countries are of course aware of the importance of natural resources and have indeed been the champions of global biodiversity conservation programs. The problem however is that the developed countries have relied more on preachments and shown no real determination to offer more than pittance sums for the protection of these natural tracts. This quote from Oluf Langhele[37] amply demonstrates point:

> The reason that most biological diversity is located in developing countries is not just due to climatic conditions, but also the fact that developed countries have substantially reduced their

[36] G. Munda, 'Environmental Economics, Ecological Economics and the Concept of Sustainable Development', *Environmental Values* **6**: 2 (1997), 213–234.

[37] O. Langhelle, 'Sustainable Development and Social justice: expanding the Rawlsian Framework of Global Justice', *Environmental Values* **9**: 3 (2000), 316.

biological diversity during the last 250 years. Demanding that natural capital must be kept constant may sound as a nice thing when there are no forests left and most people life in affluence. It is something quite different when your country consists of 74 per cent forest and a majority of people is living in severe poverty.

7. Conclusion

Present day environmental co-operation is taking place under serious conditions of North-South injustice. Although it has now been acknowledged that environmental issues such climate change implicates serious issues of inter and intra-generational justice, the global governance arrangements have not attended seriously to these issues of justice. But while ethics might not be a popular term in international affairs, it remains an inseparable aspect of every political process insofar as these demand choices among different ideas of what is right or desirable.[38] Distributional justice is not merely instrumental to, but a part of the package of environmental sustainability forming an integral part of its socio-economic and political dimensions. Hence, achieving global sustainable development would require more radical interrogations of the basic structure of the international society and of patterns of social relations between the North and South. In short, questions of environmental justice must be seen as questions about the mode of wealth creation and appropriation itself rather than as add-on optional extra. Given the equal and common dependence of human kind on one single natural system, the idea of global environmental or planetary citizenship should not be seen as a mere preachment but one that deserves to be taken as a foundation upon which the institutions for international environmental governance ought to be built. To stand any chance of meeting the aspirations of majority of the global population, international management approaches must strive harder to reflect responsible stewardship and the fact of our common inheritance and ownership of the planetary resources.

Smith School, Oxford

[38] B. Holden, 'Introduction', in *The Ethical Dimensions of Global Change*, B. Holden (ed.) (London: Macmillan Press, 1996), 4.

Aesthetic Appreciation of Nature and Environmentalism

ALLEN CARLSON

1. Introduction

There can be no doubt that aesthetic appreciation of nature has frequently been a major factor in how we regard and treat the natural environment. In his historical study of American environmental attitudes, environmental philosopher Eugene Hargrove documents the ways in which aesthetic value was extremely influential concerning the preservation of some of North America's most magnificent natural environments.[1] Other environmental philosophers agree. J. Baird Callicott claims that historically 'aesthetic evaluation... has made a terrific difference to American conservation policy and management', pointing out that one of 'the main reasons that we have set aside certain natural areas as national, state, and county parks is because they are considered beautiful', and arguing that many 'more of our conservation and management decisions have been motivated by aesthetic rather than ethical values'.[2] Likewise environmental philosopher Ned Hettinger concludes his investigation of the significance of aesthetic appreciation for the 'protection of the environment' by affirming that 'environmental ethics would benefit from taking environmental aesthetics more seriously'.[3] Callicott sums up the situation as follows: 'What kinds of country we consider to be exceptionally beautiful makes a huge difference when we come to decide which places to save, which to restore or enhance, and which to allocate to other uses' concluding that 'a sound natural

[1] Eugene C. Hargrove, 'The Historical Foundations of American Environmental Attitudes', *Environmental Ethics* **1** (1979), 209–240; reprinted in A. Carlson and S. Lintott, eds., *Nature, Aesthetics, and Environmentalism: From Beauty to Duty* (New York: Columbia University Press, 2008).

[2] J. Baird Callicott, 'Leopold's Land Aesthetic', in Carlson and Lintott, *Nature, Aesthetics, and Environmentalism*, 106.

[3] Ned Hettinger, 'Allen Carlson's Environmental Aesthetics and the Protection of the Environment', *Environmental Ethics* **27** (2005), 57–76, 76.

doi:10.1017/S1358246111000257

aesthetics is crucial to sound conservation policy and land management'.[4]

Callicott's claim is certainly true. However, it leaves open the question of the nature of 'a sound natural aesthetics'. What is a sound natural aesthetics? And what is the proper relationship between such an aesthetics and environmental thought and action? Does environmentalism itself require certain features for a natural aesthetics to be sound? If so, what are these requirements of environmentalism? In this essay I address these questions as follows: I first review two historically significant positions concerning aesthetic experience of nature, the picturesque landscape tradition and the formalist theory of art. I note that some environmentalists have found fault with the modes of aesthetic appreciation of nature that are associated with these two views, charging that they are anthropocentric, scenery-obsessed, superficial, subjective, and/or morally vacuous. On the basis of these apparent failings of traditional aesthetic approaches to nature, I suggest five requirements of environmentalism: that aesthetic appreciation of nature should be acentric, environment-focused, serious, objective, and morally engaged. I then examine two contemporary positions concerning the appropriate aesthetic appreciation of nature, the aesthetics of engagement and scientific cognitivism, assessing each with respect to the five requirements of environmentalism.

2. Traditional Aesthetics of Nature: The Picturesque and Formalism

The picturesque landscape tradition has its roots in the eighteenth century, with the acceptance of nature as an ideal object of aesthetic experience and the separation of its appreciation into three distinct modes: the beautiful, the sublime, and the picturesque. Historian John Conron summarises the differences: the beautiful tends to be small and smooth, but subtly varied, delicate, and fair in colour, while the sublime, by contrast, is powerful, vast, intense, and terrifying. The picturesque is in the middle ground between the sublime and the beautiful, being 'complex and eccentric, varied and irregular, rich and forceful, vibrant with energy'.[5] Of these three, the

[4] Op. cit., note 2, 106.

[5] John Conron, *American Picturesque* (University Park: Pennsylvania State University Press, 2000), 17–18. A classic discussion is W. J. Hipple, Jr., *The Beautiful, the Sublime and the Picturesque in Eighteenth-Century*

picturesque achieved pre-eminence as a model for nature appreciation, in part because it covers the extensive middle ground of the complex, eccentric, varied, irregular, rich, forceful, and vibrant, all of which seem well-suited to nature. Moreover, the idea had grounding in the theories of some earlier aestheticians, who thought that the 'works of nature' were more appealing when they resembled works of art.[6] Indeed, the term 'picturesque' literally means 'picture-like' and thus the idea of the picturesque gave rise to a mode of aesthetic appreciation in which nature is experienced as if divided into scenes – into blocks of scenery. Such scenes aim in subject matter and composition at ideals dictated by the arts, especially landscape painting. Picturesque-influenced appreciation was popularised by William Gilpin, Uvedale Price, and Richard Payne Knight.[7] Under their guidance, the picturesque provided the reigning aesthetic ideal for English tourists, who pursued picturesque scenery in the Lake District and the Scottish Highlands. The picturesque continued throughout the nineteenth century to have a great impact on nature appreciation. In North American, it inspired nature writing and was exemplified in landscape painting. And in the twentieth century, it remains the mode of aesthetic appreciation commonly associated with tourism – that which appreciates the natural world in light of the scenic images of travel brochures and picture postcards.

British Aesthetic Theory (Carbondale: Southern Illinois University Press, 1957).

6 Perhaps another reason for the pre-eminence of the picturesque as a model for nature appreciation is that, in spite of Conron's way of putting the three fold distinction, the beautiful and the sublime, at least initially, were seemingly intended to characterize states of the appreciator, while the picturesque appears even from the outset to be more a characterization of the object of appreciation. I thank Alex Neill for making clear the importance of this point.

7 The key works include William Gilpin, *Three Essays: On Picturesque Beauty, On Picturesque Travel, and On Sketching Landscape; to which Is Added a Poem, On Landscape Painting* (London: R. Blamire, 1792); Uvedale Price, *An Essay on the Picturesque, as Compared with the Sublime and the Beautiful; and on the Use of Studying Pictures, for the Purpose of Improving Real Landscape* (London: J. Robson, 1794); Richard Payne Knight, *The Landscape: A Didactic Poem* (London: Printed by W. Bulmer and Co. for G. Nicol, 1794), and *Analytical Inquiry into the Principles of Taste* (London: Printed by L. Hansard and Sons for T. Payne and J. White, 1805). A standard treatment is Christopher Hussey, *The Picturesque: Studies in a Point of View* (London: G. Putnam's Sons, 1927).

Even as aesthetic appreciation of nature influenced by the idea of the picturesque continued to be extremely popular in the early part of the twentieth century, a related but somewhat distinct approach to nature appreciation was spawned by that period's most influential theory of art: the formalist theory. As developed by British art critics Clive Bell and Roger Fry, formalism is basically a theory about the nature of art, which holds that what makes an object a work of art is an aesthetically moving combination of lines, shapes, and colours. Bell called this 'significant form' and argued that aesthetic appreciation of art is restricted to it, notoriously stating that to 'appreciate a work of art we need bring with us nothing but a sense of form and colour'.[8] However, even Bell, whose aesthetic interest was almost exclusively devoted to art, could find aesthetic value in nature when it is experienced, in his words, 'with the eye of an artist' by which an appreciator, 'instead of seeing it as fields and cottages… has contrived to see it as a pure formal combination of lines and colours'.[9] Like the tradition of the picturesque, Bell had in mind seeing nature as it might look in landscape paintings, but not exactly the same kind of paintings as those favoured by the picturesque. Understandably, Bell's view was more closely allied with the work of artists of his own time, such as Paul Cézanne. For example, Cézanne's landscape paintings are classics of one kind of formal treatment of the landscape, in which nature is represented as patterns of lines, shapes, and colours. Throughout the first part of the twentieth century, various artists and schools of painters developed this kind of formal approach to landscape appreciation and thus it came to dictate a popular way of aesthetically experiencing nature.

Although formalism and the tradition of the picturesque have somewhat different emphases and take different kinds of art as their models, they are yet similar enough in their overall approach to the aesthetic appreciation of nature to come together in what might be called traditional aesthetics of nature. The overall approach combines features favoured in picturesque appreciation, such as being, to return to Conron's words, 'varied and irregular', 'rich and forceful', and 'vibrant with energy', with the prominence of the bold lines, shapes, and colours privileged by formalists. In this sense, traditional aesthetics of nature is the legacy of both the picturesque tradition and formalism.[10] In popular aesthetic appreciation, this legacy has given

8 Clive Bell, *Art* [1913] (New York: G. Putnam's Sons, 1958), 30.

9 Ibid., 45.

10 Although I relate what I call traditional aesthetics of nature to the historical developments of the idea of the picturesque and the formalist theory

rise to an emphasis on striking and dramatic landscapes with scenic prospects, such as found in the Rocky Mountains of North America, where rugged mountains and clear water come together to contrast and complement one another.

The role of traditional aesthetics of nature in the development of popular appreciation of nature as well as in the growth of environmental thought and action is difficult to over-estimate. As I noted at the outset of this essay, aesthetic appreciation of nature has played a major role in North American environmentalism. And throughout environmentalism's development in the nineteenth and twentieth centuries, such aesthetic appreciation was shaped largely by the picturesque landscape tradition and later supplemented by formalism. North America's rich heritage of parks and preserves is in large part the result of the fact that these areas were found to be aesthetically appealing in light of the appreciative approach of traditional aesthetics of nature. The same is true of many other parts of the world.

3. The Failings of Traditional Aesthetics of Nature and the Requirements of Environmentalism

However, more recently the relationship between aesthetic appreciation of nature and environmentalism has become a focus of concern. Increasingly individuals interested in the preservation of natural environments have started to doubt that traditional aesthetics of nature has the resources necessary to fully carry out an

---

of art, certain aspects of this kind of view are defended in some recent work on the aesthetics of nature; for example, see Robert Stecker, 'The Correct and the Appropriate in the Appreciation of Nature', *British Journal of Aesthetics* **37** (1997), 393–402; Donald W. Crawford, 'Scenery and the Aesthetics of Nature', in A. Carlson and A. Berleant, eds., *The Aesthetics of Natural Environments* (Peterborough, Canada: Broadview Press, 2004); and Thomas Leddy, 'A Defense of Arts-Based Appreciation of Nature', *Environmental Ethics* **27** (2005), 299–315. Formal aesthetic appreciation of nature is defended in Nick Zangwill, 'Formal Natural Beauty', *Proceedings of the Aristotelian Society* **101** (2001), 209–224; for follow-up concerning formalism, see Glenn Parsons, 'Natural Functions and the Aesthetic Appreciation of Inorganic Nature', *British Journal of Aesthetics* **44** (2004), 44–56, and Nick Zangwill, 'In Defence of Extreme Formalism about Inorganic Nature: Reply to Parsons', *British Journal of Aesthetics* **45** (2005), 185–191.

environmentalist agenda. The beginnings of these doubts can be found in the middle of the last century in the writings of Aldo Leopold. In *A Sand County Almanac* published in 1949 and *Round River* in 1952, Leopold presented a vision of the relationship between aesthetic experience of nature and the natural environment that continues to shape contemporary understanding of the relevance of aesthetic appreciation to environmentalism. Nonetheless, although recognizing the historical importance of traditional aesthetics of nature, he yet expressed some concern about its role in shaping what he called the 'taste for country', which he noted 'displays the same diversity in aesthetic competence among individuals as the taste for opera, or oils'. Thus, many appreciators of nature 'are willing to be herded in droves through "scenic" places' and 'find mountains grand if they be proper mountains with waterfalls, cliffs, and lakes' but yet find 'the Kansas plains…tedious'.[11]

What Leopold came to see was that the 'taste for country' of the majority of nature appreciators, which was largely the result of traditional aesthetics of nature, had certain limitations and perhaps did not fully accord with the environmental values that were becoming clear to him as he worked out the details of his 'land ethic'. Recent environmental thinkers, following in Leopold's footsteps, have become increasingly concerned that the aesthetic values embodied in traditional aesthetics of nature have failed in a number of ways to accord with the values of environmentalism.[12] In fact, in the opinion of some contemporary environmentalists, there are at least five major failings of traditional aesthetics of nature. To put it succinctly, traditional aesthetics of nature is criticized for endorsing aesthetic appreciation of nature that is: 1. anthropocentric, 2. scenery-obsessed, 3. superficial and trivial, 4. subjective, and 5. morally vacuous.[13] In light of these failings, it is possible to indicate

[11] Aldo Leopold, *A Sand County Almanac with Essays on Conservation from Round River* [1949, 1952] (Oxford: Oxford University Press, 1966), 179–180; relevant selections are reprinted in Carlson and Lintott, *Nature, Aesthetics, and Environmentalism*.

[12] It is important to note that not all environmental thinkers agree with this assessment of traditional aesthetics of nature. Some offer a reinterpretation of the picturesque that is more in accord with environmentalism; see, for example, Isis Brook, 'Wildness in the English Garden Tradition: A Reassessment of the Picturesque from Environmental Philosophy', *Ethics and the Environment* **13** (2008), 105–119.

[13] Some of these criticisms, especially that traditional aesthetics of nature tends to be superficial and scenery-obsessed, have been noted since the beginnings of the renewed interest in the aesthetics of nature; see, for

Requirements of Environmentalism for appropriate aesthetic appreciation of nature by contrasting the failings with solutions or, perhaps better, antidotes. Thus, environmentalism seemingly requires appreciation that is: 1. acentric, 2. environment-focused, 3. serious, 4. objective, and 5. morally engaged.[14] I discuss each of the failings and the corresponding antidote in turn.

1. *Acentric rather than anthropocentric appreciation*: The charge that traditional aesthetics of nature is anthropocentric or human-centred is directed at both the picturesque tradition and formalism. There is a sense, of course, in which all aesthetic appreciation is, and must be, from the point of view of a particular human appreciator, but the criticism concerns the specific conception of nature and our relationship to it that seems implicit in traditional aesthetics of nature. Part of this conception involves the anthropocentric thought that nature exists exclusively for us and for our pleasure. For example, environmental aesthetician Yuriko Saito argues that the 'exclusive emphasis on visual design' of the 'picturesque/formalist view' encourages us to appreciate only that which is 'amusing, enjoyable, or pleasing'.[15] Landscape geographer Ronald Rees agrees, contending that 'the picturesque... simply confirmed our anthropocentrism by suggesting that nature exists to please as well as to serve us'.[16] Likewise, Canadian environmental philosopher Stan Godlovitch argues that to 'justify protecting nature as it is and not merely as it is for us... a natural aesthetic must forswear the anthropocentric limits that... define and dominate our aesthetic response'.[17] Godlovitch's antidote for anthropocentrism and thus a requirement

---

example, Mark Sagoff, 'On Preserving the Natural Environment', *Yale Law Journal* **84** (1974), 205–267, and Allen Carlson, 'On the Possibility of Quantifying Scenic Beauty', *Landscape Planning* **4** (1977), 131–172.

[14] I consider at least seriousness and objectivity to be general adequacy requirements for an aesthetics of nature; see Allen Carlson, 'The Requirements for an Adequate Aesthetics of Nature', *Environmental Philosophy* **4** (2007), 1–12.

[15] Yuriko Saito, 'Appreciating Nature on Its Own Terms', *Environmental Ethics* **20** (1998), 135–149, 138; reprinted in Carlson and Berleant, *The Aesthetics of Natural Environments*.

[16] Ronald Rees, 'The Taste for Mountain Scenery', *History Today* **25** (1975), 305–312, 312.

[17] Stan Godlovitch, 'Icebreakers: Environmentalism and Natural Aesthetics', *Journal of Applied Philosophy* **11** (1994), 15–30, 16; reprinted in Carlson and Berleant, *The Aesthetics of Natural Environments*.

of environmentalism is to attempt to achieve what he calls an acentric approach to appreciating the natural world. The idea is that an appreciator must strive for an experience that is not from any particular point of view, human or otherwise, what is sometimes called a 'view from nowhere'. It is far from clear exactly how a human appreciator can adopt such a fully non-anthropocentric viewpoint. Nonetheless, after affirming that in 'acentric positions, the value expressed... cannot reflect the point of view of the recipient', Godlovitch proposes that since 'only acentric environmentalism takes into account nature as a whole...we require a corresponding acentric natural aesthetic to ground it'.[18]

2. *Environment-focused rather than scenery-obsessed appreciation*: Although there can be no doubt that traditional aesthetics of nature, and the picturesque tradition in particular, is focused on scenery, the second criticism is that traditional aesthetics of nature goes far beyond this focus to the point of obsession. And although it may be granted that there is much of aesthetic value in the scenery favoured by traditional aesthetics of nature, when the point of view becomes an obsession, the upshot is that other less conventionally scenic environments are excluded from appreciation. The problem is especially acute concerning environments that may be ecologically valuable, but do not fit the traditional conception of scenic landscapes, such as prairies, badlands, and wetlands.[19] In 'The Aesthetics of Unscenic Nature', Yuriko Saito argues that the 'picturesque... has... encouraged us to look for and appreciate primarily the *scenically* interesting and beautiful parts of our environment' with the result that 'those environments devoid of effective pictorial composition, excitement, or amusement (that is, those not worthy of being represented in a picture) are considered lacking in aesthetic values'.[20] Here, however, the antidote is somewhat less radical than accepting a theoretical complex notion such as Godlovitch's acentrism. Rather, it involves only acknowledging any of several rather

[18] Ibid. Godlovitch's acentrism reflects some of the ideas in Thomas Nagel, *The View from Nowhere* (Oxford: Oxford University Press, 1986).

[19] On wetlands in particular, see Allen Carlson, 'Admiring Mirelands: The Difficult Beauty of Wetlands', in Heikkila-Palo, ed., *Suo on Kaunis*, (Helsinki: Maahenki Oy, 1999); Holmes Rolston, III, 'Aesthetics in the Swamps', *Perspectives in Biology and Medicine* **43** (2000), 584–597; and J. Baird Callicott, 'Wetland Gloom and Wetland Glory', *Philosophy and Geography* **6** (2003), 33–45.

[20] Yuriko Saito, 'The Aesthetics of Unscenic Nature', *Journal of Aesthetics and Art Criticism* **56** (1998), 101–111, 101; reprinted in Carlson and Lintott, *Nature, Aesthetics, and Environmentalism*.

obvious dimensions of the experience of natural environments, such as emotional arousal or intellectual curiosity, that quite naturally draw appreciators away from a focus simply on scenery or on lines, shapes, and colours. For example, according to environmental philosopher Holmes Rolston III, the requirement of environmentalism in this case involves the recognition that appreciation of nature typically 'requires embodied participation, immersion, and struggle' and that it is a mistake to think of forests, for example, 'as scenery to be looked upon' for a 'forest is entered, not viewed' and you 'do not really engage a forest until you are well within it' and once within the 'forest itself, there is no scenery'.[21]

3. *Serious rather than superficial and trivial appreciation*: The third criticism, that the appreciation endorsed by traditional aesthetics of nature is superficial and trivial, is perhaps the most grave of the five charges. After observing that 'we continue to admire and preserve primarily "landscapes", "scenery", and "views" according to essentially eighteenth century standards of taste inherited from Gilpin, Price, and their contemporaries', Callicott claims that our 'tastes in natural beauty… remain fixed on visual and formal properties' and is 'derivative from art'. The upshot is that the 'prevailing natural aesthetic, therefore, is not autonomous: it does not flow naturally from nature itself; it is not directly oriented to nature on nature's own terms… It is superficial and… trivial'.[22] As Callicott makes clear, the heart of this criticism lies in the fact that traditional aesthetics of nature is dependent on artistic models and does not treat nature as nature. Thus, the requirement that appreciation be serious rather than superficial and trivial is satisfied when it is 'true to nature' in the sense of being directed fully and deeply toward what nature is and the qualities it has. In his groundbreaking essay, 'Contemporary Aesthetics and the Neglect of Natural Beauty', Ronald Hepburn suggested this requirement of environmentalism. He contrasts appreciating a cumulo-nimbus cloud as resembling a basket of washing and amusing ourselves by dwelling upon this resemblance with appreciating it by realizing 'the inner turbulence of the cloud, the winds sweeping up within and around it, determining its structure and visible form'. Hepburn suggests that the latter experience is 'less superficial…, truer to nature, and for that reason more worth having', noting that since 'there can be a passage, in art, from easy

[21] Holmes Rolston, III, 'Aesthetic Experience in Forests', *Journal of Aesthetics and Art Criticism* **56** (1998), 157–166, 162; reprinted in Carlson and Berleant, *The Aesthetics of Natural Environments*.

[22] Op. cit., note 2, 108–109.

beauty to difficult and more serious beauty, there can also be such passage in aesthetic contemplation of nature'.[23]

4. *Objective rather than subjective appreciation*: The criticism that appreciation grounded in traditional aesthetics of nature is subjective has been directed against both the picturesque tradition and formalism. In the case of the former, the subjectivity stems from the fact that aesthetic judgements are seemingly more a reflection of the pleasurable experiences of appreciators than of the objective features of objects of appreciation, while concerning the latter subjectivity is often related to the fact that formalist such as Bell seem to provide no grounds for making such judgements other than personal experience. However, subjectivity is perhaps more of a problem for the picturesque tradition than it is for formalism.[24] Be that as it may, the problem is acute in that if traditional aesthetics of nature yields only subjective judgements about nature's aesthetic value, then individuals making environmental decisions may be reluctant to acknowledge its importance, regarding it simply as based on personal whims or on relativistic, transient, soft-headed artistic ideals. As Ned Hettinger remarks: 'If judgments of environmental beauty lack objective grounding, they seemingly provide a poor basis for justifying environmental protection'.[25] Environmental philosopher Janna Thompson concurs: 'A judgement of value that is merely personal and subjective gives us no way of arguing that everyone ought to learn to appreciate something, or at least to regard it as worthy of preservation'.[26] Thus, the objectivity requirement is a particularly important requirement of environmentalism. As Thompson further observes, the 'link... between aesthetic judgment and ethical obligation fails unless there are objective grounds – grounds that rational, sensitive people can accept – for thinking that something has value'.[27] The importance of the requirement is

[23] Ronald Hepburn, 'Contemporary Aesthetics and the Neglect of Natural Beauty', in B. Williams and A. Montefiore, eds., *British Analytical Philosophy* (London: Routledge, Kegan Paul, 1966), 305; reprinted in Carlson and Berleant, *The Aesthetics of Natural Environments.*

[24] It can be argued that formalism underwrites a degree of objectivity of aesthetic value; see Glenn Parsons, *Aesthetics and Nature* (London: Continuum, 2008), 41–43.

[25] Ned Hettinger, 'Objectivity in Environmental Aesthetics and Environmental Protection', in Carlson and Lintott, *Nature, Aesthetics, and Environmentalism*, 414.

[26] Janna Thompson, 'Aesthetics and the Value of Nature', *Environmental Ethics* **17** (1995), 291–305, 292; reprinted in Carlson and Lintott, *Nature, Aesthetics, and Environmentalism.*

[27] Ibid.

put in even stronger terms by aesthetician Noël Carroll, who contends that 'any... picture of nature appreciation, if it is to be taken seriously, must have... means... for solving the problem of... objectivity of nature appreciation'.[28]

5. *Morally engaged rather than morally vacuous appreciation*: The last charge against traditional aesthetics of nature is again especially important regarding environmental thought and action, for environmentalists wish to bring aesthetic appreciation in line with ethical obligations to preserve and maintain ecologically healthy environments. But if traditional aesthetics of nature is morally vacuous, then ultimately there is no significant way of linking, as some environmental philosophers put it, beauty and duty. Ronald Rees contends that in traditional aesthetics of nature, there is 'an unfortunate lapse' in that our 'ethics... have lagged behind our aesthetics' allowing 'us to abuse our local environments and venerate the Alps and the Rockies'.[29] Landscape historian Malcolm Andrews confirms this, arguing that 'the trouble is that the picturesque enterprise in its later stage, with its almost exclusive emphasis on visual appreciation, entailed a suppression of the spectator's moral response'.[30] The problem is that the scenery of the picturesque tradition and the lines, shapes, and colours favoured by formalist seem to support either no moral judgements or else only the emptiest ones, such as the prescription to preserve that which pleases the eye. Thus, the key to satisfying the last requirement of environmentalism, that aesthetic appreciation of nature be morally engaged, lies at least partly in the differences between art-based appreciation of nature and nature appreciation that is, to return to Hepburn's phrase, 'truer to nature'. Philosopher Patricia Matthews points out that in the latter case our 'aesthetic assessments take into consideration not only formal elements such as color and design, but also the role that an object plays within a system'. This, she concludes, 'allows for a complex, deep, and meaningful aesthetic appreciation of nature' such that 'facts about... environmental impact... can affect our

[28] Noël Carroll, 'On Being Moved by Nature: Between Religion and Natural History', in S. Kemal and I. Gaskell, eds., *Landscape, Natural Beauty and the Arts* (Cambridge: Cambridge University Press, 1993), 257; reprinted in Carlson and Berleant, *The Aesthetics of Natural Environments*.

[29] Op. cit., note 16, 312.

[30] Malcolm Andrews, *The Search for the Picturesque* (Stanford: Stanford University Press, 1989), 59.

aesthetic appreciation' and thus 'our aesthetic and ethical assessments of what ought to be preserved in nature may be more harmonious'.[31]

In sum, the requirements of environmentalism for the aesthetics of nature are that it should support aesthetic appreciation of nature that is: 1. acentric rather than simply anthropocentric, 2. environment-focused rather than scenery-obsessed, 3. serious rather than superficial and trivial, 4. objective rather than subjective, and 5. morally engaged rather than morally vacuous. The question now is whether the new approaches to the aesthetics of nature that has been developed within contemporary work in environmental aesthetics can meet these requirements and thus foster a stronger and more positive relationship with environmentalism than is possible with traditional aesthetics of nature.

4. Contemporary Aesthetics of Nature and the Requirements of Environmentalism

Contemporary approaches to the aesthetics of nature are frequently divided into two different camps, labelled in various ways, such as non-cognitive and cognitive or non-conceptual and conceptual. Positions of the first type stress emotional and feeling-related states and responses, which are taken to be the less cognitive dimensions of aesthetic experience. By contrast, positions of the second type contend that knowledge about objects of appreciation is a necessary component of their appropriate aesthetic appreciation. I first consider non-cognitive and then cognitive approaches, focusing on a

[31] Patricia Matthews, 'Scientific Knowledge and the Aesthetic Appreciation of Nature', *Journal of Aesthetics and Art Criticism* **60** (2002), 37–48, 38; reprinted in Carlson and Lintott, *Nature, Aesthetics, and Environmentalism.* Discussions concerning bringing aesthetic appreciation and moral obligation in line with one another include Jane Iverson Nassauer, 'Cultural Sustainability: Aligning Aesthetics and Ecology', in J. I. Nassauer, ed., *Placing Nature: Culture and Landscape Ecology* (Washington, DC: Island Press, 1997); Marcia Eaton, 'The Beauty that Requires Health', in Nassauer, *Placing Nature*; and Sheila Lintott, 'Toward Eco-Friendly Aesthetics', *Environmental Ethics* **28** (2006), 57–76; all reprinted in Carlson and Lintott, *Nature, Aesthetics, and Environmentalism.* On this same topic, although more focused on human environments, is Yuriko Saito, 'The Role of Aesthetics in Civic Environmentalism', in A. Berleant and A. Carlson, eds., *The Aesthetics of Human Environments* (Peterborough, Canada: Broadview Press, 2007).

prominent example of each type and assessing it in light of the five requirements of environmentalism.

There are a number of different non-cognitive approaches to the aesthetic appreciation of nature. However, 'non-cognitive' here should not be taken in its older philosophical sense meaning primarily or only 'emotive'. Rather it indicates simply that these views argue that something other than a cognitive component is the central feature of aesthetic appreciation of nature. Thus, they are grouped together mainly by their lack of emphasis on cognitive considerations. Different positions focus on different kinds of states and responses, such as arousal, affection, reverence, engagement, and mystery. For example, the arousal model is championed by Noël Carroll. Carroll holds that we may appreciate nature simply by opening ourselves to it and being emotionally aroused by it, which he contends is a legitimate way of aesthetically appreciating nature without invoking any particular knowledge about it.[32] Another alternative, sometimes called the mystery model of nature appreciation, is defended by Stan Godlovitch. He contends that neither knowledge nor emotional attachment yields appropriate appreciation of nature, for nature itself is ultimately alien, aloof, and unknowable, and thus the appropriate experience of it is a state of appreciative incomprehension involving a sense of mystery.[33]

The most fully developed non-cognitive approach is the aesthetics of engagement. This position rejects much of traditional aesthetics of nature, such as the external, distanced appreciator favoured by the

[32] See Carroll, op. cit., note 28. Despite the centrality this model grants to emotional arousal, it is considered by some to be a cognitive rather than a non-cognitive approach, since Carroll accepts what is known as the cognitive theory of emotions, by which emotional responses can be judged appropriate or inappropriate. Likewise, although Emily Brady's work, which is noteworthy for its treatment of environmental issues, is typically classified as non-cognitive, its central component, that of imagination, is not clearly non-cognitive in any straightforward sense; see Emily Brady, 'Imagination and the Aesthetic Appreciation of Nature', *Journal of Aesthetics and Art Criticism* **56** (1998), 139–147; reprinted in Carlson and Berleant, *The Aesthetics of Natural Environments*; and especially Emily Brady, 'Aesthetic Character and Aesthetic Integrity in Environmental Conservation', *Environmental Ethics* **24** (2002),75–91; reprinted in Carlson and Lintott, *Nature, Aesthetics, and Environmentalism*; and Emily Brady, *Aesthetics of the Natural Environment* (Edinburgh: Edinburgh University Press, 2003).

[33] See Godlovitch, op. cit., note 17; see also Stan Godlovitch, 'Valuing Nature and the Autonomy of Natural Aesthetics', *British Journal of Aesthetics* **38** (1998), 180–197; reprinted in Carlson and Lintott, *Nature, Aesthetics, and Environmentalism*.

picturesque tradition and formalism, arguing that these approaches involve a mistaken conception of the aesthetic and that this is most evident in aesthetic experience of nature. According to the engagement approach, the distancing and isolating gaze of traditional aesthetics of nature is out of place in nature appreciation, for it wrongly abstracts both natural objects and appreciators from the environments in which they properly belong and in which appropriate appreciation is achieved. Rather the approach recommends that traditional dichotomies, such as between the object and the subject of appreciation, be abandoned, contending that aesthetic experience involves a participatory engagement of the appreciator within the object of appreciation. Thus, it stresses the contextual dimensions of nature and our multi-sensory experience of it, taking aesthetic experience to involve a total 'sensory immersion' of the appreciator within the natural world.[34] The foremost proponent of this position, Arnold Berleant, claims that 'we cannot distance the natural world from ourselves' and that we must perceive nature from within 'looking not at it but being in it' in which case it 'is transformed into a realm in which we live as participants, not observers'. He concludes that the 'aesthetic mark of all such times is... total engagement, a sensory immersion in the natural world'.[35]

Standing in contrast to the non-cognitive approaches are a number of positions classified as cognitive, since they are united by the idea that central to appropriate aesthetic appreciation is knowledge and information about the object of appreciation. In general, they hold that, in the words of Yuriko Saito, nature must be 'appreciated on its own terms'.[36] Thus, for example, Marcia Eaton holds that in aesthetic appreciation of nature, we must carefully distinguish between facts about nature and fictions, since while knowledge of the former is necessary for appropriate aesthetic appreciation, the latter can often lead us astray and pervert our appreciation.[37] Other cognitive

[34] See Arnold Berleant, *The Aesthetics of Environment* (Philadelphia: Temple University Press, 1992), especially Chapter 11, 'The Aesthetics of Art and Nature;' reprinted in Carlson and Berleant, *The Aesthetics of Natural Environments*; Arnold Berleant, *Living in the Landscape: Toward an Aesthetics of Environment* (Lawrence: University Press of Kansas, 1997); and Arnold Berleant, *Aesthetics and Environment: Variations on a Theme* (Aldershot: Ashgate, 2005).

[35] Op. cit., note 34, *Aesthetics of Environment*, 169–170.

[36] Op. cit., note 15, 135–149.

[37] See Marcia Eaton, 'Fact and Fiction in the Aesthetic Appreciation of Nature', *Journal of Aesthetics and Art Criticism* **56** (1998), 149–156; reprinted in Carlson and Berleant, *The Aesthetics of Natural Environments*.

approaches, including Saito's, emphasize other kinds of knowledge and information, claiming that appreciating nature 'on its own terms' may involve experiencing it in light of various local, folk, or historical traditions. Thus, for appropriate aesthetic appreciation, regional narratives and even mythological stories about nature are endorsed as either complementary with or alternative to factual information.[38]

The best-known cognitive approach is scientific cognitivism. Like most cognitive positions, which in general reject the idea that aesthetic experience of art provides satisfactory models for appreciation of nature, this view stresses that nature must be appreciated as nature and not as art. Nonetheless, it holds that aesthetic appreciation of nature is analogous to that of art in its character and structure and, therefore, that art appreciation can show some of what is required in adequate appreciation of nature. In appropriate aesthetic appreciation of art, it is essential for works to be experienced as what they are and in light of knowledge about them. For instance, appropriate appreciation of a work such as Jackson Pollock's *One: Number 31, 1950* requires experiencing it as a painting and moreover as an action painting within the school of mid-twentieth century American abstract expressionism. Therefore, it must be appreciated in light of knowledge of these artistic traditions and especially of action painting. In short, in the case of art, serious, appropriate aesthetic appreciation is informed by art history and art criticism. However, since nature must be appreciated as nature and not as art, scientific cognitivism contends that, although the knowledge given by art history and art criticism is relevant to art appreciation, in nature appreciation the relevant knowledge is that provided by natural history, by the natural sciences, especially geology, biology, and ecology.[39] Thus, to appropriately appreciate nature 'on its own

[38] For example, see Saito, op. cit., note 15; Yrjö Sepänmaa, *The Beauty of Environment: A General Model for Environmental Aesthetics* (Helsinki: Annales Academiae Scientiarum Fennicae, 1986; Second Edition, Denton, TX: Environmental Ethics Books, 1993); and Thomas Heyd, 'Aesthetic Appreciation and the Many Stories about Nature', *British Journal of Aesthetics* **41** (2001), 125–137; reprinted in Carlson and Berleant, *The Aesthetics of Natural Environments*.

[39] See Allen Carlson, 'Appreciation and the Natural Environment', *Journal of Aesthetics and Art Criticism* **37** (1979), 267–276; reprinted in Carlson and Berleant, *The Aesthetics of Natural Environments*; Allen Carlson, 'Aesthetic Appreciation of the Natural Environment', in R. G. Botzler and S. J. Armstrong, eds., *Environmental Ethics: Divergence and Convergence*, Second Edition (Boston: McGraw-Hill, 1998); reprinted in

terms' is to appreciate it as it is characterised by science. In this sense, scientific cognitivism is akin to the approach attributed to Aldo Leopold, which is sometimes labelled ecological aesthetics or the 'land aesthetic'. Like scientific cognitivism, this approach is committed to the centrality of scientific knowledge in aesthetic appreciation of nature. Callicott points out that 'the land aesthetic is sophisticated and cognitive,' delineating 'a refined taste in natural environments and a cultivated natural sensibility' the basis of which is 'natural history, and more especially evolutionary and ecological biology'.[40]

How then do contemporary approaches to aesthetics of nature, as represented by the aesthetics of engagement and scientific cognitivism, fare on the requirements of environmentalism? First it seems obvious that both the aesthetics of engagement and scientific cognitivism are clearly superior to traditional aesthetics of nature in a number of ways. An appreciator who is totally sensory immersed in a natural environment and/or well informed by scientific knowledge about it contrasts dramatically with a distanced appreciator who focuses only on formalist, picturesque scenery.[41] Thus, concerning the first of the requirements of environmentalism, the acentric requirement, the aesthetics of engagement's stress on sensory immersion seems to facilitate as acentric a point of view as is humanly possible, since it explicitly calls for abandoning traditional dichotomies, such as between the object of appreciation and the appreciator, and thus it would seem that the appreciator's own particular point of view must also be abandoned. Similarly, scientific cognitivism's reliance on scientific knowledge promotes an acentric point of view similar to that of science, which is an acentric way of knowing.[42] Concerning the environment-focus requirement, the aesthetics of engagement's stress on an appreciator's engaged participation takes into consideration whole environments and explicitly not scenery or formal composition. Likewise, scientific cognitivism's emphasis on environmental sciences focuses appreciation on environments

---

Carlson and Lintott, *Nature, Aesthetics, and Environmentalism*; and Allen Carlson, *Aesthetics and the Environment: The Appreciation of Nature, Art and Architecture* (London: Routledge, 2000).

[40] Op. cit., note 2, 116.

[41] For a classic illustration of this difference, see John Muir, 'A View of the High Sierra', in *The Mountains of California* (New York: Century Company, 1894); reprinted in Carlson and Lintott, *Nature, Aesthetics, and Environmentalism*.

[42] Godlovitch explicitly challenges this claim in op. cit., note 17.

rather than on scenery or formal features. There is no ecological science of scenery or of lines, shapes, and colours. Nor can one be immersed within scenery or within a combination of lines, shapes, and colours.

However, the success of contemporary approaches in meeting the remaining three requirements of environmentalism is more mixed. For example, although total sensory immersion may result in a high level of intensity, it does not seem to require seriousness in the sense of being 'true to nature'. It only allows for this kind of serious appreciation to whatever extent such appreciation is consistent with immersion. In addition, the aesthetics of engagement's dependence on immersion seems to weaken the position concerning objectivity, for abandoning the dichotomy between the object of appreciation and the subject of appreciation will seemingly make it difficult for an appreciator to be objective. Moreover, although the aesthetics of engagement would seem to support moral engagement concerning environmental issues, the position's subjectivity undercuts the possibility of a compelling moral stance, for without objectivity, ethical assessments, even if fuelled by intense engagement, can be dismissed as only expressions of personal feelings. By contrast, scientific cognitivism's reliance on scientific knowledge promotes appreciation that is serious in the sense of being 'true to nature' by means of attending fully to what nature is and the properties it has. Moreover, this promotes an objective viewpoint, since science is a paradigm of objectivity and, although aesthetic judgements based on scientific knowledge are not necessarily as objective as that knowledge itself, they nonetheless have an objective foundation.[43] Concerning the last requirement, scientific cognitivism is less clearly successful, for although its objectivity makes possible a compelling moral stance on environmental issues, it does not require it. Moreover, it is sometimes claimed that scientific knowledge is morally neutral and therefore promotes such neutrality. Yet, it can be argued that the factual character of scientific knowledge yields an environmentally informed response to nature and thus provides a firm basis for moral judgements.[44]

[43] See Allen Carlson, 'Nature, Aesthetic Judgment, and Objectivity', *Journal of Aesthetics and Art Criticism* **40** (1981), 15–27. For follow up, see Glenn Parsons, 'Freedom and Objectivity in the Aesthetic Appreciation of Nature', *British Journal of Aesthetics* **46** (2006), 17–37.

[44] See the discussion of *Bambi* in Eaton, op. cit., note 37.

5. Conclusion

In conclusion, I suggest the following five points: First, if we must choose between non-cognitive approaches like the aesthetics of engagement and cognitive approaches such as scientific cognitivism, then, on balance, the latter scores somewhat better than the former on the requirements of environmentalism. Second and more important, however, we do not have to choose between them, since, although the two positions have different emphases, there need be no theoretical conflict between them.[45] This is because each position can be understood as defending only necessary conditions for appropriate aesthetic appreciation. Each of engagement and relevant scientific knowledge can be held to be necessary without either being claimed to be sufficient for such appreciation.[46] There is perhaps some practical tension between the two approaches, owing to the appreciative difficulty of being totally engaged within a natural environment and at the same time taking into account knowledge relevant to its appropriate appreciation. However, this kind of bringing together and balancing of feeling and knowing, of emotion and cognition, is the very heart of aesthetic experience. It is what we expect in aesthetic appreciation of art; there is no reason why we should expect less in aesthetic appreciation of nature.

The third concluding point, therefore, is that, concerning the requirements of environmentalism, since the aesthetics of engagement is especially strong regarding acentrism and environment-focus and scientific cognitivism is stronger regarding seriousness and objectivity, and perhaps moral engagement, the best alternative is to unite the two positions. This approach is endorsed by Holmes Rolston in his essay 'From Beauty to Duty: Aesthetics of Nature and Environmental Ethics'. Rolston asks 'Can aesthetics be an adequate foundation for an environmental ethic?' replying 'Yes, increasingly,

[45] Other philosophers also suggest that non-cognitive and cognitive approaches are not necessarily in conflict; for example, in presenting his arousal model, Noël Carroll remarks: 'In defending this alternative mode of nature appreciation, I am not offering it in place of Carlson's environmental model [aka scientific cognitivism]....I'm for coexistence'; see op. cit., note 28, 246.

[46] Arnold Berleant seemingly would not accept this conclusion, for he apparently holds not only that a cognitive component is not necessary for appropriate aesthetic experience, but also that engagement is both necessary *and sufficient* for such experience. I point his out and argue that engagement is not sufficient in Allen Carlson, 'Critical Notice: Aesthetics and Environment', *British Journal of Aesthetics* **46** (2006), 416–427.

where aesthetics itself comes to find and to be founded on natural history, with humans emplacing themselves appropriately on such landscapes. Does environmental ethics need such aesthetics to be adequately founded? Yes, indeed'.[47] Given a unified position, which is, as Rolston puts it, both 'founded on natural history' and has appreciators 'emplacing themselves' within natural environments, the fourth point is that, concerning the requirements of environmentalism, contemporary environmental aesthetics, as represented by the conjunction of the aesthetics of engagement and scientific cognitivism, constitutes a substantial advance over traditional picturesque-influenced and formalist aesthetics of nature.[48] Hence, fifth, unlike traditional aesthetics of nature, contemporary approaches to nature appreciation help to bring aesthetic values and environmental values in line with one another. They encourage aesthetic appreciation of not simply scenic landscapes but also less conventionally scenic, but nonetheless aesthetically magnificent and ecologically valuable environments, like deserts, savannahs, prairies, and wetlands – indeed every kind of natural environment.[49]

University of Alberta

[47] Holmes Rolston, III, 'From Beauty to Duty: Aesthetics of Nature and Environmental Ethics', in A. Berleant, ed., *Environment and the Arts: Perspectives on Environmental Aesthetics* (Aldershot: Ashgate, 2002), 141; reprinted in Carlson and Lintott, *Nature, Aesthetics, and Environmentalism.* Rolston's acceptance of the importance of both scientific knowledge and engagement in appropriate aesthetic appreciation of nature is especially evident in op. cit., note 21, in which he explicitly discusses both scientific appreciation of forests and aesthetic engagement in forests. For an overview of Rolston's aesthetics, see Allen Carlson, '"We see beauty now where we could not see it before": Rolston's Aesthetics of Nature', in C. Preston and W. Ouderkirk, eds., *Nature, Value, Duty: Life on Earth with Holmes Rolston, III* (Dordrecht: Springer, 2006).

[48] In addition to Rolston's work, some other constructive attempts to combine elements of cognitive and non-cognitive approaches include Eaton, op. cit., note 31; Robert Fudge, 'Imagination and the Science-based Aesthetic Appreciation of Unscenic Nature', *Journal of Aesthetics and Art Criticism* **59** (2001), 275–285; and especially Ronald Moore, *Natural Beauty: A Theory of Aesthetics Beyond the Arts* (Peterborough, Canada: Broadview Press, 2008).

[49] Some of the points made in this essay are treated in more detail in the introduction to Carlson and Lintott, *Nature, Aesthetics, and Environmentalism.* A longer version of the essay with the title 'Contemporary Environmental Aesthetics and the Requirements of Environmentalism' appears in *Environmental Values* **19** (2010), 289–314.

Climate Change and Causal Inefficacy: Why Go Green When It Makes No Difference?

JAMES GARVEY

Think of some environmentally unfriendly choices – taking the car instead of public transport or driving an SUV, just binning something recyclable, using lots of plastic bags, buying an enormous television, washing clothes in hot water, replacing something when you could make do with last year's model, heating rooms you don't use or leaving the heating high when you could put on another layer of clothing, flying for holidays, wasting food and water, eating a lot of beef, installing a patio heater, maybe even, as some have said lately, owning a dog.[1] Think about your own choices, instances in which you take an action which enlarges your carbon footprint when you might have done otherwise without much trouble. Is there consolation in the thought that it makes no difference what you do?

If you didn't drive an SUV, maybe someone else would. The Americans are putting more and more cars on the road, so what's one more drop in that metallic ocean? So you throw away a recyclable bottle after lunch – it doesn't matter. Doesn't it all go in the landfill anyway? Have you seen how many plastic bags other people use – your one or two won't make a difference. What difference could your widescreen make when countries like China are producing more coal-burning power plants? Leave the heating on – it's your bill after all – and what's a few hours of wasted heat anyway, given the many millions of people who heat their homes every night? Why shouldn't you fly? The plane was going there anyway, and what difference can your comparatively little weight make? So what if you throw away food? Supermarkets throw away tons of food each day. Your tiny contribution can make no difference at all.

These are the thoughts which turn up in the heads of real people when they make everyday choices. The moral case for the claim that various countries ought to take strong action on climate change is fairly easy to see. What's much harder to spot is the moral demand for individual action, for making green choices in the

[1] B. Vale and R. Vale, *Time to Eat the Dog? The Real Guide to Sustainable Living* (London: Thames and Hudson, 2009).

doi:10.1017/S1358246111000269

course of an ordinary human life. One thing which gets in the way is the thought that nothing an individual does can possibly matter. So why bother going green? This is the environmental version of the problem of causal inefficacy. It has other manifestations too, and we'll consider some of them.

I wonder whether consequentialist reflection can somehow bring the moral demand for individual action into clear view. I want to consider, as a live possibility, the following unlikely position: one might be a consequentialist, know perfectly well that recycling today's newspaper can make no difference at all to tomorrow's climate, but still hold that there is a moral demand, having to do with consequences, for taking the paper to the recycling bin. The view might not fly, but it is worth pursuing for a reason I'll come to in a moment. First let us consider the moral case for action on the part of countries and then pin down smaller questions about individual choices in ordinary lives.

1. The Problem of Causal Inefficacy

There are plenty of arguments for large-scale action on climate change. Perhaps the most straightforward one issues in the conclusion that particular states have a moral obligation to do something serious about climate change because of their history of industrialization. Coupling facts about emissions with further thoughts about moral responsibility can make the obligation stand out clearly.[2] The argument can be up and running very quickly.

Burning fossil fuels thickens the blanket of greenhouse gasses which swaddles our world and warms it up.[3] The likely effects of this increase in temperature are various and subject to different levels of certainty. There is evidence for a future characterized by

[2] Other arguments for action have nothing to do with emissions histories. See J. Garvey, 'Responsibility', *The Ethics of Climate Change*, (London: Continuum Publishing, 2008).

[3] The settled scientific view is that there is a 90% chance that human activities are changing the climate. This finding is endorsed by all of the national academies of science of the world's major industrialized countries (a total of 32 national academies) as well as more than 40 professional scientific societies and academies of science all over the world. If you are in doubt start with J. Houghton, *Global Warming: The Complete Briefing*, (Cambridge: Cambridge University Press, 2004) and the Intergovernmental Panel on Climate Change's various summaries for policy-makers, available for free at www.ipcc.ch.

hotter days and nights, rising sea levels, dwindling water supplies, altered patterns of disease, conflict over shifting resources, more dramatic weather, longer droughts, shorter growing seasons, and on and on. It seems likely that human beings are suffering and will suffer as a result of these changes – to say nothing of the suffering of our fellow creatures who will also struggle to adapt.

The pain ahead is owed to the fact that our planet's carbon sinks cannot absorb all of our emissions, and the result is dangerous anthropogenic climate change. Compared to the poor nations of the world, the richer, more developed, industrialised countries have used up the bulk of the sinks and therefore have caused more of the suffering which is underway and on the cards. A few thoughts about fairness or justice or responsibility or the importance of doing something about unnecessary suffering, coupled with these facts, issues in the conclusion that developed countries have a moral obligation to reduce emissions and help with adaptation.

Part of what makes this conclusion easy to see is the obvious causal connection between large-scale industrial activity and suffering. It's obvious in broad outline anyway.[4] The industrialized world has dumped a lot of greenhouse gasses into the atmosphere. Over the last 150 years, as human beings have really gotten on with industrialization, carbon dioxide concentrations have risen from 280 to about 390 parts per million – one source tells me 391.76 ppm for February 2011.[5] We add about one or two more ppm each year, about 1,000 tons each second.

Greenhouse gasses are changing our climate. The changes result in suffering. It is right to say that the developed world ought to go green because doing so matters – mitigation or at least adaptation will have good consequences, will make a difference to human lives. What is much harder to see, though, is the analogous conclusion when it comes to individual choices and individual lives.

One might assume that there is a fairly tight connection between thoughts about future suffering and a moral obligation to adopt a thoroughly green lifestyle. If there is a connection between greenhouse gas emissions and human suffering, then doesn't it follow that an individual ought to do all she can to reduce her carbon

[4] That's not to say that the causal chains are straightforward. See for example S. Gardiner, 'A perfect moral storm: climate change, intergenerational ethics, and the problem of corruption', *Environmental Values* **15** (2006), 397–413.

[5] Earth Systems Research Laboratory (ESRL) / National Oceanic and Atmospheric Administration (NOAA)

footprint? Isn't avoiding a hand in the suffering ahead a good personal reason for going green? The trouble is that there is a large gap between the global premises and the local conclusion.

Given the enormity and complexity of the planet's climate system, it's hard to see how a single green choice, even a whole green life, could make the slightest difference to the suffering ahead. What's my 5 tons or so of greenhouse gas emissions per year compared to 1,000 tons per second? Sort the recycling into neat piles, insulate your house, choose local produce, travel only by bicycle and on and on – in short, make a determined effort to reduce your greenhouse gas emissions to the merest whisper – and none of it can possibly make the slightest real difference to our world. An individual's teeny effects cannot matter a jot. You can be certain that the sea level will be where it will be in 2050 whether you buy the bulbs or not.

It might be true that the governments of the developed world have a moral obligation to reduce emissions. It might also be true that the world would have more happiness in it, more preferences would be satisfied, if everyone lived closer to the Earth. Given the causal inefficacy of the individual in the face of climate change, it doesn't matter that a particular person lives a life of grotesque consumption. If an individual's effects do not make a difference, doing something about climate change can't be a reason for going green. Headlines to the contrary, you can't save the planet.

There is a little disaster in this line of thought. It is hard to find a way around this disaster if you put some store in the notion that the rightness or wrongness of actions has to do with consequences. In the following paragraphs, I'll lean on this notion and see how sturdy it is. In the end, we'll have to shore it up a little, but I think it turns out that individual green actions can be motivated by reflection on consequences. I admit that it is a fractionally round-about line of thought, but maybe it is better than an alternative or two.

Why should we lean on the notion? Why not, say, just go Kantian or cultivate personal virtue in this connection? The short answer is that thoughts about consequences have a certain hold on us when it comes to doing something about environmental degradation. We see the results of climate change – not just on the news but in our gardens – and a common reaction is the desire to do something about it, to take action. Contrary to a recent dispatch from the Vatican, probably most people are not ready to see harming the environment as a kind of vice or anyway as a lack of virtue.[6]

[6] Archbishop Gianfranco Girotti in *L'Osservatore Romano*, March, 2008.

The many environmentally friendly actions one might undertake are seen as precisely that, actions, and we undertake them principally for the consequences which result from them. We think we are doing good, not being good, when we take certain steps to save energy. We have a better world in view, not a better character.

The little disaster is the possibility that we cannot really do any good at all. If you already have Kantian leanings or think of your green activities as virtuous, then maybe you're not the person I am to convince. The person I hope to persuade is one who sometimes leans on that thought about consequences, who wonders how her consequences could possibly make a relevant difference – a person on the verge of thinking that it makes no difference what she does.

The problem of causal inefficacy gets a hearing against the backdrop of utilitarian arguments for vegetarianism and further reflection on voting, and some other questions too. The plan is to make a start by using these discussions to try to get a handle on climate change and causal inefficacy. Maybe we can leapfrog to an answer to our version of the problem by making use of the good thoughts of those who have already done some work in this neighbourhood. Consider vegetarianism first.

2. Threshold Chickens

Singer has argued that there is a strong and obvious connection between the obligation to become a vegetarian and utilitarianism. He originally maintained that 'because becoming a vegetarian reduces the overall demand for animal flesh, an individual could assume that it lowered the profitability of the animal industry, and thus reduced the number of animals factory farmers would breed'. [7] The choice not to eat animals, it might be thought, saves animals from suffering. As several critics point out, though, the loss of just one meat-eater from the millions and millions of consumers in a market makes a difference too tiny to be a noticeable difference to factory farmers.[8] It's not possible to say that an individual's choice

[7] P. Singer, 'Utilitarianism and Vegetarianism', *Philosophy and Public Affairs*, **9** (1980), 335. See also *Animal Liberation*, Chapter 4, (London: Pimlico, 1995).

[8] See M. Almeida and M. Bernstein, 'Opportunistic Carnivorism', *Journal of Applied Philosophy*, **17** (2000), 205–11; H. Hudson, 'Collective Responsibility and Moral Vegetarianism', *Journal of Social Philosophy* **24** (1993), 89–104; G. Matheny, 'Expected Utility, Contributory Causation

to become a vegetarian has an effect on the number of animals killed. Just as the climate will do what it does whether or not an individual goes green, the size and complexity of the factory farming industry is such that a single individual's choices cannot possibly register.

One set of responses to this has to do with thresholds. It might be true that just one vegetarian does not make a substantial difference, but a large number of vegetarians must make a difference. Maybe for every 10,000 vegetarians one fewer 100,000-bird factory farm is needed to supply the market. If enough people become vegetarians, the demand for meat drops below a certain threshold, producers take note, and a farm closes.

This can all be interpreted in a number of ways. You might think that whether you choose to be a vegetarian or not makes no difference at all to the market, unless you happen to be the lucky person who pushes the number of chickens demanded by the market down under the critical threshold. There's a chance it might be you, and since the stakes are so very high maybe that chance is enough to nudge you away from meat. Or you could understand your tiny role in boosting the numbers of vegetarians as contributory in some sense – as maybe not pushing the numbers past a threshold but nevertheless having a not entirely inconsequential part to play in swelling the ranks and closing one big factory farm. Maybe this little hand in ending a large wrong conveys enough utility to make the choice to go veggie the right one.

Let us take the main arc of this thinking about thresholds and try to adapt it to the case of climate change. If enough of us become vegetarians, then the demand for meat has to decrease, the market has to notice, and animals have to be saved from a horrible life on a factory farm. Can we say the same sorts of things about going

---

and Vegetarianism', *Journal of Applied Philosophy* **19**.3 (2002), 293–297; and J. Rachels, 'The Moral Argument for Vegetarianism' in *Can Ethics Provide Answers?* (Lanham: Rowman & Littlefield, 1997). For discussions of vegetarianism and consequences generally, see P. Devine, 'The Moral Basis of Vegetarianism', *Philosophy* **53** (1978), 481–505; J. Garrett, 'Utilitarianism, Vegetarianism, and Human Health: A response to the Causal Impotence Objection', *Journal of Applied Philosophy* **24**.3 (2007), 223–237; N. Nobis, 'Vegetarianism and Virtue: Does Consequentialism Demand Too Little?', *Social Theory and Practice* **28**.1 (2002), 135–156; T. Regan, 'Utilitarianism, Vegetarianism and Animal Rights', *Philosophy and Public Affairs* **9** (1980), 305–24; P. Singer, 'Utilitarianism and Vegetarianism', *Philosophy and Public Affairs*, **9** (1980) and *Animal Liberation*, Chapter 4, (London: Pimlico, 1995).

green? Can we really see the same sorts of connections? Maybe there is a parallel thought with respect to climate change, but I suspect that it's too murky to help us if we are after a consequentialist motivation for environmentally responsible action. Try to get a grip on the relevant antecedent and consequent.

The antecedent – which we might render as 'If enough of us go green ...' – is hazy, partly because we do not yet have a clear take on what it means to go green. Going green is a much more amorphous proposition than going vegetarian. Certainly there are different sorts of vegetarians, and no doubt it's a complex thing, but probably there are fewer wrinkles in going vegetarian than there are in going green. If you are a vegetarian, at bottom that means that you don't eat meat. Maybe we can argue about the finer points of that statement, but certain things are just right out. But what is it, at bottom, to be green?

Probably there are things to be said about the fact that we have not yet settled on what 'going green' actually means. It's a new thought for most of us. We do not yet have a good grip on how to reduce our impact on the Earth. Consider a few very common questions. Should I throw away my old bulbs (and thus waste the energy which went in to making them) or wait until they burn out before replacing them with the environmentally friendly ones? Should I buy local produce (and save on food miles) or buy Fair Trade from abroad (and help the poor farmers in South America)? Should I avoid flying altogether or offset my emissions with a clear conscience? Should we risk nuclear power in an effort to avoid greenhouse gas emissions? I have heard someone wonder if it's better to keep the air conditioning on in a car with the windows up (and thus reduce drag) or roll down the windows and turn off the air conditioning (and lower demand on fuel). These questions range from hard to trifling, but the point is that they are many, and some answers are not obvious.

Consider the consequent. How do we fill it in? 'If enough of us go green (however we spell that out) then' ... what? An easy thought to have is that the concentrations of greenhouse gases in our atmosphere will level off or drop, but it's hard to spell out how this works in enough detail to keep a solid response to the problem of causal inefficacy in view. We know a lot about how the climate works, but there's a lot we do not know, too. I am by no means suggesting that there is uncertainty with regard to climate change where it counts. We know that human beings are causing the change, and we know a lot about the nature of that change. We do not know much about regional variations and local impacts, and we do not know much about the timing of the changes ahead. There is a lot we do not know about feedbacks and thresholds. These gaps in our knowledge add uncertainty to our reflection about our effects.

It's not just our ignorance. Even concerning some aspects of the problem where we have a good understanding of what is going on, the complexity itself is overwhelming. It can make the relevance of the threshold response fade when it comes to climate change. Don't worry about green causes or the anticipated effects, but consider what's in between. One can, nearly, think about market forces and farmers and producers and buyers and come to the conclusion that enough of a change here will cause a change there. Maybe that conclusion can lead to vegetarianism.

Can we do the same sort of thing with, say, our greenhouse gas emissions and the global effects of climate change? Bear in mind, as you think about the answer to that question, that it might take a supercomputer a quadrillion different operations and more than a month to manipulate a climate model. There are feedbacks associated with ice and snow, animal life, clouds, wind, rain and on and on. Further, our effects are smeared out not just in space, but in time as well. Our emissions join together with past and future emissions and have further effects which might well be both spatially and temporally distant from us. It is hard to see a straight line from leaving my DVD-player on standby to melting ice caps.[9]

All of this is not to say that a person cannot see her role in all of this and come to the conclusion that, if enough people take serious action on climate change, we might, together, have good effects. I have that conclusion in my head from time to time, but I think it comes from something other than reflection on thresholds and causal chains and emissions. The difficulty I want to highlight lies in turning thoughts about thresholds into a consequentialist reason for green choices. In short, the weaker our grip on our place in the causal network the more difficult it is for causal thresholds to serve as a motivating reason for action. In the case of climate change, our conception of how our actions fit into the causal network is feeble to say the least. Maybe my effects are so small, and the world so huge, that I just can't talk myself into seeing what I do as playing any role at all in crossing any sort of threshold. Although a proto-vegetarian stands a chance of getting certain thresholds in view, seeing analogous thresholds in the climate change case might well be beyond us. Let us look elsewhere for help.

[9] Op. cit., note 4.

3. The Principle of Divisibility

Glover usefully distinguishes between two sorts of thresholds: absolute and discrimination thresholds.[10] An absolute threshold exists where there is a sharp boundary between two different outcomes. As he says the clearest example is voting. It's all or nothing – either one candidate gets enough votes and is elected or not. In a sense there's no point in your voting unless the race is so close that a single vote will swing it one way or another. If you have consequentialist grounds for voting, your reasons can't have much to do with the election's outcome.

Where there is a discrimination threshold, however, an individual's single act can only nudge the situation fractionally in the direction of some outcome. Effects are widely spread out, and an individual's contribution might go unnoticed. There's no easily visible threshold to cross. Instead, 'reality is a gentle slope, and the threshold is defined by the distance apart on the slope two points have to be in order to be seen as separate by us.'[11] To borrow Glover's example, if there is a power shortage and I keep my heating on even though we're asked to conserve energy, the power cut we endure will be a fraction of a second longer than it might have been had I done my civic duty. No one will notice my misdemeanour, but things will get worse, will slide down the slope, if more people do as I do. Although Glover does not address the subject, probably we can think of climate change in terms of discrimination thresholds. It's not as though anyone can say that one more office photocopier left on at the weekend will hurl us over the brink.

In the case of absolute thresholds, we can see clear outcomes and apportion praise and blame accordingly, but with discrimination cases, we sometimes think it makes no difference what we do. However, Glover argues, one really is responsible for the fraction of the harm done in discrimination threshold cases. According to his Principle of Divisibility: 'in cases where harm is a matter of degree, sub-threshold actions are wrong to the extent that they cause harm, and where a hundred acts like mine are necessary to cause a detectable difference I have caused 1/100 of that detectable harm.'[12]

[10] J. Glover, 'It Makes No Difference Whether or Not I Do It', *Proceedings of the Aristotelian Society*, Supplementary Volume **XLIX** (1975), 171–90.

[11] Op. cit., note 10, 2.

[12] Op. cit., note 10, 173.

Glover's example, having to do with bandits and beans, draws out the absurdity in the denial of the principle – in thinking that it makes no difference what you do in discrimination cases. Suppose 100 villagers sit down to a lunch of 100 bowls containing 100 beans each. 100 hungry bandits descend on the village and take one bowl each, at gunpoint, leaving the villagers hungry. They each do a discernable amount of harm. There's an absolute line that each bandit crosses, and the result is hungry villagers.

But suppose each bandit takes just one bean from each bowl. If you reject the principle of divisibility, you might conclude that although the bandits still eat all the beans, they nevertheless do no wrong, as each one does an indiscernible bit of damage. The villagers will probably disagree with you. The point is that indiscernible damage is still damage, and one really is responsible for one's share of the wrong.

Does this help someone genuinely concerned about the morality of individual choices and climate change? We are now talking about something other than 1/100 of some detectable harm.

There are nearly 7 billion people on the planet. Together we emit 28.4 gigatons of CO2 each year.[13] A gigaton is one billion tons. By comparison, I am responsible for about 4 tons of CO2 each year. Am I to see myself as responsible for 4/28.4 * 1,000,000,000 or 0.000000000141% of the harm done to our planet this year? Should I try to do better and aim for 4/28,399,999,999?

I can go along with the Principle of Divisibility and admit that I have a share in a slow-motion disaster. Even so, in this case at least, the harm I do is so impossibly teeny that it can't figure into a real motivation for green action. I can't really see it. We'll have to look for help elsewhere.

4. Side effects and Spirals

There are other sorts of replies to the problem of causal inefficacy. Vegetarians sometimes admit that the consequences of going veggie might be difficult to see when it comes to animal welfare, but there's plenty of personal utility to be had in the health benefits of

[13] United Nations Statistics Division, Millennium Development Goals indicators http://mdgs.un.org/unsd/mdg/SeriesDetail.aspx?srid=749, accessed 23/3/2010.

becoming a vegetarian. Maybe there's enough utility in improved health to make vegetarianism a moral requirement. I suppose one might argue, in a similar spirit, that taking certain green steps will save one a bit of cash in fuel bills. Maybe you'll avoid a plane crash if you cut back on flying.

There is another, maybe more familiar thought that one's effects can spiral out into the causal network – that maybe my efforts will be seen by others who will, in turn, follow me and also be example to yet more people. Certainly some carnivores change their diets after talking things through with a committed vegetarian. Maybe others will recycle if I they see me doing it.

If it's not clear that even one animal avoids suffering as a result of an individual's dietary choices, it is possible that other, good effects can result. Maybe the same is true of individual action on climate change. Perhaps turning off the heating won't matter when it comes to the climate itself, but I'll save a bit of cash. I might even have more effects on others which, all told, add up to something with a serious consequence on the climate. Given the size of our world's planetary systems, it would have to be one impressive spiral, but maybe my going green is just the start of a huge avalanche of change. Who knows?

It all might be true, but it feels like looking away from where the moral weight ought to fall. Such thoughts are 'one thought too many', as Williams puts it.[14] Probably a vegetarian wants the rightness of her behaviour to have something to do with animal welfare, not her own welfare. Someone who turns down the thermostat wants that act to be the moral crux of things, not the money saved or the possibility that, somehow, she might be the next Al Gore. Maybe we'll be forced out of this thought, but it's the main effects, not the side-effects that should be at the very centre of our thinking, shouldn't it?

There are familiar responses having to do with utilitarianism and correcting our moral intuitions, not pandering to them. You can take this point, maybe get a feel for where the argument is headed when it comes to climate change, and keep looking for something else which lines up with your hope that the rightness or wrongness of your actions has to do with something other than side-effects and spirals. That's what we'll do.

[14] B. Williams, *Moral Luck*, Cambridge: Cambridge University Press, 1981.

5. Larger lives

As we saw a moment ago, there is a sense in which a single vote is causally impotent. The point arises also in some considerations of democracy and free riding.[15] In an electorate of sufficient size, I might anticipate a close race, but probably I cannot really think that it's going to be so close that my vote will actually break a tie. Perhaps every vote counts in the sometimes optimistic sense that every vote really is counted, but it makes no difference whether or not any particular individual votes.

If you look away from responses to this problem which sound like the ones we've already considered – and don't be too distracted by debates about the merits of act and rule utilitarianism either – what you find can strike a chord. There is the claim that one has a moral obligation to vote, and this is rooted sometimes in talk of duties which simply fall out of citizenship. Maybe other moral demands are mentioned, perhaps honouring the memories of those who fought for suffrage. It can be a complicated set of motivations.

Even more suggestive, given the consequentialist thought we want to lean on, is the claim that voting is best understood as something much more than marking a page or pulling a lever. It can be an expression of all sorts of thoughts and principles which together result in the vote itself, as well as all sorts of other actions and further thoughts, which together are part of the meaning of a life. Voting is something people do because of the people they are, the lives they live, maybe the hopes they have. You might have heard expressions of this sort of thing in the run up to the 2008 US presidential election. Votes are not just momentary acts, but consistent parts of larger lives.

This aspect of the response made by certain voters is echoed in the claims of at least some vegetarians. Singer puts it like this:

[15] See S. Gendin, (2001) 'Why Vote?' *International Journal of Politics and Ethics*, **1**.2 (2001), 123–132; A. Glazer, 'A New Theory of Voting: Why Vote When Millions of Others Do?' *Theory and Decision* **22** (1987), 257–270; A. Goldman, 'Why Citizens Should Vote: A Causal Responsibility Approach' *Social Philosophy and Policy* **16**.2 (1999), 201–217; J. Riley, 'Utilitarian Ethics and Democratic Government' *Ethics: An International Journal of Social, Political and Legal Philosophy* **100**.2 (1990), 335–248; S. Salkever, 'Who Knows Whether It's Rational to Vote?' *Ethics: An International Journal of Social, Political and Legal Philosophy* **90** (1980), 203–217; R. Hardin, 'Street level Epistemology and Democratic Participation', *The Journal of Political Philosophy* **10**.2 (2002), 212–229.

> I advocate vegetarianism as something which 'underpins, makes consistent, and gives meaning to all our other activities on behalf of animals' (*Animal Liberation*, 171).... Becoming a vegetarian is a way of attesting to the depth and sincerity of one's belief in the wrongness of what we are doing to animals.[16]

The thought is that becoming a vegetarian is something larger than simply not eating meat. Choosing to be a vegetarian creates a psychological tie not just to a certain sort of action, but to a kind of life. Maybe most importantly, thinking of vegetarianism in this sort of way makes it clear that avoiding meat is a choice consistent with various beliefs and principles. Voting can be an expression of a similar sort of consistency. Being a vegetarian is not just a momentary choice of what one might have for lunch, just as a vote is not just a mark on a page. Both actions might be thought of as consistent parts of larger agenda, hopes, practices and plans – parts of whole lives if you like.

There is something admittedly wishy-washy about all of this, and certainly no arguments have been offered to force this kind of holistic view of vegetarianism or voting on us. What I find suggestive here, though, is the notion of consistency.[17] I might have to vote or chose to eat in one way rather than another because doing so is consistent with the principles I hold or perhaps consistent with my thinking on nearby problems. If so, then I might have consequentialist grounds for acting, even though my actions probably have no relevant consequences. If that way of putting it jars too much, you can think of the grounds as nearly-consequentialist or partly-consequentialist. Let us follow this thought as it applies to climate change.

6. Consistency

Consistency isat the centre of a great deal of our thinking about morality. If someone in such and such a situation deserves a certain sort of treatment, then the demand for consistency tells us that others in that situation deserve the same treatment too. If times are tough for me, and I think you ought to share what you've got, then I know I ought to share out what I have when things are going well for me. You can be an atheist and still think that you should do unto others

16 Op. cit., note 7, 336–7.

17 Singer, for his part, goes on to say that there is nothing logically inconsistent about eating meat and campaigning for animal rights, but I have a deeper, maybe wider, notion of consistency in mind.

what you would have them to unto you. The demand for consistency leads a utilitarian to think that everyone's pleasures and pains ought to figure into our calculations, not just her own. It's part of a Kantian's reason for universalizing maxims. It makes moral debates something more than expressions of emotion. Maybe consistency is part of the reason a voter votes and a vegetarian avoids meat. Such actions are consistent expressions of a collection of attitudes and beliefs – they are consistent and coherent parts of lived human lives.

Consistency can provide a utilitarian with a reason for favouring individually green choices too. It's a round-about reason, but it's not just one thought too many, and it side-steps the problems we found with other responses to the problem of causal inefficacy. Here is a cartoon version of how this line of thinking might go. It takes a fairly common moral argument about the US and action on climate change and insists on consistency between that argument and reasons and actions in an individual life. Numbers make it a little more clear, but you can imagine doing without them. It depends on the global arguments one accepts, as well as the principles which govern a life, coupled with the demand for consistency in our thinking and acting. This generic version is only meant to be suggestive.

A consequentialist can, rightly, denounce the world's biggest polluters for failing to take strong action on climate change. The US, for example, with just 5% of the world's population, is responsible for around 25% of the planet's greenhouse gas emissions.[18] Recall that short argument for government action on climate change at the start of this paper. The developed world is causing the largest amount of damage. If you think causal responsibility is tied to moral responsibility for action, then probably you think that the biggest polluters have the largest moral obligation to do something about climate change. The US is doing a lot of damage to the climate, and this damage will cause human suffering. There are numerous consequentialist reasons for thinking that the US ought to change the way it uses energy, ought to minimize its carbon-footprint, ought to help the poor of the world to adapt to the changes already underway. In short, the biggest polluters have the biggest obligation to take meaningful action on climate change.

There are some principles operative in such thoughts, and if you apply them to an individual life, you might be drawn to a solution to the problem of causal inefficacy. The premises and principles

[18] Have a look at www.unstats.un.org for the numbers. The numbers in the paragraphs which follow come from this site. It is likely that things have since changed, but the point of the argument still stands.

operative in your thinking about the world's biggest polluters, *mutatis mutandis*, apply to you too. It might be that you ought to take strong action on climate change, and that you are doing wrong if you do nothing, for familiar reasons. Consistency provides the necessary linkage.

If, for example, the US is wrong to do nothing about climate change despite being responsible for the most emissions per country, then maybe consistency demands that we think of ourselves as wrong to do nothing about climate change, despite being responsible for the most emissions per capita. People who live in the US, Canada or Australia are responsible for about 20 metric tons of carbon dioxide on average each year. People in many EU countries, like Denmark, the UK and Germany, emit about 10 metric tons on average.

Residents of more than half of the countries on our planet emit less than 5 metric tons on average. Residents of more than a third of the countries on the planet are responsible for less than even a single metric ton each year. Many human beings are responsible for no measurable emissions at all. Compared to most people on the planet, the greenhouse gas emissions resulting from our individual lives in the West are massive. You might be doing 20 times as much damage to the planet as many other people in the world.

Think again about consistency. If you are a utilitarian with good consequentialist grounds for thinking that the world's biggest polluters ought to take strong action on climate change, then maybe consistency demands that the everyday choices in your life must be much more green.

Probably you ought to take serious action to reduce your carbon-footprint. You should not fly. Get a bike. Work out what resources you use and use only those which make a real difference to you. Let 'Reduce, reuse, recycle,' be your mantra. Turn down the thermostat right now. Unplug everything. Give money to green charities. Devote considerable time to lobbying your national government and your local representatives. Put some pressure on environmentally unfriendly corporations too. Buy the bulbs, and on and on. You even have to recycle that little coffee cup lid.

You can think all of this, perfectly consistently, right alongside the thought that it makes no difference whether or not the coffee cup lid ends up in a landfill. Your little green actions can make no real difference at all, but you still ought to undertake them. You have a moral obligation which depends on the demand of consistency in thought and action, on the reasons you have for thinking what you do about governments and what obligations they have, as well as the sort of life you hope to lead. Your reasons for this conclusion can have a lot of relevant consequences in them, consequences having to do with the Earth, large scale social change, re-powering our fossil-fuel burning world, and avoiding the suffering of human beings – even though many of those consequences have nothing to do with your particular thermostat. Your reasons can be bolstered by their consistent position in the rest of your projects, the rest of your green life. You have to do the green thing, even if doing so makes no difference at all.

7. Concluding thoughts

It might be said that there is something suspect in a line of thinking which bounces back and forth between the moral demands placed on individuals and the moral demands proper to whole governments. Plato got into trouble with that sort of thing, but I don't think the call for consistency in our thinking and acting amounts to anything as embarrassing as a shaky argument by analogy. There is the familiar thought that we are very good at spotting local, hometown wrongs but awful at working out what to do when the enormous scale of harm overwhelms us. It might somehow be true, too, that we can spot huge and obvious wrongs while missing little outrages in our own lives. Bouncing back and forth like this might end up mattering when it comes to facing up to global rights and wrongs as well as finding a way to think of ourselves in the midst of it all. It might pull us in both directions, maybe help us see both scales a little better. The bouncing back and forth might be a recommendation of this reply to the problem of causal inefficacy.

Maybe there is fast talk in this stuff about the whole of a life. I'm certainly not saying that the whole of a life has enough in the way of effects to make a difference to the planet, but what is being said is still only rough and ready. Agreed that what we have here is just the first step in what might have to be a long line of thought. It's just an argument for connecting our thoughts about the world at large to our thoughts about our individual lives. Large, global conclusions are easy to see when we look at the actions of governments, but we lose our grip when we apply those thoughts to the little specks of our lives. What's needed is a better way of understanding a whole life, and maybe reasons for thinking that a life guided by consistent moral principles is worth pursuing.

Is there something funny in the different uses of 'responsible' in the US case and in your case? In the former case it's true that the US is causally and morally responsible for a lot of damage, and in the latter case it's only true that an individual is responsible for high emissions per capita, for more damage than most people but still not much in itself. The real consequences are on just one side of the ledger. That might be true, but the point is not to show that an individual is really responsible for anything. I'm admitting that an individual's effects don't add up to much. The aim is to make a connection between our thinking about large and small responsibilities, between our judgements about the US's conduct and our own lives.

Is this all still consequentialism? I have doubts about this, but there really are still consequences in the arguments just scouted, even if the consequences aren't mine. I admit too that I get fairly close to virtue ethics when I talk about going green as being part of a larger life, choices made because of the person one wants to be, and maybe I am drawn to thoughts about virtues in the end. When I avoid a long-haul flight, I know it makes no difference whether or not I fly. I take the train partly because of my global judgements about the US and others, about the way I think the world ought to go, the hopes that I have for future human beings, and the sort of person I aim to be. There's plenty of reflection on consequences in those thoughts. If my life is to be consistent with all of that, I can't just hop on a plane.

I admit that I've been sloppy with the word 'consistency' too – I've used it in different ways. There is a kind of bedrock notion of consistency at the heart of morality, another conception at work when we talk about the consistent application of moral principles to governments and ourselves, another operative when we talk about consistency in our judging and acting. It's this last which most interests me. I'm after a conception of consistency as a demand for action based on a connection between belief, principle and behaviour – walking the walk, in other words. Montaigne says that, 'The true mirror of our discourse is the course of our lives.' There's a sense in which our words sometimes have to commit us to action. Our actions just have to be consistent with our thoughts. How and why this should be so is worth a great deal of reflection. I don't have a grip on it yet, but talk of consistency is as close as I can get at the moment.[19]

What really matters, though, is whether or not these sorts of thoughts get us past the problem of causal inefficacy with respect

[19] I'm grateful to J. Baird Callicot for helping me see that consistency isn't the whole of morality. It's not a Vulcan view I'm pressing for with talk of consistency, just an insistence on local action in accord with global conclusions.

to climate change. I don't think that the consistency move will work for everyone troubled by the problem. Most human beings need to pile up a lot of reasons before they start doing all that a green life demands, but I am hopeful that plenty of reasons are out there. Maybe the demand for consistency is one of them. Talk of consistency does strike me as more promising, more convincing than talk of thresholds, spirals and the like. It still leans on consequentialist thinking, but shores those thoughts up with something very solid, something at the heart of a great many good thoughts on morality.

If the argument works, it does so by thinking of environmentally friendly choices as something other than little, individual actions which might have good or bad consequences. Being green, however we settle on the meaning of it, is something like a way of life – going on in one way rather than another, as Wittgenstein put it. Choosing to live in a certain green way, a way consistent with various judgements, principles and facts, will make no difference at all to the sea level in 2050. It is, nevertheless, the right thing to do.[20]

Royal Institute of Philosophy

[20] Thanks are owed to Anthony O'Hear for a very thought-provoking lecture series. I'm also grateful to the speakers and audience members for interesting talks, questions and comments.

A Reasonable Frugality*

DAVID WIGGINS

1. I begin with a citation from *Our Final Century*.[1] Its author is Sir Martin Rees, the current President of the Royal Society.

> A race of scientifically advanced extra-terrestrials watching our solar system could confidently [have predicted] that Earth would face doom in another 6 billion years, when the sun in its death throes swells up into a 'red giant' and vaporizes everything remaining on our planet's surface. But could they have predicted this unprecedented spasm [visible already] less than half way through Earth's life – these million human-induced alterations occupying, overall, less than a millionth of our planet's elapsed lifetime and seemingly occurring with runaway speed? ....
>
> It may not be absurd hyperbole – indeed, it may not be an overstatement – to assert that the most crucial location in space and time (apart from the big bang itself) could be here and now. I think that the odds are no better than 50-50 that our present civilization on Earth will survive to the end of the present century without a serious setback....
>
> Our choices and actions could ensure the perpetual future of life... or, in contrast, through malign intent or through misadventure, misdirected technology could jeopardize life's potential, foreclosing its human and post-human future.[2]

So, where the earth is concerned, what line of action will humanity pursue? At the end of his first chapter (page 24), Rees describes a position he calls realism, according to which the best prospect of our surviving beyond a century is for 'all nations [to] adopt low risk and sustainable policies based on present technology'. That is one kind of realism, he remarks, but another sort of realism says that policies such as these would:

* In writing and revising this paper, I have incurred a great debt of gratitude to Gareth Jenkins, especially in sections 4, 7 and 9, but also at other points where he drew my attention to oversights, mistakes or misconceptions. Other acknowledgements and thanks are due to Terence Bendixon, Roger Scruton, Cameron Hepburn, Tony Curzon-Price.

[1] William Heinemann, London 2003.

[2] Ibid, 7–8.

doi:10.1017/S1358246111000270

> require an infeasible brake on new discoveries and inventions. A more realistic forecast is that society's survival on Earth will, within this century, be exposed to new challenges so threatening that the radioactivity level in Nevada thousands of years from now will seem supremely irrelevant.[3]
>
> Indeed ... we have been lucky to survive the last fifty years without catastrophe.

2. But what about policy? The first kind of realism, if it were to be translated into a way forward that was saner and safer than either of the two realisms that Rees describes, would have to cultivate new technologies studiously – though not in the spirit of the second possibility that Rees describes, where technology comes loose (one might say) from essential needs. Aspiring only to encourage others to think further about such a median policy, I shall point out (towards the end) that there are all sorts of things that we have incontrovertibly good reasons to alter in our present way of living, reasons independent of ecological considerations. I begin by arguing that, once the ecological threat to human civilization becomes yet plainer and the prospect comes into focus of a world population of nine billion, Rees's two realisms will have to coalesce in a perception of our environmental circumstances that is less dismissive of Malthusian warnings than the cheerful rebuttals and wild past-to-future extrapolations you will find in the textbooks. More specifically though – and here I move towards the particular case where I want to begin – these attitudes or outlooks will have to come together in an all-embracing effort (of reflection, discovery, invention and funding) to free us from our dependence upon setting fire to carbon and releasing it into the atmosphere.

Assertions such as this last are apt to provoke either a feeling of fatigue that long antedates recent events in Copenhagen or outright disbelief – or else the blind anger that comes upon us from feelings of utter helplessness. But, in this paper, having set out the scientific argument that I accept for the claim concerning carbon-dependence, I shall dissent from some of the received responses to it. In their place, I shall describe a position that accords better (I believe) with a new perception of our true circumstances and better (I believe) with that which human beings can become ready to will and to do.

[3] The state of Nevada contains the nuclear waste dump for the USA.

3. The burning of fossil fuels[4] increases the carbon dioxide-concentration in the atmosphere. Carbon dioxide absorbs the infrared radiation which is sent out from the earth, and this raises the temperature at which the earth is in thermal equilibrium with its surroundings. As a result, land and sea rise gradually in temperature. On the level of theory, this process (sometimes described by an analogy with the way in which a quilt traps heat and slows its escape from one who lies beneath the quilt) has been understood since well before the twentieth century (by the labours of Joseph Fourier, John Tyndall and Svante Arrhenius). On the level of observation and reconstruction (from tree rings, ice-cores, etc.), it is now known that since 1769, when James Watt patented the steam engine, carbon dioxide concentration in the atmosphere has increased from 280 parts per million to more than 380 parts per million. It is now increasing at more than 2 parts per million every year. Looking forward upon this rate of increase, it is expected that, when the 1769 concentration of carbon dioxide[5] is doubled, that will have the same eventual effect as increasing the intensity of the sun by at least 2 percent and raising global mean temperature by at least 3 degrees.[6] Among the likely consequences are a rise in sea levels which will be simply calamitous for many millions of coast dwellers; the misery of millions upon millions of refugees; serious and unpredictable (already incipiently evident) disruptions of the seasonal patterns on which farming and much else depends; greater frequency of hurricanes and other high energy weather events; and the shrinkage or disappearance of numerous glaciers that supply the rivers upon which some billions of human beings have largely to rely for fresh water…

These predictions arise from a larger picture that places the 26 gigatons of CO_2 per annum that our burning of fossil fuels adds to the atmosphere alongside the 440 gigatons the rest of the biosphere emits and the 330 gigatons the oceans add to it. These other emissions belong to a cycle that long pre-existed human emissions. Within that

[4] Here I shall lean not upon Rees, whose preoccupations cover a much wider area, but upon chapters 1 and 31 of David J. C. MacKay's book *Sustainable Energy without the Hot Air* (UIT Cambridge Ltd, 2009).

[5] And of other gases, CFCs, HFCs, methane, nitrous oxide etc., as measured in terms of the number of molecules of CO_2 it would require to produce the same greenhouse effect. Taking these into account the current figure is not 380 but 400.

For another way and importantly different way of looking at the link between CO_2 emissions and global temperature, see Myles R. Allen *et al.*, pages 1163–6 in *Nature* **458** (30 April 2009).

[6] MacKay, 10.

cycle, flows of carbon out of soil, vegetation or atmosphere more or less balanced flows into soil, vegetation or atmosphere, even as the atmosphere equilibrated with the surface waters of the oceans.

Such were the conditions under which, long ago, human civilization came into being. The thing that is relatively new is the imbalance between the CO_2 being emitted into the atmosphere from fossil fuels etc. and the CO_2 that is taken up from this by the forests and oceans.[7] It has been suggested that, as things are now, roughly half of the CO_2 emissions from our burning of fossil fuels are staying in the atmosphere. But even that figure gives a poor basis for extrapolation into a future where there will be less rainforest and the acidification of the oceans is likely to have diminished their capacity to take up CO_2 from the atmosphere. Some such diminution appears already in a 40% decrease in plankton since 1950.

Human life as we live it is slowly but surely disrupting the conditions that make that life possible. So much is more certain than any specific meteorological or geographical prediction can be. The things that are almost beyond dispute are, first, that CO_2 in the atmosphere is already at a concentration never exceeded at any time in the last 400,000 years; second, that the atmosphere's capacity to carry CO_2 (relatively) safely is comparable in its way to any other natural resource. It is at once precious and exhaustible.[8]

4. If economic theory or 'ethical theory' as we now have it find difficulty with the question how much any of this must matter to us – living as comfortably as we do here and now in the cheerful way that is natural to us, then so much the worse, I say, for these forms of 'theory'.

Each of us knows that our concerns with other human beings are not confined to ourselves or our own offspring. We are disturbed, for instance, if we perceive that something we are doing will either deprive other people of that in which they reasonably expect to share or else endanger them seriously.[9] It need not matter who these people are. Wherever we can see how to do so, moreover, we

7 MacKay, 242.

8 Indeed we are well on the way to the point where, with the burning (say) of the trillionth tonne of CO_2, it will be exhausted and the accumulated emissions will make the earth uninhabitable. See again here Myles R. Allen, op. cit., note 3.

9 Consider wasting water during a drought. Consider the acts of leaving behind unmarked radioactive waste, unexploded ordnance or landmines or, less perilously, something that people are almost certain to stumble over.

are aware of an obligation to remedy the bad act we have done or to put matters right for the future. But, in so far as that is so, our convictions have long since reached a point where we cannot, consistently with demands that we already recognize, be indifferent to the damage that we do to the biosphere. After all, we have only to rehearse to ourselves the thought that the biosphere is something we inhabit in common with others who rely upon it no less than we do, either directly or indirectly, for the satisfaction of their every vital need. This last idea, already evident in old invocations of a mother earth the provider, surely lies close to the origin of an ordinary human concern for the earth.[10]

For many or most people, however, the concern for the earth goes further still:

> My mother was certainly not an environmentalist in the way we would understand the concept today, but she knew the beauty of nature when she saw it and how it made her feel. My mother told me a story of when she was a young woman. She used to walk through the forests from Nyeri to Naivasha on the western side of the Aberdare range [in Kenya]. As she walked she crossed numerous tributaries of the Gura River which I could hear from our house in Ihithe when I was a child. The Gura and all the other tributaries, known collectively as Magura, flowed down the Aberdares and my mother told me they were teeming with trout. Kikuyus didn't eat fish at that time so there was no fishing. But she and her friends would rest by the streams, watch the trout, and marvel at how beautiful they were.
>
> My mother is gone, as are many of those rivers and with them the trout and a way of life that knew and honoured the abundance of the natural world. Now, because of the devastation of the hillsides [by logging or conversion to cash crops], instead of rivers there are only little streams and the Gura River no longer roars. Its waters don't pass over the stones so much as seep into the riverbed, and even when I stand next to it, the river says nothing … its roar has slowly been silenced.[11]

[10] Cf. Hume's comparison at *Enquiry Concerning the Principles of Morals*, section VI, part 1, ad fin. '…the happiness and misery of others are not spectacles entirely indifferent to us… the view of the former, whether in its causes or effects, like sunshine or the prospect of well-cultivated plains communicates a secret joy and satisfaction.' The comparison works both ways.

[11] Wangari Maathai, *Unbowed: One Woman's Story* (Heinemann, 2007, London), 275–6.

I cannot of course be certain that absolutely everyone will respond to such words in the way in which I find myself doing. What *is* certain is that, if we will not invest the biosphere itself with a significance transcending our concern with the fate of particular people (as well as see its present and future resources as a matter of concern in which all mankind will have to share), then we shall be strangers to the only frame of mind that offers any chance of humanity's evading Rees's gloomy predictions. (See below section 17.) This is not to say that nobody can refuse to invest the earth with the significance that one finds implicit in Maathai's utterance. It does however require considerable sophistication – or else single-mindedness of a special kind – to refuse to do so.

Among economists and philosophers of a consequentialist or quasi-utilitarian bent, there is a tendency to suppose that the practical problem Rees describes is to be understood in terms of the 'net present value' (that is the value estimated now on the basis of its temporal distance from now) of the income streams of future generations. I shall return at the end of section 9 to the internal difficulties of any such view. But here, in advance of those difficulties, I want to complain against it, first, that the economistic view depends on the highly questionable idea that our concern with the earth is exhausted by our concern for human welfare.[12] My second and more general complaint, which prescinds entirely from the first complaint, is that any such view has the effect of making the care that we owe to the condition of the earth come down to a question of our altruism or benevolence towards those whom the earth will have to support. It comes down to that because, when the net present value is to be determined of those future income streams, the question then becomes: what should be the rate of discount? Shamed by Frank Ramsey who challenges us to consult our imaginations,[13] shall we adopt a zero rate of discount? Or, cleaving to the dictum of Aristotle at *Nicomachean Ethics* 1168b8, shall we insist that the knee is closer than the shin? And if we prefer Aristotle, then what discount rate are we to

[12] Compare Wangari Maathai, quoted above; compare Bernard Williams 'Must a concern with the environment be centred on human beings?' in *Making Sense of Humanity* (Cambridge, 1995); and my 'Nature, respect for nature and the human scale of values', *Proceedings of the Aristotelian Society* **100** (corrected text to be found only in the bound volume), 2000.

[13] Compare Frank Ramsey 'Discounting is a practice which is ethically indefensible and arises merely from weakness of the imagination', in *Foundations: Essays in Philosophy, Logic, Mathematics and Economics*, ed. D. H., Mellor, (RKP, 1978), 261.

choose? How much benevolence must we expect of ourselves? What is the 'rational' way of answering such a question? Or are these the wrong questions?

The objection I want to bring against all of this is that we are losing hold of the real point. The thing that is wrong with despoiling the earth, like the thing that is wrong with doing positive harm to others, has almost nothing to do with failure in positive benevolence or altruism.[14] After all, there is nothing wrong with being indifferent to a person to whom we have no relation or tie. That does not make it all right gratuitously to wound a person we do not care about, to kill him or to destroy that whereby he lives. Where benevolence is concerned, we have relatively few not specifically contractual *duties* and almost everything is properly subject to Aristotle's dictum. But (as Aristotle knew) that leaves over countless other duties – the negative ones, without which, if they were not recognized, human life would be almost unrecognizable. In continuity with this, I suggest that, on any sensible view, most of our obligations to the civilization of the future and to the future condition of the earth itself are essentially negative and prohibitive. They concern what we must *not* do. The earth is not ours to despoil or to do what we like with. Our benevolence or lack of it has almost nothing to do with the matter. (For more on the content of the negative duty, see below section 8.) Ramsey and Aristotle make very different claims, but there is no real conflict between them.

You may ask how a morality such as the ordinary morality that I am appealing to, and which I seek to ground in familiar human concerns and feelings, can advance so far beyond the immediate reach of those concerns and feelings. I reply by agreeing that it is indeed human concerns, feelings and prohibitive aversions (these last insufficiently explored by Hume) that give us our first understanding of values and obligations. It is these things which, by the aid of reason (as Hume insisted), furnish us with the wherewithal to arrive at a Standard of Morals.[15] (The phrase is Hume's.) Once we explore these concerns and feelings, moreover – and once we permit them to extend themselves, if they will, to the biosphere itself – sentiment and reason

14 See my 'Solidarity and the Root of the Ethical', *Tijdschrift voor Filosofie*, 71/2009, 239–269, developing what I say in *Ethics: Twelve Lectures on the Philosophy of Morality*, Penguin and Harvard, 2006. See pages 11, 15 and the Index sub 'prohibitive aversions'.

15 I enlarge upon all this at *Ethics: Twelve Lectures*. See pages 46–50, 11–12. For one of Hume's claims concerning the role of reason, see (for instance) *Enquiry into the Principles of Morals* V, part 2, footnote.

can combine to force us to think much harder about the harms we ought not to do, either to others or to the earth. Where the habitability or beauty of the earth are concerned, moreover, the demand that I say we ought to find growing upon us is to act as if human civilization and the habitable earth have an entirely open future – even if the best we can do is to delay, as if indefinitely, their destruction or demise.

5. In the face of these findings and all the responsibilities that flow from them, what are human beings now thinking and doing?

At the 2009 Summit meeting in Copenhagen, there was general agreement that steps should be taken to limit any further increase in global temperature to below 2 degrees. This was widely taken to mean limiting emission of greenhouse gases to the CO_2 equivalent of 500 parts per million, which is the halfway point in the 450–550 range proposed in the 2007 *Stern Review on the Economics of Climate Change*.[16] (Some countries wanted a ceiling far below 500 and Stern himself now favours a limit of 450 ppm.) Despite that consensus, however, it proved impossible to arrive at 'legally enforcible' international treaty to replace the Kyoto protocol which expires in 2012.

Such a treaty might perhaps have come into being if some sufficiency of First World countries had been prepared to offer Third World countries something along the lines of the 'contraction and convergence' proposals advocated by the Global Commons Institute.[17] This would have involved drawing up a 'contraction budget' for greenhouse gas emissions and assigning entitlements to each country on the basis of its population in a baseline year, agreeing at the same time two dates – a date by which the entitlements of all countries would converge to being equal per capita (relative to the baseline year) and a further date by which there would be no further increase in the carbon concentration of the atmosphere. It would have been a question whether the United States negotiators were in a position to promise a treaty.[18] It would have been a question whether Third World countries would persist in the objection that,

[16] In effect, the UK committee on climate change aims not to do better than to respect this limit. See Stephen Plowden, 'Trust the People on Climate Change', *Oxford Magazine*, no. **299**, Trinity Term 2010, 4–5.

[17] See Aubrey Meyer, *Contraction and Convergence: The Global Solution to Climate Change*, Schumacher Briefing No. 5, Green Books, Dartington, Devon. See also Aubrey Meyer, 'The Case for Contraction and Convergence', 29–56, in *Surviving Climate Change*, ed. David Cromwell and Mark Levane (Pluto Press, London 2007).

[18] In 2008 the US administration did try to offer the rest of the world an 80% reduction in CO_2 emissions by the year 2050. It put legislation before

even under this proposal, there is insufficient recognition of their substantial innocence of the noxious emissions that have brought the atmosphere to its present state. But in the end, even the simple but fundamental thoughts that prompt such proposals were effectively obscured.

In Europe after Copenhagen one might have hoped that, with the question of convergence adjourned, the emphasis could shift to absolute contraction. Yet the main focus is not upon absolute contraction. Still less is it upon allowing the necessity for that contraction to impinge at full force upon the awareness either of the public at large or of policy makers. In Britain at least, the focus is upon the mechanics of 'cap and trade' (see section 6 below); it is upon the endlessly debatable subtleties of discounting (8 below); and, distracting attention and resources from urgent research or development, it is upon the so-called Renewables Obligation (9 below). Each deserves some commentary.

6. The first distraction from the urgency of absolute reduction – the reality of contraction, I mean, all sources included – is a fixation upon its simulacrum. It is upon the merits, scope and detailed workings of a system of 'carbon trading' – 'cap and trade' – already in partial operation, which requires larger companies whose activities involve substantial emissions either to reduce emissions or else to buy 'carbon credits' to a value proportionate to those emissions. The claim is that, by making carbon credit 'tradeable', the scheme directs new resources to wherever carbon intensive activities can best be modified or replaced. The claim is that, given a cap upon emissions, the trading scheme identifies the most efficient way of containing emissions within that cap.[19] The words 'the most efficient way' mean here the way of staying below the cap that costs least in respect of human 'income'.

Was this scheme worth the ten or more years of effort it took to develop and gain favour for it? I think – and I said at the time –

Congress to achieve this. The legislation passed the lower house but was rejected by the Senate.

[19] Analogous claims were plausible enough when made on behalf of the US Environmental Protection Agency's cap and trade scheme for controlling sulphur dioxide emissions. This was the endlessly fascinating Coasean paradigm for the EU and UN carbon trading scheme. But, depending as it did on the surveyability of a relatively restricted field of operation and a uniform rule of law under a single sovereignty, it is a strikingly poor paradigm for a worldwide system of carbon trading. Indeed, even within one territory, the surveyability problems relating to CO_2 emissions and SO_2 emissions are of altogether different orders of magnitude.

that these years could have been more properly spent in arriving at a better public appreciation of the possibilities for a civilization that made fewer demands on the energy we derive from carbon, not in circumventing the need for this better appreciation. But advancing now to the particular merits or demerits of carbon trading, I remark that it makes a difference whether one supposes that there is a global cap upon emissions or one supposes that it is for each country to determine its own cap.[20]

If each country fixes its own cap but is empowered to issue carbon permits which are valid everywhere, that is likely to prolong and diversify the kinds of exploitation and abuse in which carbon trading and the 'Clean Development Mechanism' have already been so heavily implicated.[21]

If, on the other hand, there is a global cap and efforts are made to see that it is globally enforced – a managerial fantasy perhaps, and pregnant with sinister possibilities, to judge by the way in which the World Trade Organization is reported to have impinged upon some of the poorest among Third World countries – then carbon permits will rise steadily in price to match the severity of the cap. But that will not prevent the richer nations from protecting some of their most wasteful and irresponsible uses of fossil fuels. Rather than modify their emissions substantially, they will see the opportunity to pay poorer nations to reduce *their* emissions. (For any abatement is equivalent to any other abatement given similar reductions of CO_2. That is the doctrine.) The efficiency that is claimed for carbon trading is blind to the difference between wasteful activities and (emission-equivalent) activities which are indispensable or nearly indispensable as things are at a given time to human life at that time.[22] To this extent carbon trading is blind to opportunities

[20] Gareth Jenkins made me see the importance of distinguishing these cases and helped me to demarcate the two objections that follow.

[21] For recent reportage of some prevalent scams, see page 26 of *The Guardian*, Wednesday 27th October 2010. No doubt steps will be taken to counter this particular fraud. Another puncture, another patch. See further 'A realistic policy on international carbon offsets' by Michael W. Wara and David G. Victor, Working Paper 74, April 2008, http://pesd.stanford.edu.

[22] This distinction rests on a moral judgment, someone will say. Yes, I reply, but at some point every practical argument in this area has to rest on some sort of moral judgment. Why try to postpone it?

It is a thought too rarely entertained that the methodological requirement to minimize or postpone ethical considerations is not necessarily 'ethically neutral' or promotive of objectivity. Why try to be neutral for as long as

to close down emissions which needlessly and wastefully damage the biosphere (cp. section 4). It is not to be denied that carbon trading makes transfers from richer to poorer nations. But there are many other ways to do this. Some even promise something in return – e.g. the solar energy in which so many poor nations have a comparative advantage. See section 10 below.

Such doubts about cap and trade point in the direction of a further disquiet. The efficiency claimed for cap and trade amounts to its restrictions costing less in respect of human 'income'/overall marginal satisfaction than any other system for controlling emissions of CO_2. Even as it stands, this contention is doubtful, in so far as taxes, regulations and prohibitions may reach down to many more wasteful carbon-emitting activities than does cap and trade. (See below, sections 16–17.) More fundamentally though, the unfavourable comparison presupposes that a system to tax and regulate must have exactly the same aim as the carbon trading system. It need not. Tax and regulate may set itself the aim to produce the largest possible absolute decrease in emissions (which may turn out to be a larger decrease than cap and trade will achieve) that is consistent with an ongoing or emergent sense of fairness, at the same time promoting the effort to divert every resource that may be spared from the vital and immediate needs of human life into the business of making green energy affordable enough for it to displace carbon.

Tax and regulate differs politically, practically and motivationally from cap and trade. Unlike cap and trade (in the short term), tax and regulate will depend upon public opinion. In that respect, its advantage lies in its avoiding the abstractions I have criticized in section 6 and its speaking directly to ordinary moral awareness. Cap and trade need not seek either to promote or to engage human awareness of the fragility of the ecosystems on which human civilization depends. Cap and trade does not even seek to ensure that a rise in the price at which carbon trades here and now will amount to sufficient motivation here and now, where delay is indefensible, to speed long-term research and investment into carbon-sequestration at coal-fired power stations such as the economies of China and India apparently depend upon. Compare MacKay page 222. (It is noteworthy that in Britain, where 'the price of carbon' has been a talking

---

possible between just and unjust or good and evil? As regards the *objectivity* at t of the standards at t of vital need presupposed by judgments of wastefulness, see my *Needs, Values, Truth* (amended Third Edition Oxford, 2002), Essay One.

point for at least 15 years, such research has accounted for an almost negligible fraction of GDP. Is this an accident?)

7. This is as good a place as any to point out how dangerous and lazy is the widespread acquiescence in a limit of 500 or, as some say, 500–550 parts per million. Those who do acquiesce and institutionalize that acquiescence in their determinations of the cap that controls the market in carbon too easily forget the terms in which Jim Hansen and other scientists have described the peril that attaches to settling for any concentration of greenhouse gas emissions beyond 400 parts per million (as measured in CO_2 equivalents). One of their several arguments is this: that, where the permafrost melts, this releases methane, a gas whose greenhouse effect is 21 times more pernicious than that of CO_2. If such a tipping point is reached, it will be almost impossible to 'reconsider' (this is UN speak) the limit chiefly under discussion at Copenhagen or to conceive of 'long term stabilization' (this is Stern speak) at a level of greenhouse gas concentration less than the limitation proposed in the *Stern Review*. It is not clear that those who are content to think in terms of 450 or 500 or 550 parts per million have any *scientific* answer to Hansen, or any practical response for the outcome where he is proved right.[23] It would also appear that they are assuming recklessly that ocean and forest will continue to absorb CO_2 from the atmosphere in the same quantities as they do now.

8. The pros and cons of the carbon trading mechanism are not the only distraction from post-Copenhagen realities. Another distraction derives from continuing controversy and confusion concerning not the means but the proximate end itself of present action. A line of policy that is based on the idea that what has to be at issue is the net present value of the income streams of future generations represents a confused and confusing substitute for the simpler and truer perception that we are now at a point in the diminution of natural resources – including the capacity of atmosphere and ocean to absorb CO_2 (relatively) safely, the variety and plenitude of plant and animal species, the fertility of the soil and the purity of our sources of fresh water... where the act of wasting, polluting or destroying these things becomes comparable to the act of raiding or

[23] For one set of responses to Hansen, see Nicholas Stern, *A Blueprint for a Safer Planet* (Bodley Head, London 2009), 150–152, 39. For more on the said acquiescence, see Stephen Plowden, op. cit. and Myles R. Allen, cited at note 3 above.

plundering a common store. Conjoining that last claim with the commonsensical finding that we do not know how to live without to *some* appreciable extent diminishing those resources, we arrive, not at a contradiction (neither logic nor ordinary morality nor the two together can turn this conjunction into a contradiction), but at a practical conclusion[24]: we must look always for any means consistent with our ordinary happiness and ordinary justice to reduce our demands upon resources which are not in any realistic sense renewable. In this matter we have to see what we can do, prefer the more sustainable way of living over the less, and profit from the example of countries which find ways better than ours to do these things.

Here (as in sections 4 and 6) it may be complained by persons of a managerial or technical disposition that formulations such as these are too vague to constitute any effective basis for action as they envisage action. (They are too vague for instance to fix a carbon cap.) But the formulations we have used give expression to ordinary ideas that have a clear hold upon us and a dialectical point – a hold and a point that might transfer to the political realm if politicians and statesmen had any trust at all in the democratic process that they praise in other connections. *In a given context* formulations such as these can combine year on year with vague, defeasible but (so far as they go) accurate descriptions of actual states of affairs to yield definite and increasingly persuasive (however defeasible) conclusions in that context.

What then is the way forward? Prescinding from convergence under treaty, prescinding for the moment from all internationalist hopes, and concentrating for the moment on contraction, we might say this: let each country do its own utmost to reduce absolutely what it sends into the atmosphere. By placing taxes upon carbon-emitting activities differentially (lower if they are essential to vital human needs and higher if they are inessential) while forbidding entirely activities that are at once profligate and pointless, let each country secure that end, so far as possible, without damage or detriment to human solidarity.[25] Apart from countries such as Sweden and any other small countries

[24] Some say that *ought* implies *can*. Do they mean that, if I live irresponsibly enough, I can release myself from my obligations to my debtors? A careful statement of the connection between *ought* and *can* will not affect the claim in the text.

[25] More specifically, let the objective be to do everything we find we reasonably can do while respecting so far as possible the ideal that looks always to a state of affairs where each and everyone will want each and everyone else to be protected in his/her efforts to pursue (through means constrained by the same ideal) his/her own most in his/her circumstances unforsakeable vital needs. See here my 'Solidarity', op cit, 265.

which are similarly sensible, why has almost every nation supposed that it must wait for every other nation to do something?

By way of reply, someone is sure to assert that it is in the interests of each party that *someone else* reduce emissions. But, on the true view, which can be explained to almost anyone anywhere on the basis of a less impoverished notion of self-interest – and soon will be explained, I hope – it is in the interests of each and all countries that *every possible* reduction in emissions be attempted. For that is the nature of the emergency we are arriving at. On a true view, no nation or country can know when or how it will itself be stricken by the effects of climate change, deterioration of the soil, or of the acidification of the oceans. It is a strange idea of self-interest that makes it nothing better than short-sighted idiocy.

From all this it follows, I conclude, that if we look at things from the viewpoint of an ordinary prudence which does not exclude morality, then the sustainability of the demands that we make on the biosphere ought to be determined by the experience of living responsibly, not stipulated top-down by the fiat of boffins and consultants. If we look at matters instead from the point of view of the kind of 'theory' I criticized in section 6, then it will seem we are told that we have first to concern ourselves with the income streams available to our posterity and then (God help us) to adjoin to economic theory another theory, namely the theory of justice – equal concern for all, inequalities only justifiable where they result in a larger benefit for all, especially those who have least... or whatever else is your favourite theory. Once we allow ourselves to be drawn into this line of thinking, however, and we lift the artificial restrictions that frame current studies of the problem, we arrive almost immediately at the question how many more billions than our own billions of people there will then be, enjoying what income stream... in 10 years, 50 years, 100 years, 1000 years... time. Faced with the uncertainty and controversy to which such thoughts lead, one may see the philosophical attractions of some older and more commonplace account of justice, drawing upon a larger plurality of intuitive ideas.[26] This will prompt us to concentrate our thoughts upon the harm or damage we do to our descendants, whoever they may be, if we help ourselves to more than we vitally need of the earth's resources at risk of prejudicing their renewal or we inflict upon our descendants arrangements that deprive them of all resilience against the kinds of problem that mankind is heir to, water-, energy-, or food- shortage, the passionate hostility of neighbours, armed struggle for natural resources....

26 For one version of this, see *Ethics: Twelve Lectures*, op. cit. Chapter 10.

9. In countries such as Britain, yet other things have drawn attention away from the duty to reduce emissions absolutely. Among these further distractions I shall mention just two.

The first is the marvellous illusion of absolute contraction already achieved, an illusion that we owe to the fact that, in this country, manufacturing industry has been allowed or encouraged to migrate elsewhere and we rely now upon imports without assuming any responsibility for the emissions that arise from their manufacture.[27]

A second distraction has been HMG's preoccupation with an EU directive requiring every member country to produce at least 15% of its energy by the year 2020 from renewables – and the feeling of intense engagement and prolonged activity against climate change which ministers and their civil servants derive from seeking to meet this target. The target has taken on a life of its own which has come loose from any call for absolute reduction. I do not deny that, in so far as householders have been encouraged (singly or in concert) to contrive their own small-scale wind or solar installations, this interest in renewables has served some extremely valuable purposes. But large-scale projects such as on-shore and off-shore wind turbines with huge connection and construction costs together with massive (recorded or unrecorded) emissions of CO_2 are another matter altogether. Dieter Helm writes:

> A study by the National Audit Office has found that the Renewables Obligation 'is several times more expensive than other measures currently being implemented by the government'. Compared with the EU ETS carbon prices in the range £20–£30 per tonne of carbon, the UK renewables programme is staggeringly expensive. Perhaps only the Italian renewables programme looks more expensive. Recently it has begun to be appreciated that current biofuels policy may be even worse – not only in terms of cost, but also in terms of the very limited carbon savings and the impact on agriculture.

The thing that is needed is not a new crop of wind and off-shore schemes but a careful study, not only of the future competence of householders to subsidise these schemes through their payments for utilities, but of the results of a proper carbon audit. What is the *net* saving of CO_2 per kilowatt? How would it compare with the

[27] See Dieter Helm, 'Climate-change policy: why has so little been achieved', *Oxford Review of Economic Policy*, Volume **24**, No. 2, 2008, 211–238. I am indebted to this article.

saving that could be effected by interim conversion of power stations from coal and oil to gas?

10. So much for the distractions from real reduction. We come now to the larger picture into which renewables and everything else has to fit.

Focusing on Britain as an example, let me lean again upon David MacKay. In outline, MacKay formulates five alternative energy plans (and then a sixth), insisting throughout that, whatever strategy one considers, the projected supply must measure up to some recognizable summation of the actual demand – unless demand is to be reduced (see section 12 following). Each plan involves some particular combination of clean, carbon-sequestered coal, wind, hydro, wood, nuclear, tide, wave, pumped heat, solar, biofuel, etc.[28] Each plan, dispensing almost entirely with the burning of fossil fuels, involves a near-tripling of electricity generation. Or so it seems *if we treat the demand for energy as a simple given*. Taken in conjunction, Mackay's explorations of these plans point collectively towards a simple conclusion: Britain will never come anywhere close to living by its own renewables. In Britain – as in Europe, MacKay goes on to show – a 'low-carbon economy' would have to depend radically on one, the other, or both of nuclear energy and solar energy, the latter to be purchased (in some just imaginable future) from other people's deserts, e.g. the deserts of the Sahara, and delivered northwards by high-voltage, direct current transmission lines.[29]

On the evidence MacKay provides, it appears nearly impossible, so long as we treat the demand for energy as a simple given, to supplant this conclusion. That is what is so useful about MacKay's analysis and the discipline which insists that the policies should add up to the demand. With heavy heart and the utmost reluctance, the reader of MacKay's book – unless driven (with me) to think that demand itself simply has to be reduced more radically than most of his readers will be ready yet to contemplate – is led to the conclusion that Britain has no alternative but to build one more generation of

[28] It is a pity that MacKay, like Stern, says little or nothing about agriculture and its dependence upon fertilizers derived from fossil fuels, but let us supply this deficit by supposing that they have undergone a quiet conversion to organic agriculture, permaculture or whatever. As the paper goes to press, I note that a United Nations report has aligned itself with the same thinking and claims that this is the way for poor farmers to double their food production claiming that these are in fact the way for poor farmers to double their food production. (Reuters report, March 8th, 2011.)

[29] See MacKay, 233, 178–9.

nuclear-power stations. But that could be the last generation, it might still be hoped, if enough technological and diplomatic ingenuity, and enough material resources were to be put into some sort of Sahara plan or some other plan still to be devised.

Speaking personally, I find some consolation for this awful conclusion about the (however conditional) need for nuclear power generation in another thought prompted by MacKay, but not his responsibility. Nuclear and solar apart, small scale domestic or municipal wind power, pumped heat and carbon sequestration of coal-fired power must all be worth persisting in. But, *if there is no alternative to nuclear and nuclear will have to happen anyway*, why persist in wind farms which will alienate (not to say despoil) great stretches of land, will depend forever upon hidden subsidies, and abstract resources from more effective measures? And why persist in offshore wind and wave schemes where unforeseen engineering difficulty and expense can only be increased by the uncertainty of future sea levels?

11. Sticking to the need for absolute reduction of CO_2 emissions but at risk of seeming to go backwards, I revert here for one moment to the international scene and Copenhagen (2009).

If what I have said so far is right, then such a summit might have done better to avoid the idea that everything but everything, absolutely everything, depended on the effort to arrive at 'legally binding' agreements concerning future emissions. Negotiations apart, it might have taken the opportunity for the free exchange of ideas. Such a summit might have more time to explore what it would take for the rest of the world to induce, bribe or help Brazil, Paraguay, Guyana, Indonesia, Burma, Australia and other countries with rainforest still standing to treasure and conserve it and to implement a total ban on road-building there. So far as CO_2 is concerned, nothing could be more urgent. Such a ban might at least help to safeguard or prolong the present capacity, such as it is, of the carbon sinks which have served us up to now. Next, without waiting for a binding agreement on any of these things, the First and Second World countries might have expressed their willingness not only to reduce almost all their emissions absolutely (by whatever means they devise) but also to put all their available resources into exploring *with* Third World countries the full variety of technological and political possibilities for the collection and transmission of solar energy. Who knows? Once real progress were made with all that, solar energy might even become cheap enough for African and other countries themselves to desalinate water from the oceans and seek to afforest the desert. That is pure fantasy perhaps. The solid point is that Third World countries would see the prospect of huge capital flows from the First World to the Third World, and a sustainable rent upon which they could go forward in their own way. (Let us hope or pray that that way will not be a copy of our way.)[30]

12. I promised in section 2 to try to say something about how Martin Rees's first kind of realism might be turned into a policy of sustainability, measured risk and the training of human effort upon the ends of life which we can pursue by means of carbon-free enhancements or replacements of present technologies. There is room here for a huge variety of contributions. My own, such as it is, starts out from certain things that reading MacKay makes evident to reflection (and he anticipates at his page 213): namely, the cost at present demand levels of carbon-free energy; the cost – in consumption forgone, natural resources unsustainably consumed or natural beauty destroyed – of wasting energy; and the large unknown potential of that which some environmentalists have called the forgotten fuel. They mean by that the fuel we waste but don't need to waste in pursuing ends we do need to pursue and the fuel we could save in abandoning certain other ends that we might decide to abandon.

13. Like so much else that is at issue here, such thoughts involve changes in the way we live now, changes we should consider before they are forced upon us. Above all, they involve examples. In some of the more benign cases, they involve going back to ways of living that were familiar to our mothers and fathers or to our younger selves. In other cases they will involve possibilities we shall have to discover. I begin however with changes which, even now, have much to be said for them, both positively (I mean) and independently of climate change – either because they steer us away from things which seem crazy in their own terms once we see that they result

30 At a summit rather different from Copenhagen, to which nations came without specific negotiating positions fixed in advance, and where they could listen to one another in a spirit less defensive and more inquisitive, one might have hoped for an open-ended discussion of world population trends and of the unwisdom or idiocy of employment taxes and policies which have the effect of displacing human labour at a time when there is a massive excess of human labour. Attending for a moment to the question of feeding the billions, it might have dwelt on forms of agriculture less dispersive of CO_2 and less destructive of soil than those now generally practised. It might also have attended to the ways in which the world's fisheries are being destroyed by greed and destructive technology, even as the acidification of the oceans not only destroys the plankton on which marine life depends.but also threatens carbon sink.

from unsolved co-ordination problems, or else because they help to secure the self-sufficiency and the resilience of regions or localities.

Why do I mention self-sufficiency? Because, even if (despite the grounds Martin Rees gives for pessimism) our present civilization on earth will in fact survive up to 2100, it is a fallacious and gratuitous extrapolation from the prosperity of the twentieth century to suppose that civilization of the future will be exempt from new kinds of economic collapse, exempt from so far (relatively) unfamiliar disputes over natural resources, or exempt from other major disruption issuing in armed conflict, or other upheaval. Why suppose that everywhere some arm of central government will always be in a position to ensure, in whatever way it has so far, that every place have sufficiently secure supplies of money, food, manufactures or other essentials that it now relies upon coming to them from elsewhere? What a pity it is that the political architects in London and Brussels of farming and industrial policy never look beyond the dogmas of 'trade liberalization' to ancient history. Here let me quote from the author of *The Fall of Rome and the End of Civilization*, Bryan Ward-Perkins:

> [By 450 AD] the Romano-British population had grown used to buying their pottery, nails and other basic goods from specialist producers, based often miles away, and these producers in their turn relied on widespread markets to sustain their specialised production. When insecurity came in the 5th century, this impressive house of cards collapsed, leaving a population without the goods they wanted and without the skills and infrastructure needed to produce them locally. It took centuries to reconstruct networks of specialization and exchange comparable to those of the Roman period. The more complex an economy is the more fragile it is and the more cataclysmic its disintegration can be.

14. This matter of self-sufficiency or resilience is closely connected with an example or eminent instance by which I hope to illustrate another inherently desirable kind of change that might in the names of realism and economy be forced upon us by the exigencies of environmental degradation and climate change. I introduce that example with the words of a former captain of industry, Sir Daniel Pettit, speaking as long as 35 years ago, at the Mercedes Benz Conference in Eastbourne, 18–20th June 1975:

> Responding to the freedom and the new opportunities that road transport has given it, industry has moved steadily away from locations near a railhead, port or inland waterways and has evolved a new, more dispersed approach to Land Use than was

> evident in the 19th Century with its emphasis on consolidation in metropolis and conurbation. Much new light industry is situated either on industrial estates on the outskirts of established towns, or in new towns. Warehouses in which goods are prepared for final delivery are often located in rural or semi-rural areas where land prices are lowest and supplies of labour are still reasonably consistent and of quality. Research into this area consistently underlines and reflects the irrefutable hold which road transport now has secured over the channels of supply, illustrated by the Mercedes Blue Book and the FTA Handbook and studies in my own organization and the ever-increasing and well justified need for road infrastructure as a prerequisite for growth ... there can be little doubt that growth will continue and, while it will extend the pleasures of increased affluence to more sections of the populations, it will also make more pressing the problems that affluence brings, and highlight the less attractive aspects of the road transport industry as it responds to the increasing demands made on it...
>
> We must give a great deal more thought and determination to developing the concept of the dispersed society, one which in both its appeal to individual liberty and mobility and its use of land is more attuned to the motorcar and the lorry responding to individual needs than the concentration and conurbation developments of the 19th century dependent on and conditioned by the railways, providing for the pattern of supply in commodity terms to the population en masse.

When he spoke of the growth and power of the system he was anatomizing, Pettit was a true prophet – as he was when he spoke of the need 'to give more thought to the concept of the dispersed society'.

To engage with this matter, the contrast we need is not exactly that between the dispersed and the not dispersed but the contrast between a settlement pattern created lengthwise and/or radially by local bus, foot, bicycle or train[31] and a settlement pattern that brings together consumers, producers, workers, employers, goods and services in the manner that Pettit describes (free that is from any of the limitations of older modes of travel), where we end up with a huge

[31] Think, for instance, of 'Metroland' – the large area north and north west of London (Baker Street) opened out in the earlier twentieth century to new habitation and new commerce by the Metropolitan Railway. Think how it was *before* the motor car dispersed dwellings and commerce in every direction in the way Pettit describes, gradually filling all the spaces that lay between separate lines and stations.

demand for unrestricted movement in almost any direction, from almost any point to almost any other point.

In the last 20 or 25 years alone, at once enlarging and ministering to that kind of demand, Departments/Ministries of Transport have expended more than £100 billion at current prices on roads and huge further sums I do not know how to calculate on other modes, all in the name of saving time spent on travel.[32] Result: average speeds have risen by 50%. But the average amount of time spent travelling has scarcely altered by more than one minute. It seems that within the duration of the length of time they are ready to spend travelling, people simply rearrange their lives to travel further.[33] It is a fair guess that they are poised to take up any further improvements in just the same way. At the place where they now are, they have new mobility desiderata, no doubt. But, once these are satisfied, others will no doubt replace them. More and more vehicles will continue to get in the way of more and more other vehicles. No wonder that decade after decade transport occupies a larger and larger share of GDP, takes a larger share of natural resources, and pre-empts a larger share of public expenditure...[34]

15. There is no need to try to sit in judgment on the individual citizens who respond in this way to new opportunities that lie in front of them. That is not the question. The question relates to changes in our present way of living which might both save carbon emissions and have something positive to be said for them in the present or immediate future. The question relates also to the wisdom or unwisdom of the public policies which have shaped the unconcerted choices that individual citizens make. It is rarely or never considered where such policies are leading. (The Town and Country Act of 1946 marks a rare moment of wisdom in this regard.) Still less are they

[32] Meanwhile in London, the capital of one of the most capitalocentric countries of the world, planners have been reluctant to allow congestion on roads or tube lines to constrain demand or prompt businesses to see for themselves whether the time has come for them to expand elsewhere into places where economic activity is conspicuously lacking and housing cheaper and more plentiful. Such a policy has railway implications, to which let the response have proper regard for freight transport.

[33] See David Metz, 'The Myth of Travel Time Saving' *Transport Reviews*, 2007.

[34] I do not understand the arguments offered against recouping this expenditure by levying tolls on the motorway sections of the new network. Why should not such tolls reflect the engine capacities and CO_2 emissions of the vehicles paying the tolls?

considered in the light of problems of coordination which are inaccessible to individual choice.

Such questions are not new. For instance, the distinction has long been familiar between simple mobility and access to facilities, not least the access of those too old, too young or too poor to drive or without access to the car which goes away each day with a wage earner. The question became visible in HMG's 1976 consultation document *On Transport Policy*:

> At the same time as mobility has been reduced for those without a car, [the] advantages [of car-mobility] have increased. For as car ownership spreads, schools become larger, hospitals are regionalized, out of town shopping centres multiply and the Council Offices are situated further away; meanwhile the local shop and post office disappeared [and local bus or railway services are diminished or, in some cases, never existed because whole neighbourhoods are themselves the creature of the pattern that Pettit has described for us.] Mobility becomes ever more necessary; but command over it for the minority grows less. This is perhaps the most important problem which emerges from our review of the Transport scene.

'Important' though this problem seems to have seemed to the government of that day, the same tendencies still continue almost unrestrained. Doctors are still encouraged (or almost compelled) to set up group practices. Hospital services are still amalgamated or sadly neglected in the expectation of imminent amalgamation. Thousands of post offices have closed. Policies for school education are still insensitive to such questions.

16. There is no way back to a universal way of life in which many an ordinary adult's everyday travel hardly exceeded eight miles a day and a huge generality of people found ways to locate their work and their dwelling-place (not to mention their doctor, dentist, shopping and recreation) along a good line of public transportation or at a walkable distance.[35] But there is every reason for public policies not to *aggravate* the problem we have made for ourselves (for it can still be

[35] It is worth adding that at the time we are recalling such lives were nevertheless not confined within that narrow horizon. Almost any place in the UK was within reach of almost any other place in the UK by public transport. Contrast a journey made at nearly 200 mph for two-thirds or four-fifths of the way only to find no more public transport at all for the rest of the journey.

aggravated enormously), not to acquiesce so readily or any further in the dispersed patterns of development that Pettit describes, and not to discourage a significant minority who might decide that that old way is the way they would positively like to live.[36] It is hard to resist the thought that it would not only reduce our carbon dependence but bring about something else that is desirable in itself if public policies were reoriented to take advantage of the divers ways in which, even now, in a vast variety of places (not only the large city), human lives can still be lived without radical or near total dependence on the car. Too little thought has been given to the large public benefits of making ordinary life possible for a potentially numerous minority who might choose to live, or to continue to live, without dependence upon the car.

Another thought it is hard to resist is how little we should lose if we simply dropped all that talk about 'getting people out of cars or aeroplanes' and doing so by spending billions upon billions on high-speed railway lines. Cannot the new preoccupation with high speed as such be moderated by a much closer concern with the first and last stages of a journey. Suppose that instead some smallish fraction of the money and resources saved from these projects were spent on restoring rural railway connections to the main lines and reinstating railway stations which have been removed to make headways for very high speed traffics.[37] So far as getting people out of aeroplanes is concerned, moreover, there is no need for an expensive subsidy. Let HMG simply tax more heavily (but not without making first a careful carbon audit) those who suppose they absolutely have to make some rapid inland journey by aeroplane.

17. In what I have said, however breathlessly, about the particular examples I have chosen in order to illustrate the possibility of changes which might be desirable independently of climate change, you may perceive a drift, or a further drift, towards the centralized or managed economy (as if we did not already have one). For

[36] The suggestion is offered in full awareness of countless differences between town, suburb, exurb and country.

[37] See here more generally David Wiggins and Mayer Hillman, 'Railways, Settlement and Access', in Anthony Barnett and Roger Scruton eds, *Town and Country*, (Jonathan Cape, 1997).

It is noteworthy that in the same epoch in which rural public transport was dismantled hundreds of thousands of people were moving outwards towards rural areas. Witness the rise in house prices there and the lamentable effects for the rural economy of both these changes.

emergencies such as war or earthquake, flood or drought ... that is what you must hope for. But your must also hope that those who direct from the centre will begin to concentrate more unsentimentally on bare essentials, which will be numerous enough. For in truth top-down policy-initiatives are only one small fraction of the answer. Indeed, if top-down policies now multiply and take on the forms of regulation that we see all about us, then we are doomed.

Almost everyone whom one speaks to on this subject reports the waste of heat, light and capital they see all about them, reports the unintended energy consequences of every visit by Health and Safety (and the even larger consequences of the fear of such a visit) – just as they report how every 'improvement' they see in the office, schoolroom, club premises ... that they frequent has resulted in a net increase in the light or heat used or in air-conditioning. Until some idea or notion reaches every citizen about the nature and magnitude of the problem that confronts us all – until some new awareness comes to be expressed in all the ingenuity and enterprise they can bring to bear upon everyday life – we shall never know properly how much carbon we can save now *or* what energy we shall need in the future.[38] In the case of policy-makers, might not such an awareness, combining with a little common sense, fill the vacuum which has made politicians call for 'joined-up thinking' (at the centre)? In the case of town-planners, such an awareness might prompt them to think of the carbon cost of the building works and extensions they so often approve or even prescribe. In the case of architects, might not such an awareness prompt them to think of the carbon cost of the horrible material which they put down everywhere between London and Dubai and then beyond? I mean concrete. Five percent of human-originated carbon dioxide emissions result from freeing calcium carbonate previously kept safe within limestone and cooking the result to 800 centigrade.

These are simply examples. Is there any limit to the number of such observations which could be made? I doubt it. During the time when I was writing this paper, and within one square mile of central London abuzz with the sound of oil-driven machinery, I have witnessed road-sweeping machines deputizing (rather ineffectively in many situations) for brooms and human hands; helicopters idling endlessly back and forth over sporting events their hirers were promoting in a Royal Park; police helicopters hunting back and forth for one knows not what reason and police trucks lifting up private cars from expired parking spaces to take them to an official pound several

[38] See MacKay, 233, 178–9.

miles away in South London (do the police have to buy carbon credits?); the semi-pedestrianization (price tag £26 million) of 1000 yards of a London street by the laying of a quarter of a million tiles which are shaped either off-site or there on the spot by a petrol-driven cutting machine to make them fit into an abstract mosaic; a host of gardeners in two London squares either collecting leaves not with brushes or effectively but with motor-driven blowers or else mulching fallen branches with a petrol engine; the rearing over Hyde Park of yet another cliff in steel and concrete of luxury apartments far beyond the means of anyone poorer than a Russian olearch; the huge and unprecedentedly destructive surface and sub-surface works of a £17 billion 'Cross-Rail' project which will perpetuate and enlarge the magnificent supremacy of the Greater London region over all other regions in Britain, but continue the processes which are depriving the capital itself of the low-cost neighbourhoods that Jane Jacobs so eloquently describes as essential to the creativity and small-scale enterprise of the city...[39]

Who shall keep track here of the distinction between essential and inessential or measure the distance these activities take human civilization towards the trillionth tonne of CO_2 emitted into the atmosphere?[40] Cap and trade? It does not even claim to be that sort of scheme. An agency or arm of the state implementing by yet further powers of selective prohibition an assemblage of abstract targets whose proper rationale will all too easily be lost to view? A parliament already possessed of the power to pass a law prohibiting almost anything, but scarcely equipped to forbid in precise legal terms that which is involved in the more wasteful of the activities here described? A far better instrument, better designed to keep a constant watch upon the world and to forestall many ill-considered projects, lies within human beings themselves. I mean their eyes and ears, their minds and their rational capacity, given only the right conditions, to exercise the licence to ask what the thing they are doing is *for*. I mean also their innate capacity to embrace and enter into an *ethos*, mentality or way of being which can be animated by the understanding of something seriously at issue.[41]

[39] See *The Death and Life of the Great American City*, 1962.

[40] For the symbolic and real significance of the trillionth tonne, see again Myles R. Allen op. cit., note 3.

[41] Here too belongs a frame of mind, which in his forthcoming *Green Philosophy: Turning for Home*, (Grove Atlantic, 2011), Roger Scruton calls *oikophilia*, the love of home/homeland.

18. In 1939–40 when HMG was expecting the Blitz and a blackout was instituted in order to confuse the navigation of enemy bombers and fighters, it took only two or three weeks for everyone to catch on to the idea and to be ready to tap on their neighbour's door to tell them in friendly fashion if they were showing even a small chink of light. Citizens caught on effortlessly to the mentality that was expressed in posters put out by the government: 'Dig for victory', 'If you know something keep it under your hat'. What organized the thoughts and dispositions of citizens was the fear of destruction or invasion by a hostile power and an idea of liberty and human decency which they had resolved to uphold to the end. In the present what should organize our awareness and dispositions? A new awareness among the citizen body at large of the fragility and huge complexity of the life systems on which we depend and a concern for what remains of the beauty of the earth. But, in the place of 'Keep calm and carry on', I hope we may prefer some version of Hume's wonderful sentence,

> All prospects of success in life or even of tolerable subsistence must fail where reasonable frugality is wanting.

Postscript March 2011.

As the typescript goes to the printer, one year after the lecture was delivered, the official estimate of danger from the nuclear accident caused by the earthquake in north eastern Japan has risen from level 4 to level 5 (out of 7). Apart from the danger of explosion or meltdown, drinking water and vegetable supplies are now radioactively contaminated in places as far south as Tokyo. This must be the moment to reconsider what I say in section 10 and think much harder too about the implications for the nuclear option of the political and ideological turbulence of a world constantly subject to war, civil war, terrorism and the fiat of dictators. I underestimated the strength of the case against nuclear energy. This mistake does not enhance the economics of the enormous on-shore and off-shore wind schemes currently projected. The case it enhances is for natural gas in the short term, for carbon-sequestered coal in the longer term, for solar in the longest term – and for the refusal to take as a simple given current demands for energy generation. Above all it helps the case (as I said) for a reasonable frugality.

New College, Oxford

Carbon Trading: Unethical, Unjust and Ineffective?

SIMON CANEY[a] AND CAMERON HEPBURN[b]*

Cap-and-trade systems for greenhouse gas emissions are an important part of the climate change policies of the EU, Japan, New Zealand, among others, as well as China (soon) and Australia (potentially). However, concerns have been raised on a variety of ethical grounds about the use of markets to reduce emissions. For example, some people worry that emissions trading allows the wealthy to evade their responsibilities. Others are concerned that it puts a price on the natural environment. Concerns have also been raised about the distributional justice of emissions trading. Finally, some commentators have questioned the actual effectiveness of emissions trading in reducing emissions. This paper considers these three categories of objections – ethics, justice and effectiveness – through the lens of moral philosophy and economics. It is concluded that only the objections based on distributional justice can be sustained. This points to reform of the carbon market system, rather than its elimination.

1. Introduction

The design of climate-change policy involves underappreciated ethical dimensions. Greenhouse gas emissions might be reduced by

We are grateful to David Frame for helpful discussions and to Timmons Roberts and Henry Shue for their very instructive comments on the paper presented by Caney at the 'Commodifying Carbon' Conference (Oxford, 16 July 2007); to Dale Jamieson and participants the Environmental Studies Research Seminar at New York University for comments on the paper presented by Hepburn on 21 April 2009; to members of the Royal Institute of Philosophy for comments on the paper presented by Hepburn on 11 February 2010; and to Luc Bovens, John Broome, and David Wiggins for their written comments. We are also grateful to Wilfred Beckerman, Rufus Black, Simon Dietz, Mike Mason, Dieter Helm, Nicholas Stern and Ed Page for useful discussions. Caney undertook research on this while holding an ESRC Climate Change Leadership fellowship and is grateful to the ESRC for its support.

* Corresponding author. *E-mail address:* c.j.hepburn@lse.ac.uk

doi:10.1017/S1358246111000282

several main approaches, each of which raise different considerations of ethics and justice. For instance, governments might provide information about the science and economics of climate change, price greenhouse gas emissions through a 'carbon tax', subsidise clean technology, establish a 'cap-and-trade scheme' in which a limit is placed on total emissions which declines over time (e.g. as per notions of 'contraction and convergence'), and/or implement 'command-and-control' regulation requiring firms and individuals to take certain action, such using specific cleaner technologies. These approaches have various levels of effectiveness (that is, of successfully reducing emissions) and of efficiency (in terms of reducing emissions at least cost). They also have distributional implications (in that there will inevitably be losers and winners). Implementing climate-change policies is also likely to, and indeed will need to, change our relationship with the natural environment.

This paper focuses on cap-and-trade systems, which are argued by some to be a vital component of the attempt to prevent 'dangerous anthropogenic forcing'[1] and dangerous temperature increases.[2] Indeed, greenhouse gas emissions trading was provided for by Article 17 of the Kyoto Protocol.[3] Many environmentalists support a cap-and-trade system because it is the only policy that places an absolute limit on the level of emissions. This allows emissions to fall over time consistent with the notion of 'contraction and convergence', for instance.[4] Other policies such as carbon taxes might, with luck, achieve the same effect of controlling and reducing emissions, but they do not provide the level of guarantee provided by a cap-and-trade system. Unless emissions are reduced, moreover, business-as-usual economic activity will increase the concentrations of greenhouse gases in the atmosphere, leading to temperature increases of perhaps four degrees Celsius by the end of the century, and serious risks of dangerous changes in precipitation and climate.

Several cap-and-trade systems for greenhouse gases have been implemented around the world. The most notable is the EU

[1] United Nations Framework Convention on Climate Change (UNFCCC): 1992, Article 2, text available at http://www.unfccc.int.

[2] We focus on carbon dioxide emissions given their sheer volume and contribution to climate change but we should note, of course, that carbon dioxide is not the only greenhouse gas.

[3] Cameron Hepburn, 'Carbon trading: a review of the Kyoto mechanisms', *Annual Review of Environment and Resources*, **32** (2007), 375–393.

[4] Aubrey Meyer, 'Contraction and Convergence: The global solution to climate change' *Schumacher Briefing* 5, 2000, Foxhole, UK: Green Books Ltd.

Emissions Trading Scheme (EU ETS), which came into effect on 1 January 2005 and is now in its second phase (2008–2012).[5] Other countries are establishing emissions trading, and some countries such as Australia are engaging in vigorous debates about the merits of emissions trading schemes compared with other approaches. The USA passed legislation in the House of Representatives which would cap emissions, with the cap reducing to 80% below 2005 levels by 2050, but passage of the legislation through the Senate was blocked. China has recently announced it will pilot carbon trading in five provinces and eight large cities in the coming years.[6] Long before the implementation of cap-and-trade systems for reducing greenhouse gas emissions, there were other kinds of environmental trading schemes. Perhaps the best known is the trading scheme for sulphur dioxide (SO_2) in the USA under Title IV of the 1990 amendments to the Clean Air Act, which has successfully reduced acid rain at low cost.[7]

As cap-and-trade systems to limit carbon dioxide pollution have actually been implemented, so too have criticisms emerged. The most aggressive criticisms of cap-and-trade emerge from climate-change sceptics, who would prefer to see no government response to climate change, and who consider cap-and-trade the most likely policy to succeed in passing through the relevant legislatures. More sober criticisms include arguments that emissions trading is inherently ethically objectionable. For instance, Michael Sandel argued that:

> turning pollution into a commodity to be bought and sold removes the moral stigma that is properly associated with it...[and] may undermine the sense of shared responsibility that increased global cooperation requires.[8]

The merit of such criticisms can depend upon the specific form of emissions trading under consideration. Trading within a cap-and-trade system could occur between countries (e.g. as occurs under

[5] For an overview of the EU ETS see the special issue of *Climate Policy*, vol.6 no.1 (2006).

[6] Global Times, 'Five provinces, eight cities selected for gas-emission cut off', 11 August 2010. http://business.globaltimes.cn/china-economy/2010-08/562368.html

[7] Robert N Stavins, 'What Can We Learn from the Grand Policy Experiment? Lessons from SO_2 Allowance Trading' *Journal of Economic Perspectives* **12**:3 (1998), 69–88.

[8] Michael Sandel 'Should we Buy the Right to Pollute?' in *Public Philosophy: Essays on Morality in Politics* (Cambridge: Massachusetts: Harvard University Press, 2005), 94 & 95.

the Kyoto Protocol), between firms (e.g. as occurs in the EU ETS), or potentially even between individuals. The implications for the sense of shared responsibility vary in each case. Furthermore, policy choices about the allocation of tradable allowances, whether given away to regulated entities for free or else sold, affect the justice of an emissions trading scheme.

This paper examines various ethical and moral objections to emissions trading. We examine these considerations in relation to a simple emissions trading scheme (ETS), rather than with respect to 'add-on' policies like carbon offsetting. While carbon offsets are beyond the ambit of this paper, we simply note here that offsets have two important moral virtues, – namely minimising waste and transferring climate finance to poorer countries to help them reduce emissions – but they also face challenges of 'asymmetric information' which opens the way to potential gaming and fraud. By considering its moral virtues, Section 2 examines why emissions trading might be thought to be a suitable policy response to climate change. Section 3 reviews and elaborates on a general taxonomy of ethical reasons for caution in the use of markets, engaging with the literature on the moral limits to markets. Section 4 employs this taxonomy to assess the view that carbon trading is unethical. Section 5 examines the notion that carbon trading may lead to unjust outcomes, and section 6 reviews arguments that carbon trading has not so far been effective at reducing emissions. Policy implications are suggested in the conclusion (section 7).

2. The moral virtues of cap-and-trade

2.1 Ensuring environmental protection

Cap-and-trade systems for pollution control can guarantee that pollution will be limited to the quantity specified by the 'cap', if it is suitably enforced.[9] The pollution cap is reduced from one period (often several years) to the next, thereby reducing total emissions over time. In the EU, for instance, the cap in the 2008–2012 period was set so that emissions would be reduced by 5% compared with 1990 levels, and the cap for the next period (2012–2020) has been set to reduce

[9] Enforcement requires independently verified measurements of emissions (with sensors or flowmeters) or independent calculations of those emissions based on the measured output produced and its emissions intensity, coupled with spot checks by verification agencies.

emissions by at least 20% compared with 1990 levels, although the EU commission is currently contemplating tightening the cap to a 30% reduction by 2020, a position which has the support of the United Kingdom, France and Germany, among others.

In this way, cap-and-trade systems provide policymakers and environmentalists with the certainty that a given emissions target will be met. Other policies, such as carbon taxes, subsidies or specific regulations, can make good progress towards reducing emissions, provided they are designed and enforced appropriately, but do not provide the same confidence as cap-and-trade systems. Cap-and-trade systems, like taxes, also provide a price signal. When the total level of emissions (and thus permits allocated) is fixed below business-as-usual levels, the permits become 'scarce' and trade with a positive price. Regulated entities can trade permits amongst themselves, establishing a 'carbon price'. This price fluctuates with time, providing information about whether it is cheaper for companies to reduce emissions internally, or whether it is cheaper to purchase allowances from another firm which has reduced its emissions below its allocation.

2.2 Minimising waste

Cap-and-trade schemes therefore ensure that the cheapest short-run sources of abatement are undertaken first, because firms have an incentive to reduce their emissions whenever they can do this for less than the market price. There will be many different ways firms can economise on their emissions. The market price ensures that firms are rewarded if they do make reductions and penalised if they don't. Just as the 'cap' supports environmental integrity, the 'trade' supports minimum cost. This is true too of carbon taxes, which provides a similar economic incentive for firms to seek out abatement opportunities in a manner which minimises waste.

In contrast, government will rarely know where the cheapest sources of abatement are to be found, because opportunities to reduce emissions are often at the operational level of individual firms. Even if government had access to data on individual operational decisions (which it generally does not), it would be a mammoth task to attempt to specify the 'optimal' actions for each firm. If government does attempt to do this, it will doubtless make mistakes. If it doesn't, and instead applies a uniform regulatory standard, this is likely to be wasteful, because one firm can often comply more cheaply than another.

To take an example, suppose that firm A and B are both required to reduce emissions by 1 million tonnes of CO_2. If firm A can reduce emissions for £10/tonne, while for Firm B it costs £20/tonne, then £10 million is wasted if trade between Firm A and Firm B is prevented. These wasted funds might have been used to develop new low-carbon technologies and products, increased staff wages, been passed onto shareholders or simply given to charity. Trade creates these benefits by minimising waste.

2.3 Maintaining liberty

A final moral virtue of economic instruments, including both carbon trading and taxes, is that these policies allow regulated entities (whether countries, firms or individuals) the liberty to reduce their emissions using the methods they see fit. In the (relatively unlikely) event that government actually knew more cost-effective ways to reduce emissions than individuals, there would still be value in allowing individuals to make their own choices, and indeed to make (and learn from) their own mistakes. Regulatory approaches which stipulate the specific actions to be taken deny people this liberty and deny them the creativity to arrive at different and original ways of cutting back on emissions or other ways which, even if they are more expensive, may be preferred by the individuals concerned.

There is a further benefit from allowing this liberty. If environmental groups take the view that the cap is not tight enough, they can purchase allowances and then retire them, thus preventing firms from using them to pollute. In this way, non-governmental organisations can voluntarily choose to tighten the cap. Indeed, in the EU ETS this is precisely what occurs, and there are various non-profit and indeed for-profit organisations that offer individuals the opportunity to force companies to reduce emissions by more than the government limits.

3. A general taxonomy

We have seen that moral virtues attach to carbon trading. This is one of the reasons why legislatures around the world have introduced such systems as a means of controlling emissions. Yet there are important moral arguments against emissions trading, and in order to give a comprehensive account of such arguments, we present in this section a taxonomy of the kinds of reasons that one might have for thinking that certain goods or services should not be traded. In section 4, we draw on this taxonomy to examine several different arguments against emissions trading. By doing so we hope to provide as systematic an account as possible of the different reasons one might have for rejecting emissions trading.

Our taxonomy draws on an account developed by Judith Andre in her instructive analysis of Michael Walzer's well known but rather unsystematic discussion of goods that should not be transferred for money.[10] Andre seeks to provide a more rigorous categorisation of the different kinds of reasons that can be given for thinking that certain burdens or benefits should not be bought and sold.[11] Drawing on her work, we distinguish between five types of case where trading a benefit or a burden is morally problematic.

First, there are goods which 'by their nature cannot be owned'.[12] Well-known examples might include love, friendship, respect and admiration.

Second, there are some things that it is possible to own but which we think it would be wrong to own.[13] Again there are well-known examples. It is possible to own human beings but, of course, we now think that this is an indefensible practice, as this fails to respect the dignity and moral standing we attach to other human beings.

A third case where a trade in goods or services is problematic arises when it is impossible to alienate a good or a responsibility.[14] First, consider goods. There are goods which a person can possess but which he or she conceptually cannot transfer to others. An example would be an honour (such as the Nobel prize).[15] This honour belongs to the person awarded it and she cannot bestow it on someone else. It is not possible to alienate it. The same can be said of academic qualifications. People can only acquire these in a certain kind of way. For example, they must have been admitted onto the course in question, complied with the regulations, and passed the relevant examinations. The pedigree matters and this

[10] Michael Walzer *Spheres of Justice: A Defence of Pluralism and Equality* (Oxford: Basil Blackwell, 1983), 100–103.

[11] Judith Andre 'Blocked Exchanges: A Taxonomy' in *Pluralism, Justice, and Equality* (Oxford: Oxford University Press, 1995) edited by David Miller and Michael Walzer, 171–196.

[12] Andre 'Blocked Exchanges', 175: cf 175–176.

[13] Ibid., 176: cf 176–178.

[14] Ibid., 178–179.

[15] Ibid., 179.

entails that it is not possible simply to transfer the good to others. Consider now responsibilities: there are some responsibilities which only the original duty bearer can honour and which it is not possible for others to honour. For a clear example of this kind of responsibility, suppose that a spouse has a duty of sexual fidelity to their partner. In such a case, this is a responsibility that they alone can honour. Compliance with that duty requires that particular person to personally discharge the duty. They cannot outsource that obligation to others in some way (though others can, of course, assist them in their performance of the duty).

In addition to the first three categories, there are also cases where it is possible to alienate a good or a responsibility but we might think that it is wrong to alienate such a benefit or a burden to other people.[16] Again we can distinguish between two cases here. The first is when someone alienates a responsibility to someone else but we think it is wrong for him or to do so. Machiavelli, for example, argued that it would be wrong for citizens to delegate the responsibility to protect their state or fight their wars to others, notably mercenaries. In his view, citizens should defend the state themselves.[17] Another example would be someone who seeks to alienate a civic responsibility (like doing jury service) to someone else. One might think that this is their job: they should do it and should not pass it on to others. We shall refer to these as 'non-delegable duties'. These are duties one can alienate but should not. A second kind of case involves alienating a 'benefit'. To take one example, some like John Stuart Mill, hold that people should not be allowed to alienate their own liberty.[18] They have inalienable rights. Another case is voting rights. It is widely held that it is wrong to transfer this benefit to others.[19]

Let us turn finally to a fifth category. This fifth type of argument maintains that certain goods (or responsibilities) should not be alienated for money.[20] It does not object to someone exchanging a good or service but it does object to someone exchanging it for

[16] Andre 'Blocked Exchanges', 179–180.

[17] Machiavelli *The Discourses* (Middlesex: Penguin, [1531] 1970) edited with an introduction by Bernard Crick, Book 1, Discourse 43, 218.

[18] John Stuart Mill, *On Liberty* (Middlesex: Penguin, (1859) 1974, 173.

[19] The case of voting rights has an extra complication for one might think that although it is a benefit to the citizen it also comes with a duty too (for example, to cast it in the public interest) and that this duty in part explains why it should not be transferred.

[20] Andre 'Blocked Exchanges', 180–187.

financial gain. Consider, for example, prostitution. Some, for example, would argue that whilst there is nothing wrong with having sex *per se*, and indeed sex as part of a loving relationship is normally considered to be good, it would be wrong to exchange sexual favours for money. Some argue along similar lines against commercial surrogate motherhood.

We can sum up the preceding discussion with the following table.[21]

Table 1: Arguments against trading certain burdens and benefits

Type	Description	Illustrative Examples
1	Goods which cannot be owned	Love, friendship
2	Goods which should not be owned	Persons
3	Goods and responsibilities that cannot be alienated	Honours
4	Goods and responsibilities that should not be alienated	Civic responsibilities, votes
5	Goods and responsibilities that should not be alienated for money	Sex

4. Five ethical arguments against emissions trading

Having presented this taxonomy of the kinds of objections one might make to trading in general, we now turn to examine the case against trading allowances to emit greenhouse gases.[22] Not all of the categories outlined in the previous section lend themselves to a critique of emissions trading. In particular, we set aside the first and third type of argument. There do not seem to be any reasons why one cannot own an emissions allowance (so the first kind of argument

[21] This table captures, we hope, the logical possibilities but it obviously does not describe all the kinds of issues that might arise under the various headings. For excellent discussion of the kinds of issues that arise and the relevant normative consideration see Debra Satz, *Why Some Things Should Not Be for Sale: The Moral Limits of Markets* (New York: Oxford University Press, 2010).

[22] For an excellent discussion of arguments against markets in permits 'to pollute' see Robert Goodin 'Selling Environmental Indulgences', *Kyklos* **47**:4 (1994), 573–596. For a contrary view and response see Wilfred Beckerman and Joanna Pasek 'The Morality of Market Mechanisms to Control Pollution', *World Economy* **4**:3 (2003), 191–207.

does not apply) and one can easily transfer this good to others (so the third kind of argument does not apply).

We shall therefore focus on arguments 2, 4 and 5. More precisely, we shall consider one type 2 argument, two type 4 arguments, and two type 5 arguments.

Before beginning the normative analysis it is worth distinguishing between two separate questions. The first question is whether it is permissible for states and other political institutions to set up emissions trading schemes. Let us call this the *institutional question.* The second question is whether it is ethically appropriate for individuals to buy or sell emissions permits. Let us call this the *individual question.* These two questions are importantly different. One might, for example, argue that it is appropriate for the state to allow this kind of trading even if one thinks that such trading is immoral. On a liberal conception of the role of the state, the duty of the state is to treat people justly and respect their rights. This can include granting persons rights to do things which one believes to be immoral. For example, one might think – at the institutional level – that persons should be allowed to sell sexual services for money and yet also think – at the individual level – that persons ought not do so.

Our concern is primarily with the first type of question. The arguments from environmental outcomes, waste minimization and liberty give us *prima facie* reasons to endorse such a scheme. Our view is quite compatible with the view that persons are under a moral obligation to reduce their emissions, not to use energy wastefully and unnecessarily and, more generally to adopt an ethic of frugality of the sort advanced by David Wiggins in his paper.[23] Let us now consider five anti-market arguments to see whether the reasons in favour of emissions trading can be outweighed.

Argument A: Owning what should not be owned

One argument that might be made against emissions trading is that it involves owning a kind of good that, while it is possible to own it, should not be owned.[24] Emissions trading assumes that humans have property rights in the natural world. It might be argued that this is undesirable. The natural world (or perhaps, more plausibly, particular features of the natural world like the Earth's atmosphere) should not be treated as people's private property. Anti-commodification arguments are familiar, and in many cases, have force. For

23 Wiggins 'A Reasonable Frugality' this volume.

24 For this line of reasoning see also Goodin 'Selling Environmental Indulgences', 578–579.

example, as noted above, we surely think that humans should not be owned. However, these types of arguments are unpersuasive in the context of emissions trading.

One central problem with the argument is that emissions trading does not rely on the assumption that persons own the atmosphere.[25] Emissions trading involves a right to use up some natural resource but a 'use right' is not the same as a 'property right'.[26] An example might bring out the point. Consider someone who purchases a permit to camp on a certain plot of land. He or she does not, thereby, gain a private property right in the land. Rather they have a 'use right' – a right to use that piece of land for a fixed period of time. Emissions permits can be understood in a similar way. They entail a right to use, for a period of time, a certain proportion of the absorptive capacity of the atmosphere. After some time (maybe several hundred years in the case of greenhouse gases) the impact of the emission of greenhouse gases, like the impact of the camper, will effectively disappear.

Further evidence for the claim that emissions trading does not assume that persons own the atmosphere can be found once we note that emissions trading is quite compatible with the idea of stewardship. It is often said that humanity should act as 'stewards' or 'trustees' of the natural world rather than as private owners of it.[27] The concept of stewardship or trusteeship (we use the two interchangeably) might be said to include three components. First, those who are trustees of some particular designated natural resources may have a right to use that resource (*use rights*). Second, however,

[25] For further discussion see Caney 'Markets, Morality and Climate Change: What, if anything, is Wrong with Emissions Trading?', *New Political Economy* **15**:2 (2010), 204–205. See also Caney 'Justice, Morality and Carbon Trading', *Ragion Pratica* **32** (2009) for a discussion of this and other anti-market arguments.

[26] Hermann E. Ott and Wolfgang Sachs 'The Ethics of International Emissions Trading' in *Ethics, Equity and International Negotiations on Climate Change* (Cheltenham: Edward Elgar, 2002) edited by Luiz Pinguelli-Rosa and Mohan Munasinghe, 171.

[27] For example, Brian Barry writes that 'those alive at any time are custodians rather than owners of the planet, and ought to pass it on in at least no worse shape than they found it in', 'Justice Between Generations' in *Liberty and Justice: Essays in Political Theory Volume 2* (Oxford: Clarendon, 1991), 258. For discussion of the concepts of 'stewardship' and 'trusteeship' see Robin Attfield *Environmental Ethics* (Cambridge: Polity, 2003) chapter 2 and Attfield *The Ethics of the Global Environment* (Edinburgh: Edinburgh University Press, 1999), chapter 3.

those who hold the natural resources in trust are not entitled to destroy the natural resources (*no right to destroy*). As Tony Honoré notes in his seminal analysis of ownership,[28] the right to destroy is one of the key eleven 'incidents' of private property, so this second feature distinguishes trusteeship from ownership. A third, and related, component can best be explicated by using a distinction coined by John Passmore in his seminal *Man's Responsibility for Nature*. Passmore distinguishes between 'conservation', which he defines as 'the saving of natural resources for later consumption',[29] and 'preservation', which he defines as 'the attempt to maintain in their present condition such areas of the earth's surface as do not yet bear the obvious marks of man's handiwork and to protect from the risk of extinction those species of living beings which man has not yet destroyed'.[30] Utilising this distinction one might say that a third aspect of stewardship includes duties to conserve and/or preserve certain resources and features of the natural world for those who follow them (*duty to conserve or preserve*).

Now emissions trading is compatible with this ideal. Someone committed to the ideal of stewardship may think that we are stewards of Earth's climate and, therefore, may not destroy it and indeed must conserve or preserve it for future generations (thereby complying with the second and third features of 'stewardship'). However, she may also quite consistently think that, within limits specified by the duty not to destroy, humans and non-human animals may use the absorptive capacity of the atmosphere (thereby conforming to the first feature of stewardship). This requires setting a budget specifying a safe level of emissions. With this in mind the proponent of a stewardship approach must then consider what policy instruments – including carbon taxes or emissions markets or regulations – would best protect this atmosphere. She might then quite consistently propose an emissions trading scheme for those permissible emissions. Emissions trading is, thus, not reliant on the private ownership of Earth's atmosphere and is fully compatible with a commitment to global stewardship.

Before we turn to consider a second argument against emissions trading we should, however, note an objection that might be levelled against our response to the first argument.[31] A critic might reply that

28 Tony Honoré 'Ownership' in *Making Law Bind: Essays Legal and Philosophical* (Oxford: Clarendon Press, 1987), 161–192 at 170.

29 John Passmore *Man's Responsibility for Nature: Ecological Problems and Western Traditions* (London: Duckworth, 1974), 73.

30 Passmore *Man's Responsibility for Nature*, 101.

31 We are grateful to Luc Bovens for raising this objection.

though we are correct that emissions trading does not require the 'ownership rights' over the natural world, our appeal to 'use rights' over the natural world is not sufficient to exonerate emissions trading, for use rights can be morally problematic too. Consider, for example, a form of slavery in which persons do not have full ownership relations over others (and so may not destroy them) but they can 'use' those others as they see fit and without their consent. Suppose, for example, that they can (i) require them to work for no pay and control what they do and when they do it, and that they can (ii) sell or lend these persons to others for their use. (Let us term this slavery*.) Consider, similarly, a system of marriage in which men have 'use rights' over their wives (and so may have sex with their wives without their consent), and may (like Michael Henchard in Thomas Hardy's *The Mayor of Casterbridge*) sell their wife at an auction, but may not destroy them (and so strictly speaking does not own them in Honoré's sense). (Let us term this marriage*.) It follows from these examples that a system of 'use rights' can be deeply morally unacceptable too.[32]

In reply: we agree that some kinds of use right are morally indefensible. Clearly slavery* and marriage* are objectionable. Two points, however, can be made. First, the problem with both of these institutions is that the 'use rights' involved in both slavery* and marriage* directly violate the fundamental and basic rights that all persons have over themselves. This explains why these kinds of use rights are morally unacceptable. By contrast, we see no reason to think that the natural world possesses an analogous right that would preclude human beings from having use rights over it. To challenge our position the critic would have to provide an argument that establishes both (i) that Nature can be a right-holder, and, moreover, (ii) that the rights that it possesses disallow persons from using it in anyway whatsoever without its consent (whatever that would mean). This seems to us a tall order and we are unaware of any argument that could establish this. Second, not only do we lack any reason to deny humans some use rights over the natural world, we also have positive reason to ascribe such use rights to persons. To withhold from persons any use rights over the natural world (unlike denying people use rights over other human beings without the latter's consent) would have catastrophic effects. It would deny people the

[32] Note, incidentally, that this argument does not object solely or even primarily to the 'trading' of permits. Rather its concern seems to be with a system which distributes 'rights to use the atmosphere' whether or not they are tradeable.

land they need to live on, food to eat, water to drink, energy for heat and so on. It is, in effect, to call for the end of human life on earth. We, of course, place a limit on how much persons can use the natural world but see no reason to withhold from them any use rights at all, and plenty of reason to affirm such restricted use rights (including use rights over the atmosphere).

Argument B: Alienating responsibilities that one should perform oneself
Having considered a type 2 argument, and having argued that type 1 and type 3 arguments do not apply to the trading of permits to emit greenhouse gases, let us consider a type 4 argument. These, recall, maintain that certain goods (such as one's liberty or voting rights) and certain responsibilities (such as one's civic responsibilities) should not be alienated.

This kind of argument has been applied in a number of different ways to emissions trading. One common variant of this approach argues that creating a system with emissions trading is objectionable because it allows people to alienate responsibilities that it is inappropriate for them to alienate. This argument – what might be termed the *Collective Sacrifice Argument* – appeals to what we earlier termed 'non-delegable duties'. If we focus on the distribution of emissions within a state, the claim is that each citizen should 'do their bit' and should not delegate their tasks to others. They themselves should constrain their own emissions and not pay for someone else to lower their emissions. At the international level, this argument would hold that each state should shoulder 'its' burden and that high-emitting countries should not pay others to discharge 'their' duty.[33]

Note that this argument does not claim that those who purchase permits to emit greenhouse gases are not making a sacrifice. Clearly

[33] Michael Sandel has given this kind of argument. See 'Should we Buy the Right to Pollute?', 95. Sandel's argument against emissions trading is a part of a more general civic republican concern about the role of markets and the way they encroach into many domains in human life. See Michael J. Sandel *Justice: What's the Right Thing to do?* (London: Penguin Books, 2009), 84–91 and his discussion of 'republican citizenship' in Sandel 'What Money Can't Buy: The Moral Limits of Markets', *The Tanner Lectures on Human Values* delivered at Brasenose College, Oxford, May 11 and 12, 1998, 107ff. This is available at: http://www.tannerlectures.utah.edu/lectures/documents/sandel00.pdf (last accessed on 8 September 2010). See also his first Reith Lecture ('Markets and Morals') at http://www.bbc.co.uk/programmes/b00kt7rg (last accessed on 8 September 2010).

they are. The complaint is that they are not making the *right kind* of sacrifice. Paying a financial burden is not the way to discharge one's duty. One must discharge one's duty by keeping one's emissions within a pre-specified limit.

The idea of a shared sacrifice is a powerful one. However, this argument only has force against certain kinds of systems of emissions trading.[34] For example, if the government were to allocate permits to individuals and require them to control their own emissions as a matter of public duty, it would then be problematic to allow some people to pay to be exempted from this particular sacrifice. This would be akin to having a system of national military service and then allowing some to pay for others to substitute for them in discharging their public duty. However, it is crucial to note that emissions trading schemes do not necessarily have this character. An emissions trading scheme which allocates permits to firms, who either reduce their emissions or trade with other firms who have done so, can protect the environment without creating an individual civic responsibility to reduce emissions. Emissions trading need not involve the creation of civic duties, only to then allow *individuals* to escape their own *duty* by paying a sum of money. They can instead be a system which does not directly ascribe responsibilities to reduce emissions to its citizens, but which nevertheless achieves the collective environmental objective.

At this point a proponent of the *Collective Sacrifice Argument* may, of course, reply that we ought to address the challenge of reducing greenhouse gas emissions by creating a system of civic responsibilities. They might argue that we should adopt the same kind of approach that is normally adopted during in wartime – one in which there is rationing and a ban on trading. However, it is far from clear why this is the best way to deal with emissions reductions. In very many cases we allocate responsibilities to the state rather than to each individual citizen. For example, we often require government to remove household waste (rather than call for a system in which everyone takes their own waste to the rubbish tip) and we expect governments to provide an army to defend us (rather than have a military force entirely constituted by compulsory national service) and we then pay for the state to perform these tasks. Furthermore, in other cases, we might rely on other individuals to perform various tasks (e.g. look after our children). We discharge our responsibilities by paying the money that is required, rather than personally performing

[34] For further discussion see Caney 'Markets, Morality and Climate Change', 208.

those responsibilities. But if we accept that kind of reasoning in these other cases, why should we insist that the task of emissions reduction must not be done in this kind of way? As Jeremy Waldron writes, '[w]artime conscription – together perhaps with jury service – is virtually the only example of the state's discharging its functions by exacting service rather than money from its citizens. Since the dawn of the modern era, states have relied for the most part on cash rather than in-kind contributions.'[35]

At this point one final point might be made: a proponent of the *Collective Sacrifice Argument* might argue that our analysis of the *Collective Sacrifice Argument* overlooks an important distinction between two kinds of case.[36] They might reason as follows. Consider, first, a case where, say, two agents (A and B) are emitting greenhouse gases and it is much more expensive for A to reduce emissions than B. In such a case it seems reasonable to allow A to perform her duty by paying B to reduce emissions on A's behalf. Consider, however, a case where A and B both have exactly the same costs of reducing emissions. Suppose, however, that A does not feel like reducing her emissions and so would like to pay B instead. This, it might be argued, brings out the moral appeal of the *Collective Sacrifice Argument*. When applied to emissions trading, the thought might be that it is acceptable for a rich western country to pay China to reduce its emissions more cheaply by switching to more efficient technologies already in use in the west, but that it would be wrong for a rich western country, because it can't really be bothered, to pay the Chinese to reduce emissions by, for instance, not using a technology that westerners still continue to use.

Two points can be made in reply. First, it is not clear why it would be wrong for countries to express different attitudes to the way in which they bear their burden of reducing emissions, provided that all countries do indeed bear this burden. To give an analogy: consider two neighbours. Why would it be wrong for one to pay the other for the use of the other's front drive if the other consents to it and thinks the sum is a reasonable one? One neighbour no longer has the use of

[35] Jeremy Waldron, 'Money and Complex Equality' in *Pluralism, Justice, and Equality* (Oxford: Oxford University Press, 1995) edited by David Miller and Michael Walzer, 152. Waldron's statement may overstate the exceptional nature of in-kind contributions. The challenge, nonetheless, remains: we need an argument for the claim that we must discharge our environmental duty in an in-kind form when there are other possibilities.

[36] We are grateful to Luc Bovens for raising the objection presented in this paragraph and the example we use to illustrate it.

their front drive, and perhaps would find this inconvenient, but by foregoing the use of one resource (the front drive) but they simultaneously gain the use of another one (the money) in its stead.

Second, it is arguable that this kind of argument, and, moreover, the 'West v China' example given above, gains whatever intuitive appeal it has because it invokes separate extraneous factors – namely the respective wealth of the contracting parties and the fairness of the distribution of emission permits. That is, it might seem problematic for the wealthy to pay the poor to forego a good that the wealthy continue to enjoy. It is noticeable, for example, that the example that Sandel employs to illustrate the *Collective Sacrifice Argument* involves a rich family ('[t]he family in the mansion on the hill') paying its poorer neighbours to do some work for them.[37] This, however, cannot give us reason to reject emissions trading *tout court*. Rather it draws our attention rather to ensuring that there is a fair distribution of resources, including a fair share of emissions permits (an issue we discuss below in section 5).

Argument C: Emissions trading and the vulnerable

Consider now a third argument. Like the preceding argument it maintains that emissions trading involves alienating what should not be alienated (a type 4 argument). However, unlike the previous argument it focuses not on the person buying extra permits but on those who sell the permits. It maintains that to create a system in which permits to emit greenhouse gases were traded would allow trades which are disadvantageous to the most vulnerable and, as such, should not be allowed.

One can distinguish between two versions of this argument, what might be called the *Paternalist Argument* and the *Unreliable Trustees Argument*. The *Paternalist Argument* maintains that allowing persons to trade emissions may be undesirable because people will make poor judgements about their own interests and so they should be protected from themselves.[38] This argument is hard to sustain. Though there

[37] Sandel 'Should we Buy the Right to Pollute', 95. See also Goodin's discussion of the related, but distinct, argument that it is wrong to have a scheme that allows 'some but not all' to be exempt from some burden or to enjoy some benefit, 'Selling Environmental Indulgences', 584–585. How objectionable we find such schemes will depend heavily on whether the allocation of the scarce good is fair.

[38] James Tobin defends restrictions on trade for this reason: 'On Limiting the Domain of Inequality', *Journal of Law and Economics*, **13**:2 (1970), 266.

may be cases where a degree of paternalism is justified, it is not at all clear why: (a) we should assume that adults will make dire choices about their energy needs, and (b) even if they do it is not at all clear why the value of self-determination would be outweighed here. Furthermore, (c) the argument has no force against emissions trading between companies, as in the EU ETS. For paternalism to be justified there must be a case for protecting an actor (in this case, a company) from its own decisions. This can be plausible – in restrictive conditions – when that actor has an independent moral value and when protecting their well-being is of great importance and when they are likely to make errors in judgement. However, companies – unlike persons – do not have fundamental moral status; their importance stems from their contribution to consumers, owners, shareholders and employees. It is thus hard to see why we should prevent a company from making poor decisions about how many emissions permits to purchase or sell.[39]

A more plausible argument is what we have termed the *Unreliable Trustees Argument*. This argument runs as follows: there are cases where it is either impossible or undesirable to allocate permits to emit greenhouse gases to certain groups of people, and we therefore have reason to create trustees to care for their interests. However, these trustees are sometimes unreliable (either because they are not motivated to care for those in their trust or because they are sometimes incompetent). Given this, rather than distribute money to these unreliable trustees to care for those in their charge (which they might spend inappropriately) there is a case for placing limits on how the trustees can use the resources allocated to them.

It may be helpful to give some concrete illustrations of this kind of reasoning. One example is provided by James Tobin who makes an *Unreliable Trustees Argument* when he defends allocating educational vouchers (rather than money) to parents.[40] This is a form of non-tradable good; it can only be used for one purpose and cannot be sold for profit. The case for vouchers is that these are the best way to ensure that children receive the goods we want them to receive. Now someone may argue on similar grounds that emissions trading may be morally problematic in cases where one has to use trustees, but cannot be sufficiently confident that they will use any permits allocated to them for the benefit of their charges. Henry Shue appears to endorse this kind of reasoning and argues that states should not

39 We are grateful to Luc Bovens for pressing us on this point.

40 James Tobin 'On Limiting the Domain of Inequality', 271. He makes the same point in a discussion of food vouchers (268).

be allowed to sell all of their emission rights because that would risk harming their citizens. Some emissions, he claims, should be regarded as 'inalienable'.[41]

Note, however, that Shue does not claim that this rules out all emissions trading.[42] At most, it would entail that emissions trading be impermissible where that would jeopardise vital energy and other needs. It thus does not give us any reason to condemn an emissions trading scheme in the European community or within states that one can assume will take a responsible approach to the emissions needs of their own population. It comes into play only in countries which distribute the emission rights (or the proceeds of selling emissions rights) in such an egregiously unjust way that interfering with sovereignty is unwarranted.[43] Thus it might, for example, apply in a regime that withholds emissions necessary for a decent standard of living from its citizens.[44]

[41] See Henry Shue 'Subsistence Emissions and Luxury Emissions', *Law and Policy* **15**:1 (1993), 58, and Shue 'Climate' in *A Companion to Environmental Philosophy* (Oxford: Blackwell, 2001) edited by Dale Jamieson, 455–456. This kind of argument is also endorsed by Hyams 'A Just Response to Climate Change: Personal Carbon Allowances and the Normal-Functioning Approach', *Journal of Social Philosophy* **40**:2 (2009), 244. See also 243–244 for further discussion where Hyams discusses what we term the *Paternalism* and the *Unreliable Trustee Arguments*. Hyams appears to think that Shue's claims are a paternalistic claim about whether to prevent individuals from selling their own emission rights. Shue, however, is not discussing individual carbon permits and rejecting them for being paternalistic. His point rather is about the dangers of letting states sell all 'their' emissions permits, thereby jeopardising the needs of their citizens. See also Shue 'Equity and Social Considerations related to Climate Change', Papers presented at the IPCC Working Group III Workshop on Equity and Social Considerations Related to Climate Change, Nairobi, Kenya 18–22 July (1994) especially 389.

[42] Shue 'Subsistence Emissions and Luxury Emissions', 58 and 'Climate', 455.

[43] On the moral limits of state sovereignty see Simon Caney *Justice Beyond Borders: A Global Political Theory* (Oxford: Oxford University Press, 2005), chapter 5.

[44] What about states that do not deny their subjects the emissions needed for a decent standard of living but which nonetheless distribute them unjustly? This raises a number of complex issues that we cannot hope to resolve here. Much depends on factors such as (i) whether emissions trading with this unjust state improves or worsens the condition of the unjustly treated within that state at all, (ii) whether withholding trade incentivises the unjust government to engage in reform or whether, by contrast,

Argument D: Putting a price on the natural world?
Having considered two type-4 arguments, let us turn now to a type-5 argument. Some may object to emissions trading on the grounds that it puts a price on carbon dioxide emissions. They may argue that what is objectionable about emissions trading is not that it allows people to alienate their responsibilities or exchange benefits, but rather that emissions trading puts a monetary value on carbon dioxide (and other greenhouse gases). This, they may object, is an inappropriate attitude to take to the natural world, because its value simply cannot be captured in monetary terms.

A defender of emissions trading can, however, reply that emissions trading does not necessarily involve any expression of the value of the natural world. One might, for example, quite consistently adhere to both of the following tenets:

(a) the natural world is of intrinsic value and its value cannot be captured by monetary estimates, and
(b) the most efficacious way of protecting the natural world involves setting strict limits on the extent to which humans emit greenhouse gases and then allocating the remaining legitimate emissions through the operation of an emissions trading scheme.

To hold that market mechanisms are an effective way of protecting the natural world does not entail anything about why the natural world has value. Emissions trading here is simply a means to an end and is not in any way a statement about why the natural world has value.[45]

This point might be put in another way: it is often said (and we endorse the claim) that political actors should 'put a price on carbon'. Cap-and-Trade schemes are obviously one way (though not the only one) of putting a price on carbon. It is, however, crucially important to be clear on what this does and does not entail. On the one hand it clearly entails that to emit a certain quantity of greenhouse gases will cost a certain amount of money and hence these emissions permits have a price tag. However, putting a price on (a) emissions

---

engaging in trade is a more effective way of encouraging improvements, and (iii) how much weight we accord to self-determination as compared with securing an internally just distributions. See, further, Caney *Justice Beyond Borders*, chapter 5 and 7.

45 For further discussion see Caney 'Markets, Morality and Climate Change', 206.

permits does **not** entail putting a price on (b) the protection of the earth's atmosphere. Emissions trading schemes, thus, put a price on the use of a certain amount of the absorptive capacity of the atmosphere; they do not thereby put a price on the maintenance of a climate that is hospitable to human and non-human life. To give an analogy one might think that some ancient ruins are of great intrinsic value and therefore must be protected. And one might think that the best and fairest way of achieving this is to regulate access to these vulnerable ruins and to charge people if they wish to visit them. In doing so the scheme will put a price on 'visiting the ruins'. But by doing so it does not thereby put a price on 'the protection of the ruins'. The same is true of emissions trading schemes. To put a price on one thing (the right to use the atmosphere) is not to put a price on another thing (the preservation of our climate system).

Argument E: Does emissions trading convert what ought to be a fine into a fee?

Let us turn now to a fifth argument against emissions trading. Like the preceding argument, this argument also makes a type 5 objection. It runs as follows: emissions trading grants people permission to pollute so long as they pay a financial fee but, so the argument runs, this is profoundly mistaken. Emitting greenhouse gases is a wrong that should be fined: it is not something that one should be allowed to do if one pays a fee. The core idea is nicely captured by Sandel in a short critique of emissions trading. Sandel writes:

> The distinction between a fine and a fee for despoiling the environment is not one we should give up too easily. Suppose there were a $100 fine for throwing a beer can into the Grand Canyon, and a wealthy hiker decided to pay $100 for the convenience. Would there be nothing wrong in his treating the fine as if it were simply an expensive dumping charge?[46]

Sandel's answer is 'no'. It would be wrong in this case to treat the 'fine' as if it were a 'fee'. Similarly it would be wrong for an able bodied person to park in a disabled car parking space with a view simply to paying the ensuing fine and treating the latter as a reasonable price to pay for the privilege.[47] Sandel then applies this kind of thinking to greenhouse gas emissions.[48] Persons should restrict

[46] Sandel 'Should we Buy the Right to Pollute?', 94.
[47] Ibid., 95.
[48] Ibid., 94–95. See also Goodin 'Selling Environmental Indulgences', 581–583.

themselves to a fixed quota and for any of them to exceed their individual quota is a crime that should be punished with a fine, not an option which they can pay for (as would be the case with a fee). Let us term this the *Fines/Fee Argument*.[49]

Sandel's argument is, however, unpersuasive. It applies to cases where an individual act brings about a wrong (as it does in the hiker case and the car parking case), but it does not apply to cases where a wrong is only caused by a large number of individual actions when they hit a certain threshold. Sandel's claim that it would be wrong for the hiker to treat the $100 as a fee rather than a fine is plausible. But one cannot move from this example to conclude that emissions trading is similarly inappropriate. If one individual throws a single beer can, then she despoils the environment. However, if one individual purchases allowances so that she can emit more than her quota (however that is defined) then that in itself does not necessarily constitute a wrong if others, in line with the terms of the transaction, emit correspondingly less than their quota. A system of fees is not necessarily inappropriate.[50] Allowing people to exchange emissions permits for money is not therefore a case of wrongfully alienating responsibilities for money.

In sum, none of the five ethical arguments against climate change are seen to be compelling. First, emissions trading does not rely upon the private ownership of Earth's atmosphere and is compatible with a commitment to global stewardship. Second, the *Collective Sacrifice Argument* is unpersuasive because trading between firms and/or states can protect the environmental without creating civic duties; environmental goals and stewardship can be achieved by allocating the responsibility to states, rather than to individual citizens. The *Paternalistic Argument* is not applicable to emissions trading between firms, and there is no particular reason to think it would be persuasive even if trading took place between individuals. Third, the *Unreliable Trustees Argument* might entail that emissions trading be impermissible with corrupt states where this might jeopardize vital energy and other needs. However, it is not an argument against emissions trading per se and does not rule out emissions trading such as the EU ETS or systems in other well-governed

49 For an interesting study of how people may treat what are intended as fines as if they were fees see Uri Gneezy and Aldo Rustichini's well-known paper 'A Fine is a Price', *Journal of Legal Studies* **29**:1 (2000), 1–17.

50 On this point see Caney 'Justice, Morality and Carbon Trading', 210. This point is also made by Hyams 'A Just Response to Climate Change', 243.

countries. Fourth, while emissions trading puts a price on carbon dioxide emissions, this is not an expression of the value of the natural environment. Fifth, Sandels' *Fines/Fee Argument* is unpersuasive because each individual tonne of carbon dioxide emitted does not constitute a moral wrong — it is the aggregate damage that is problematic. An emissions trading or a system of taxes is able to prevent this damage, without the need to criminalise the activity of emitting and impose a system of fines.

5. The (distributive) justice of emissions trading

Section 4 considered the five strongest arguments for the claim that it would be intrinsically objectionable to create a system of emissions trading, and found them to be relatively weak. However, even if there is nothing intrinsically unethical about trading emissions permits, this does not necessarily imply that emissions trading will lead to just outcomes. In this section, we consider the impacts of emissions trading on distributive justice and the distribution of wealth. In focussing on this issue we are not assuming that distributive justice is the only relevant consideration in determining whether a policy is just. It is, however, an important consideration and it is the focus of this section.

We start from the assumption that, other things being equal, a more equal distribution of wealth is preferable to a less equal distribution. In general, market systems have a tendency at best to perpetuate existing distributions of wealth, and at worst to exacerbate wealth differences between rich and poor. Market economies involve greater uncertainty than planned economies, and the skilled and the fortunate are the beneficiaries, while the unskilled and the unlucky tend to suffer bad outcomes. While market economies tend to generate aggregate wealth and promote liberty, they can and do lead to highly unequal outcomes.

As with markets generally, environmental markets should not necessarily be expected to promote distributive justice or reduce inequality. Other things being equal, one might therefore expect the move to emissions trading to generate more unequal outcomes. However, the distributional consequences of an individual ETS are a function of the specific rules for allocating permits. Indeed, there is no reason in principle for an ETS to lead to more unequal distribution of wealth. It will depend on how the scheme is designed. The key point is this: whatever account of distributive justice one favours, the ETS can be designed to deliver a just outcome, either by specifying the allocation of permits in line with this favoured principle or by auctioning the permits and then distributing the revenues in line with this favoured principle.

In practice, two considerations will determine whether an ETS exacerbates or reduces inequality: first, the impact of increasing the cost of emitting pollution on different segments of the population and second, the transfers of wealth involved in the sale or free allocation of emissions allowances.

Controlling pollution directly or indirectly leads to an increase in the cost of pollution so that individuals and firms produce less of it. The evidence available strongly suggests that controlling carbon dioxide emissions is regressive, which is to say that the impacts are worse for low-income households (as a proportion of their income) than high-income households. This effect can be neutralised or reversed if the policy (whether emissions trading or taxes or otherwise) raises government revenue which is recycled to compensate poorer households.[51] In Australia, for instance, the Garnaut Review notes that roughly 10 per cent of income is spent on transport fuel, gas and electricity by low-income households, while high-income households spend only 5 per cent on these goods.[52] Pricing pollution thus hits poorer people relatively harder. Further, poorer households often rent, rather than own, their accommodation, which further constrains their ability to respond by adopting low-emissions substitutes, such as insulation, efficient space heating, hot water systems and cooking appliances. Similar effects are found in other countries.

For emissions trading to avoid regressive impacts, allowances must be sold to firms with a portion of the revenues directed to provide compensation to poorer households. This compensation could be a

[51] On the regressivity of carbon taxes, see James M. Poterba 'Tax Policy to Combat Global Warming: On Designing a Carbon Tax' in Rudiger Dornbusch and James M. Poterba (eds.) *Global Warming: Economic Policy Responses*. MIT Press, Cambridge, MA, 1991 and Gilbert E. Metcalf, 'A Distributional Analysis of Green Tax Reforms', *National Tax Journal* **52** (1999), 665–681. But for the opposite conclusion see Thomas Sterner, 'Fuel taxes: An important instrument for climate policy', *Energy Policy* **35** (2007), 3194–3202. On the distributional consequences of command and control policies, see Leonard P. Gianessi, Henry M. Peskin and Edward N. Wolff 'The Distributional Effects of Uniform Air Pollution Policy in the United States', *Quarterly Journal of Economics*, **93** (1979), 281–301 and David H. Robison, 'Who Pays for Industrial Pollution Abatement?' *Review of Economics and Statistics* **67** (1985), 702–706.

[52] Ross Garnaut, *The Garnaut Climate Change Review*, Cambridge: Cambridge University Press, 2008, ch. 16.

function of the costs required to adjust to a low-carbon economy, or could simply be given to low-income households through the tax system.

In addition to the fact that pollution control increases the price of pollution, a second consideration is that pollution policies transfer wealth from some individuals to other individuals, depending upon the particular policy and how it is implemented. For instance, carbon taxes on industrial firms normally transfer wealth from their shareholders back to the government. Carbon taxes need not have a regressive effect, provided the government doesn't give the funds back to the same firms, or earmark the funds for particular pet programmes (which often occurs in practice for political reasons). If funds are used to reform and reduce the burden of taxation on the poor, the impact of carbon taxes could be progressive. Similarly, auctioned permits under a cap-and-trade scheme transfer wealth from firms to governments, and again provided these funds are used sensibly, the effect need not be regressive and could be progressive.

However, for the most part – for the political reasons discussed above – governments have not auctioned off permits or used tax revenues for progressive reforms of the tax system. Rather, as in the EU ETS, the vast majority of 'European allowances', or EUAs, have been given to firms for free, rather than auctioned.[53] This has created windfall profits for firms, because (a) the emissions trading scheme creates a price which increases marginal costs of all units of production, which is often largely passed on to consumers in the form of higher goods prices, depending on the market structure; but (b) the firms are given most of the EUAs for free. In other words, marginal costs of production on all units increase, because firms need to retire a permit for every unit of production. However, firms (a) pass the cost increase onto consumers in the form of higher prices, and (b) they are compensated by government for the cost increase by being granted permits – which are a substantial financial asset – for free.[54] Thus, the EU ETS has created large-scale wealth transfers from

[53] Cameron Hepburn, Michael Grubb,Karsten Neuhoff,Felix Matthes, and Max Tse., 'Auctioning of EU ETS Phase II allowances: how and why?' *Climate Policy*, **6**:1 (2006), 135–158.

[54] See Robin Smale, Murray Hartley, Cameron Hepburn, John Ward, and Michael Grubb, 'The impact of CO_2 emissions trading on firm profits and market prices', *Climate Policy*, **6**:1 (2006), 31–48 and Cameron Hepburn, John K.-H. Quah, Robert A. Ritz. 'Emissions trading and profit-neutral grandfathering', *Economics Papers* 2008-W12, Economics Group, Nuffield College, University of Oxford.

taxpayers to firms, who have reaped substantial windfall profits. Rather than support suppliers, customers, or employees, these windfalls have largely been retained by shareholders, who are wealthier than the average taxpayer. The consequence is that it seems almost certain that the EU ETS has been significantly regressive. Similarly, in the USA, Parry argues that the free allocation of permits to industry would be regressive, redistributing income from poorer to richer households.[55]

The conclusion is that climate-change policies are likely to create regressive impacts without other compensatory measures, and the EU ETS is certainly no exception so far. However, the design of the EU ETS has been improving as policymakers have learned from their mistakes. For instance, in the third phase of the system (2013–2020), the cap is much tighter (at least 20% and possibly 30% reductions from 1990 levels), and the proportion of EUAs sold at auction will increase substantially. However, even with these effects, it would seem that the EU ETS is likely to remain a regressive way of reducing emissions, at least until 2020. A policy that puts a price on emissions will only be progressive if it also raises significant amounts of government revenue to compensate low-income households. As this has apparently been too difficult for politicians to achieve so far, we conclude that emissions trading as currently implemented has had negative consequences for distributive justice.

6. The effectiveness of cap-and-trade

The effectiveness of any climate-change policy is also an ethical matter. If climate policies are not able to reduce emissions at the appropriate rate and scale, the risks imposed upon future generations would likely be considered to contravene intergenerational justice. Previous experience with cap-and-trade systems has shown that such systems can make significant contributions to environmental protection, provided that they are designed and implemented correctly.

6.1 Is cap-and-trade politically feasible?

One critically important question to ask of any proposed climate policy is whether it is actually politically feasible. Over the last 40

[55] Ian W H Parry, 2004. Are emission permits regressive? *Journal of Environmental Economics and Management*, **47**:2, 364–387.

years, climate-change policies have proven extremely difficult to put in place. Because these policies provide a global public good, every country, particularly smaller countries, have an incentive to free-ride on others' efforts. Furthermore, achieving domestic political agreement on tackling climate change is challenging because there are many powerful losers and relatively few winners (unless other nations take similar action). Furthermore, the science continues to have important uncertainties, and the costs are incurred now while the benefits accrue decades and centuries into the future. Given these perspectives, instead of asking 'why has so little been achieved?'[56] some sceptical economists often find it remarkable that any action has occurred at all, and consider the real puzzle to be why anything at all has been achieved.[57]

Cap-and-trade systems have the virtue that they are almost the only deliberate climate-change policy to actually reduce emissions to any significant degree so far.[58] Half of the European economy is subject to the EU ETS, with a revealed price of around €10–20/tCO_2, significantly higher than any other serious direct price signal elsewhere in the world. Other cap-and-trade schemes include the Regional Greenhouse Gas Initiative in the north-eastern USA, the Western Climate Initiative in several western USA states and Canadian provinces, and those adopted in the Australian state of New South Wales, Switzerland, Norway, Japan, New Zealand. As noted above, both China and India have also recently announced that they will be implementing cap-and-trade systems to reduce their absolute level of emissions.

The reason why some states and regions have been able to put a price on greenhouse gas emissions with emissions trading, whereas efforts to date with carbon taxes have not been as successful, is that cap-and-trade systems are able to garner political support from a wide spectrum of relevant actors. Environmentalists have supported cap-and-trade systems because the cap on emissions, which gets tighter over time, is the best method of securing a good environmental outcome. Industry has

[56] Dieter Helm, 2010. 'Climate-change policy: why has so little been achieved?' in Dieter Helm and Cameron Hepburn. (eds) *The Economics and Politics of Climate Change*. Oxford: Oxford University Press.

[57] Scott Barrett. 2003. *Environment and Statecraft*, Oxford: Oxford University Press.

[58] Greenhouse gas emissions have been reduced by non-deliberate events or policies, such as the recent recession and the Montreal Protocol on Substances That Deplete the Ozone Layer (1989) to the Vienna Convention for the Protection of the Ozone Layer (1985).

supported cap-and-trade ahead of direct regulation because it is cheaper and minimises the costs of compliance, and industry prefers cap-and-trade to taxes because, as discussed above, cap-and-trade allows a proportion of allowances to be given to firms for free. Finally, cap-and-trade systems have a natural constituency once they are up and running. The industrial firms which own the permits will see the value of that asset increase as the cap is tightened. Financial firms who trade the asset also have an interest in rising carbon prices. Unlike a carbon tax, where there is no strong constituent to support them, cap-and-trade systems have, rightly or wrongly, found support across a cross-section of environmentalists and business that make them more politically feasible.

6.2 Defining effectiveness

Only once a system has been implemented can its effectiveness be assessed. The effectiveness of emissions trading depends on the question which it is intended to answer. Is emissions trading intended to deliver global emission reductions of over 50% by 2050, without other policy interventions? Or is emissions trading intended to be part of a package of climate policies, so that its effectiveness is measured by whether it has made a sufficiently substantial contribution to reducing emissions?

In addition to measuring effectiveness of emissions trading according to the appropriate objective, effectiveness must also be measured by reference to a 'counterfactual', namely a baseline scenario describing what would have happened if the emissions trading scheme had not been introduced. Emissions trading can guarantee a specific limit on *emissions*, but it cannot guarantee a specific *reduction in emissions* compared to business-as-usual, because business-as-usual emissions are uncertain. For instance, a given emissions target might be achieved not because of emissions trading, but because of a severe economic recession which caused a fall in business-as-usual emissions. In a recession, economic activity falls and emissions fall, so the demand for permits could fall to the extent that the permit price could end up at zero. In such circumstances, it would be difficult to conclude that the ETS is working to reduce emissions. In contrast, if the price of emissions allowances is positive, then it follows that emissions trading is probably reducing emissions. The higher the allowance price, the greater the relative impact of the emissions trading scheme, and the lower the relative contribution of business-as-usual changes to reducing emissions.

6.3 Has cap-and-trade reduced emissions?

Cap-and-trade systems have been successfully used in the United States to phase out leaded gasoline in the 1980s,[59] reduce sulphur dioxide (SO_2) and nitrogen oxides (NO_x) emissions from power plants from 1995 onwards,[60] and the phase-out of chlorofluorocarbons (CFCs).[61] The leaded gasoline programme achieved environmental targets with an estimated cost saving of $250 million per annum.[62] The SO_2 programme also achieved environmental targets, saving $1 billion per annum compared with the estimated costs of other regulatory approaches.[63]

The fact that a particular policy intervention has worked for one environmental problem does not imply that it will necessarily work for others. Climate change is a particularly vexing environmental challenge because it is international, intergenerational, based on complex and uncertain science, and involves almost every aspect of production and consumption around the world. Many economists express the view that emissions trading (or some other form of emissions pricing, such as international carbon taxes) is a necessary but not sufficient component of overall climate-change policy. Other policies are needed because of the presence of multiple 'market failures'.

The most significant experiment with cap-and-trade systems for greenhouse gases to date began with the launch of the EU ETS in 2005. In the first phase of the scheme, from 2005–2007, carbon prices rose to highs of above €30/tCO_2 and then crashed to near zero for most of 2007. Zero prices arose when it became clear in the

[59] Suzi Kerr, and David Maré 'Efficient Regulation Through Tradeable Permit Markets: The United States Lead Phasedown', Department of Agricultural and Resource Economics, University of Maryland. Working Paper 96–06 (January); Albert L. Nichols, 'Lead in Gasoline', in Richard D. Morgenstern, ed., *Economic Analyses at EPA: Assessing Regulatory Impact* Resources for the Future, Washington, D.C. 1997, 49–86.

[60] A. Denny Ellerman, Paul L. Joskow, Richard Schmalensee Juan-Pablo Montero, and Elizabeth M. Bailey. (2000), *Markets for Clean Air: The US Acid Rain Program*, New York, Cambridge University Press.

[61] Robert N Stavins, 'Addressing climate change with a comprehensive US cap-and-trade system', *Oxford Review of Economic Policy* **24**:2 (2008), 298–321.

[62] Albert L. Nichols, 'Lead in Gasoline', 49–86.

[63] Carlson, Curtis, Dallas Burtraw, Maureen Cropper, and Karen Palmer. 2000. 'SO_2 Control by Electric Utilities: What are the Gains from Trade?' *Journal of Political Economy*, **108**:6 (2000), 1272–1326.

third and final year of the phase that that aggregate emissions were well below the number of allowances issued. This surplus of allowances implied that they were worthless. The period of zero prices in 2007 was problematic for several reasons; most importantly the incentive to continue reducing emissions was dramatically weakened.

The price collapse was caused by a combination of two things. First, firms actually reduced their emissions in the first two years of the phase, motivated by high prices in the 2005 and 2006 period, so that they didn't need as many allowances in 2007. Second, regulators handed out too many EUAs in the first place, as a result of uncertainty about business-as-usual emissions and sustained lobbying by individual firms and EU Member States for additional allowances. What is the overall balance between these two considerations? Ellerman and Buchner review the EU ETS over 2005 and 2006, when emissions were 60 million tonnes (or 3 per cent) below the allocation levels.[64] After a careful econometric analysis, they conclude that, although there is considerable uncertainty, emissions were probably reduced compared to business-as-usual by 50 to 100 million tCO_2 in each of those two years by the EU ETS, amounting to several percent of total emissions in the scheme. This is a considerable achievement; by comparison, the entire UK economy (which is partially covered by the EU ETS) emits around 500 million tCO_2 in any given year. This suggests that, even with the manifest design flaws in the first phase of the EU ETS, and in a system that had zero prices for a considerable period, significant reductions in emissions compared were achieved compared to business-as-usual.

More recent analysis supports this view. Anderson and di Maria (2010) find that over the three trading years of the pilot phase from 2005–2007, total abatement was 247 million tonnes, or just over 80 million tonnes per year.[65] Consistently, a separate study by Delarue et al. (2008) found reductions in the power sector alone of 30–60 million tonnes in 2005 and 20–35 million tonnes in 2006.[66]

[64] Denny Ellerman, and Barbara Buchner. 'Over-Allocation or Abatement? A Preliminary Analysis of the EU ETS Based on the 2005–06 Emissions Data', *Environmental and Resource Economics*, **41** (2008), 267–287.

[65] Barry Anderson and Corrado di Maria. 'Abatement and allocation in the pilot phase', *Environmental and Resource Economics*, 2010. DOI: 10.1007/s10640-010-9399-9.

[66] Erik Delarue, Kris Voorspools, William D, D'haeseleer. 'Fuel switching in the electricity sector under the EU ETS: review and prospective'. *Journal of Energy Engineering*, **134**:2 (2008), 40–46.

Indeed, even though the price in the first Phase (from 2005–2007) ultimately did fall to zero, Ellerman and Buchner (2008) point out that it is unsurprising that emissions were reduced given the following three observations:[67]

1. The price of EUAs was positive and significant during the 2005–2006 period, providing firms with an incentive to reduce emissions;
2. Real output in the EU rose over those two years, and improvements in CO_2 intensity had been declining which implies a baseline of increasing CO_2 emissions prior to 2005; and
3. Historical emissions data indicate a reduction in absolute emissions over the relevant period, allowing for plausible bias.

6.4 Will cap-and-trade reduce emissions in future?

Even if the EU ETS has been successful at reducing emissions to date, it must do so at much greater scale in the future if it is to provide a policy response commensurate with the scale of the challenge. There have been several changes in the design of the EU ETS between Phase 1 and the current Phase 2 (from 2008–2012), with further improvements in place for Phase 3 (from 2013–2020). Current allowance prices are around €10–20/tCO_2, significantly higher than any economy-wide carbon tax, and market participants who publish forecasts of future prices expect prices to increase substantially over the coming years. To some extent, companies take these future prices into account when making their investment decisions.

Some of the more significant changes since Phase 1 have been as follows:

- The EU commission has been more resistant to lobbying by firms, and has insisted on greater cuts in emissions than requested by EU Member States and their firms;
- A higher proportion of EU allowances (EUAs) are being auctioned to firms rather than given away for free;
- Banking of allowances is possible from Phase 2 to Phase 3. This promotes confidence that carbon market prices will not fall to zero. Indeed, prices were positive even during the recent

[67] Denny Ellerman, and Barbara Buchner. 'Over-Allocation or Abatement? A Preliminary Analysis of the EU ETS Based on the 2005–06 Emissions Data'.

> financial crises and recession, which reduced output and baseline emissions. This is because the market price reflects the effort required by market participants to achieve the agreed emission reductions through to 2020.

These changes suggest that emission reductions created through the 2008–2012 phase are likely to be significantly greater than those in the so-called 'learning' phase from 2005–2007. Furthermore, emissions reductions in the 2013–2020 phase will take the European economy substantially below business-as-usual, and indeed 20–30% below emissions in 1990.

7. Conclusion

Cap-and-trade systems for greenhouse gas emissions have been put in place in several countries over the last decade. While the evidence so far suggests that they have been successful in reducing emissions, they have been subject to increasing criticism by climate-change sceptics. Over the course of 2010, they were also tarred with the same brush of dissatisfaction addressed towards the United Nations negotiations, which failed to deliver a binding agreement at the international conference in Copenhagen in December 2009, but which appears to have achieved greater progress at Cancún in December 2010. In this paper we hope to have identified key ethical criteria by which one can evaluate such schemes. More specifically, we have defended four conclusions.

First, we have noted in their favour that emissions trading schemes may minimize waste and recognize person' interest in liberty.

Second, we have provided a taxonomy of ethical objections to the market. Drawing on this we have examined five different attempts to show that emissions trading schemes are inherently unethical and have found each of these attempts wanting. Emissions trading schemes, so we have argued, are not committed to either 'ownership' rights or unacceptable 'use rights' over the atmosphere as a whole and are compatible with an ideal of environmental stewardship (Argument A). In addition to this, while the *Collective Sacrifice Argument* has force in some contexts, we have no reason to apply it to this particular context (Argument B). A third argument – that one may restrict emissions trading in order to protect the vulnerable – can take two forms, but neither rule out emissions trading entirely (Argument C). Such arguments (in particular what we termed the *Unreliable Trustees Argument*) draw our attention to the important issues of who should possess the legal rights to emit greenhouse gases and how one can best ensure that the permits (or the revenues of auctions) should reach the people entitled to them. Such concerns do not, however, undermine many emissions trading schemes (Argument D). Finally, we have argued that emissions trading schemes do not elide the distinction between a 'fee' and 'fine' (Argument E). Emissions trading schemes are, thus, not in principle objectionable.

Having considered these five root-and-branch critiques of emissions trading we then turned to two other criteria relevant to the evaluation of emissions trading schemes. The first critical issue is the effect of emissions trading schemes on the distribution of wealth. This takes us to our third conclusion which is that while cap-and-trade systems are not intrinsically unethical, they (like other policies that put a price on greenhouse gas emissions) are likely to hit poorer households harder than richer households, with unwelcome implications for distributional justice. The current EU ETS puts a price on pollution without providing adequate compensation for poor households and, as a result, it has had a greater impact on the poor relative to the rich. This is not a necessary outcome,[68] and in principle it is possible to design an ETS so that the revenues from auctioning permits are used to produce a progressive result. Indeed, companies in the EU ETS will have to pay for a greater proportion of their allowances over time, so there is some possibility that this problem will be resolved as the ETS matures. That said, it is unlikely that the EU ETS will be progressive for at least another decade.

This leaves the final crucial consideration, namely 'are emissions trading schemes an effective means of mitigating climate change?'. Our conclusion here is that a careful analysis of cap-and-trade systems shows that they are more effective at reducing emissions than many of their critics appear to believe. As noted above, even in the 2005–2007 learning phase of the EU ETS, discredited as having 'failed' by some critics, it is estimated that 50–100 million tonnes of CO_2 a year were reduced compared to business-as-usual. The current phase (2008–2012) of the EU ETS will deliver greater reductions, notwithstanding the recession, and the reductions delivered in the next phase (2013–2020) depend upon whether the EU commits to a 20% or a 30% target in the course of the next year or so.

Given the moral virtues of cap-and-trade systems and the absence of compelling moral objections relative to other policy possibilities,

[68] Indeed, research suggests that fuel taxes might not be regressive in developing countries: Thomas Sterner, 'Fuel taxes: An important instrument for climate policy', *Energy Policy* **35** (2007), 3194–3202.

we conclude that emissions trading remains a valuable policy tool with which to address climate change. Carbon taxes have some advantages over cap-and-trade,[69] but in other ways are worse, not least in the fact that they provide no guarantee of environmental outcomes, and are significantly more difficult to establish politically. Indeed, carbon taxes are likely to continue to be politically difficult, especially in the USA, to implement and maintain at a level that will achieve reductions in emissions at the necessary rate to provide a just outcome for future generations. Direct regulation is inferior to an ETS or a carbon tax because it increases costs of compliance, increases wastage and reduces liberty of individuals and companies to adapt to a low-carbon economy in the manner most suitable to them. In an ETS, the possibility of *trade* minimises waste, the *cap* ensures environmental integrity over time, potentially according to a gradual 'contraction and convergence' pathway,[70] and the *allocation* of the permits determines the distributive justice (and political success). None of this is to suggest that a single cap-and-trade system would alone be an adequate response to climate change. Nevertheless, it is a morally valuable, rather than a morally suspect, contribution to moving at speed and at scale to the low-carbon economy required for humans to continue to flourish on Earth into the next century and beyond.

[a]*Magdalen College, Oxford*
[b]*New College and Smith School, Oxford*

[69] Cameron Hepburn, 'Regulation by prices, quantities or both: A review of instrument choice', *Oxford Review of Economic Policy* **22**:2 (2006), 226–247.

[70] Aubrey Meyer, 'Contraction and Convergence: The global solution to climate change'.

Sustainable Consumption, Climate Change and Future Generations

DIETER HELM[1]

1. Introduction

What makes climate change such a difficult problem to solve is that it is so pervasive: it is global but with very different effects on regions and nations. It stretches through time to many future generations. Its causes are ultimately the growth of population, the structure of production and growing consumption: greater numbers require ever more to make them happy.

The pervasiveness of the problem has been matched by the plurality of 'solutions'. One response with a long pedigree is essentially anti-growth and anti-consumption. 'Deep greens' argue that climate change is but one manifestation of the destruction wrought by humans on the planet, and that we should radically reduce consumption (and population), so that we can live in greater harmony with our environment. Variants on this position add cultural and spiritual dimensions arguing that we should 'get back to nature'. The Enlightenment idea of progress is rejected, along with capitalism as an economic system.[2]

An alternative view has been presented, primarily by mainstream economists. It is argued that climate change is a problem that arises because of 'market failures', and it can be 'solved' by correcting these market failures.[3] The challenge is to create a market in which carbon is priced (or taxed), and to intervene to support the technical progress to provide for new low carbon energy sources. The spirit of

[1] I have greatly benefitted from comments and discussions with David Wiggins and Cameron Hepburn. The views and errors here remain mine alone.

[2] There are of course numerous shades of green, depending on the view taken of the hardness of the constraints on economic growth. Here a simplified and stylised 'straw man' is used for exposition purposes.

[3] The concept of market failure begs the question: failure in respect of what? In mainstream neo-classical economics, the answer is: the Walrasian general equilibrium model of perfect competition, which is also Pareto optimal.

doi:10.1017/S1358246111000294

the Enlightenment – the expansion of ideas and inventions in the context of free and democratic societies – is embedded within the capitalist system and, suitably regulated, the problem can (and will) be overcome. Climate change is just another challenge for capitalism to overcome.

The gap between these two broad views is enormous: ultimately they are grounded in fundamentally different views of human nature. One attempt to bridge the gap has been provided by marrying up the economists' view with a particular ethical position that owes much to the environmentalists' position. This attempt has been best exemplified in the Brundtland report[4] and subsequently the Stern Review.[5] Brundtland – in a north/south developmental context – promoted the idea of an ethical constraint on consumption: that people in the future should be no worse off that those now. Utility should be non-decreasing over time for all future generations. Stern borrowed an earlier and more radical concept from Ramsey[6]: that utility should not be discounted over time. Stern quotes with approval Ramsey's famous remark that pure time discounting is 'ethically indefensible' arising 'from the weakness of the imagination'.[7]

This paper is very much focussed on the attempt to marry up an ethical position with the conventional economists' view. It will be argued that whilst policy problems always entail some ethical content, the position arrived at by Stern is so radical as to undermine any notion that the usual economics toolbox of correcting for market failures could meet the challenge. Stern's position is extreme: far from 'lacking imagination', the time discounting of utility is fundamental to human nature. That does not of course render Stern 'wrong', but his position to time discount at zero is so divorced from human nature as to render it a hopeless base for the design of climate change policy. Indeed it is likely to be counterproductive. The breakdown of the Copenhagen climate talks in December 2009 and the subsequent slow progress at Cancùn was in part a consequence of far too demanding an ethical claim.

[4] Brundtland Commission, *Our common future: Report of the World Commission on Environment and Development* (Oxford: Oxford University Press, 1987).

[5] N. Stern, *The Economics of Climate Change: The Stern Review*, (Cambridge: Cambridge University Press, 2007).

[6] F.P. Ramsey, 'A Mathematical Theory of Saving', *Economic Journal*, **38** (1928), 543–59.

[7] Op. cit., 543.

An alternative approach is to ground the ethics of climate change more securely on human nature, and whilst Stern is swift to dismiss a more Humean naturalistic approach, it is more likely to provide a guide to policy. It may not in consequence 'solve' climate change – but this is, under almost any scenario, going to be a matter of mitigation, technical progress and adaptation. Climate change is inevitable. The questions are: how much ought we to mitigate? and: how should we design climate change policy most efficiently?

The structure of the paper is as follows. Section two grounds the climate change problem in consumption, and sets out a framework for considering what level of consumption would be sustainable over time. This loosely accords with the Brundtland approach, though it makes no claim about the distribution of that consumption. Section three turns to Stern's more radical proposal and the concept of equality that is embedded in it. It contrasts this rationalistic approach with one loosely derived from Hume. Section four sets out the case for basing policy on pragmatism rather than idealism, howbeit one grounded on moral sentiments. Section five draws out some of the implications for climate change policy. Section six concludes.

2. Sustainable consumption: assigning responsibility

The proximate cause of climate change is a change in the composition of the atmosphere. Increased emissions of greenhouse gases (here, for simplicity, all lumped together as 'carbon') as a result of human activities are claimed to be the main culprit. Hence the 'solution' is to reduce these emissions. It is assumed that climate change is a 'bad thing', and that it is especially bad if average temperatures increase above 2 degrees centigrade in this century, and catastrophic if they rise much more.

Packed into the above paragraph is an enormous amount of science and scientific uncertainty about climate change, and a lot of economics in the estimation of the consequences. For the moment we leave aside that uncertainty – returning to it when we come to policy at the end of the paper.

What causes the increase in emissions? An obvious answer is the burning of fossil fuels, to which can be added the destruction of the great carbon sinks – the rain forests, oceans and soils. But what causes these? The answer is greater human consumption – based upon the continuous process of economic growth and population increases. To set the context for the period to 2050, over which the requirement indicated by scientists to stay within the two degrees warming is effective decarbonisation, these trends in growth and population need to be extrapolated. On economic growth, it is assumed that the developed economies continue their trend GDP growth rates of about 2–3% GDP per annum. Europe plus the US currently equate to about 25% each of world GDP, and at these rates, they will double by 2050 (and quadruple by the end of the century). Translating growth into consumption, Europeans and Americans can expect to have twice their current standard of living by 2050.

But it is in the developing countries where the effects are most dramatic. China and India are both currently growing at about 7–10% GDP per annum, and with the economic crisis making a mere dent in the trend line. If these rates continue, both will roughly quadruple their GDP by 2050 and roughly quadruple their consumption too. Brazil may also follow the same path.

This growth will be accompanied by a further expansion of world population – from around 6 billion now to around 9 billion by 2050. The increase represents an addition equal to the entire world population in 1950. These extra 3 billion will be distributed largely in China, India and Africa – roughly one billion each. There will be large increases in the Middle East too, relative to their current populations, but China and India dwarf the others.

Translating this economic growth and population increases into future consumption using current evidence of preferences indicates hundreds of millions of new cars, a major shift towards meat-based diets, massive expansion of aviation and shipping, and the conversion of much land into housing. To support this consumption, energy demand will rise sharply, as will agricultural demand. It is not hard to envisage as a result very considerable destruction of the remaining rainforests, significant freshwater constraints (with large scale, energy intensive desalination), acidification and large scale pollution of the oceans, and a major deterioration of soils, as marginal lands are brought under cultivation and existing agricultural land witnesses a major (agri-chemical based) intensification of production.

This enormous wall of consumption lies at the heart of the climate change problem – and indeed more general environmental destruction. The question is whether it can be sustained. Deep greens await confirmation of their claim that it cannot, and wait for the expiry of the global resources that will be needed to support it. They start with a model of the world's ecological systems and economy in which resources are in *fixed* supply. As they are used up, we run out of them. It is claimed by some in this camp that we have already passed the peak of oil production, and that we will run out soon, and that we will face acute shortages before 2050. As the oil runs out (and the other core minerals), the capitalist economies will face crises and, some argue, ultimately collapse. Armageddon awaits, unless we rapidly switch to lower consumption, renewables and radically reduce our energy consumption.

Fortunately or unfortunately according to one's starting point, on fossil fuels at least, this is in large measure nonsense.[8] It is not only a very static view, with implicitly an assumption of fixed technologies, but it also relies on the empirical forecast expiry of resources in the given time period. Both assumptions are suspect. Technological change is encouraged as the price of a resource rises. Thus despite warnings of a crisis as the coal 'ran out' in the late nineteenth century (famously by Jevons in 1865),[9] in fact oil-based engines came along, and oil displaced coal especially for transportation. Coal remained (extremely) abundant and for the subsequent century provided the main fuel for electricity generation. Indeed there is probably at least around 200 years left of coal burning should it be needed and should we be foolish enough to burn it. Technological progress leads to substitution, and there are lots of substitutes available. In the electricity sector, nuclear has displaced some coal, and gas has made major inroads.

Turning to oil, the marginal demand is from transport. Yet there are rapidly developing technologies that electrify transport. And electricity can be produced from nuclear, hydro, solar, wind and, importantly, gas. Contrary to the view up to the end of the 1980s that natural gas was so scarce that it should be preserved for the petrochemical industry, recent developments in unconventional gases (shales, coal-based methane and tight gas) indicate that we are, and may remain, awash with gas reserves for at least the rest of the century.

Thus, contrary to the deep greens, the problem is not scarcity of fossil fuels (the burning of which is a key cause of climate change), but rather their abundance, and if we were to use these resources, the science predicts that we will end up with a serious risk of catastrophic climate change. The case is less clear cut when it comes to land use, water and soils, but here again it is foolhardy to

[8] Helm, D.R. (2011), 'Peak Oil and Energy Policy – a critique', Forthcoming in *Oxford Review of Economic Policy*, Vol 26, Issue 4.

[9] W. Jevons, *The Coal Question: An Inquiry Concerning the Progress of the Nation, and the Probable Exhaustion of Our Coal-Mines* (London: Macmillan and Co. 1865).

underestimate the ability to continue the consumption expansion for a very considerable time. The rainforests could be felled, providing a lot more agricultural land. There is no shortage of (salt) water, and desalination opens up almost infinite fresh-water supplies. Chemicals will almost certainly stretch out the yields from soils. Again, resources are unlikely to run out (thereby stopping consumption) within the time period that climate change needs to be tackled. On the contrary, the destruction of the environment can probably run on well beyond the relevant time period for action.

Yet beyond fossil fuels the deep greens have a point in the long run. The environment is not infinite: the processes that lie behind the increase in consumption come with great destruction, and eventually the impacts will probably constrain human expansion in both numbers and consumption. In this century, the destruction of biodiversity – perhaps half of all species – will have inevitable feedbacks. Renewable resources are being so rapidly depleted that they may become non-renewable. A feature of the economists' approach is to take account of this destruction by trading it off against the growth in 'man-made capital'. So we might lose the swallows and the tigers, but we can compensate for this loss with more houses, cars and iPods. Substitution between environmental and man-made capital is assumed.

A further twist is to argue that in any event future people will probably not miss the swallows and the tigers: if they have never seen them, how can they experience a sense of loss – other than as we do now for the dodo? Compared with the sense of loss from taking a pay-cut, or not being able to take a holiday, it is for most consumers, irrelevant.

This substitution assumption goes to the core of the concept of sustainability and sustainable consumption. If environmental and man-made capital are perfect substitutes, then consumption for future generations goes up as long as we compensate for the environmental damage to the climate and biodiversity with enough man-made stuff. Deep greens would want to deny there is a trade off. Conventional economists might want to claim that the substitution is close to unity. Neither is likely to be right: to deny any substitution is to deny that there has been any progress in human history in a material sense; to claim complete substitution is to deny that there is anything special about the environment.[10]

10 The range of views between the two extremes is represented by different green positions.

Thus to establish what is 'sustainable consumption' requires an empirical estimate of this substitution. Such estimates are complicated by the fact that there is a lot of variance between cases. Indeed in extreme cases, like some viruses, the substitution is more than unity – we want to eradicate them. Many resources are renewable; many are renewable up to a particular depletion rate. There is also the problem of uncertainty: we often do not know what is a safe rate to exploit a resource, and we know little about future possible uses. Hence it might be sensible to apply a precautionary approach to identifying safe depletion rates.

In theory then, the sustainable consumption path could be defined by sorting out the substitution assumptions, and there will be a debate between environmentalists and others about how much risk we can take whilst giving future generations consumption at least as high as our own. What however is clear is that Gross Domestic Product (GDP) does not measure sustainable consumption, and indeed it takes little or no account of these limits to substitution. It follows that the GDP growth predicted for the period to 2050 is likely to be unsustainable.

GDP measures gross not net output. It takes no account of changes in asset values (natural or otherwise), and most of the pollution caused in realising GDP (including carbon emissions and biodiversity loss) is not taken into account. In order to measure sustainable consumption, pollution needs to be priced, and the increase or decrease in asset values needs to be incorporated.[11] It is immediately obvious that, were these aspects of economic growth to be incorporated into the calculation, the sustainable level would be much lower. China's growth rate in particular, based upon the depletion of fossil fuels, growing carbon emissions, and the destruction of its agricultural land and water, would probably be much lower.

None of the above indicates that people in the future cannot be better off – that growth cannot continue. The causes of growth, once the above adjustments have been made, arise from finding more productive ways of producing the things people want to consume. The main source is technological progress – science and its application. In addition, the quality of the labour force can be enhanced through better education and health provision. Governments and other institutions can be improved too. All these improvements come through the processes of discovery, learning and experimentation. They do not come from simply depleting resources faster.

[11] Helm, D.R. (2010), 'Rethinking the Economic Borders of the State', London, *Social Market Foundation*, November.

Growth is about getting more out of existing resources, having proper regard to making good their depreciation. The internet, mobile phones, and widespread computing are examples of enormous technical progress which in themselves are not necessarily more resource intensive. Smart grids, active power systems, and electric cars have the potential to transform the energy sector.

There is no evidence that the human history of ever-expanding knowledge is about to stop. Hence there is in principle no limit to growth. However, given we have done considerable damage in our pursuit of GDP and hence not taken account of the depreciation of natural (and other) assets, there is much reparation to be done. Recent debt-financed consumption has almost certainly been in excess of the sustainable level, and hence living standards may have to adjust down to the sustainable level, before resuming an upward path.

Once it is accepted that (over) consumption and a failure to take proper account of natural capital in the development of man-made capital are the ultimate causes of climate change and biodiversity, it is a relatively straightforward step to argue that responsibility for the past excess emissions of carbon lies with those who have been doing the consumption and over-exploiting the natural capital of the climate. This simple step has radical consequences: to date almost all carbon policy has been based upon the reduction of carbon *production* rather than consumption.

The assignment of responsibility is an important step in reaching any international agreement about climate change policy. It is not just about who caused the past emissions – now part of the stock of carbon in the atmosphere – but who is the ultimate cause of additional marginal emissions going forward. If China produces goods for export to the US and Europe, then the carbon produced in China is *on behalf of* consumers in the US and Europe. Indeed, it may be that the goods would have been produced in countries like Britain had not carbon production in Britain been the policy target. Rather than produce steel, chemicals and cement in Britain (and pay the price of carbon), the companies locate oversees and then export back to Britain.

The effects are dramatic. The 'carbon footprint' of the British is much higher than reported under Kyoto-based carbon production measures. Between 1990 and 2005, carbon emissions *production* fell by an impressive 15%. But on a *consumption* base, emissions went up around 19%.[12] Now consider the sustainability criterion described

[12] D. R. Helm, R. Smale, and J. Phillips, *Too Good to be True? The UK's Climate Change Record* (2007, December).

above: if GDP is adjusted to take account of the pollution (the carbon emissions) and the depreciation of the atmospheric assets (measured by increases in the carbon stock), then the measured carbon performance of the British economy looks a lot worse. The corollary is that our standard of living is considerably above the sustainable level.

3. Future Generations

The sustainability criterion gets us a long way from our current polluting consumption. To meet it would indeed be radical. No mainstream political party considers it wise to explain this to their electorates. None advocate a carbon-driven (or biodiversity-driven) reduction in current standards of living. Indeed, political debate in Britain (and most developed countries) is framed to a considerable extent on how much extra consumption now can be financed by borrowing from the future. Yet curiously some economists – notably Stern – argue we should go much further. He argues, following Ramsey, that we should be impartial between the times that people live. We should not discount utility over time. 'We take a simple approach in this Review: if a future generation will be present, we suppose that it has the same claim on our ethical attention as the current one'.[13]

Zero time preference discounting is a radical idea – and indeed it is far from clear what it means. It is based on a rationalistic application of the idea of impartiality, itself based on a concept of justice. In turn, it derives from social contract theory: that rational individuals abstracted from their places in society (and their initial endowments) would select such a principle.

This is not the place to review theories of justice. Rather we consider two objections to this sort of approach to climate change: that it is so radically different from what people actually choose as to have little chance of guiding policy; and that abstracting individuals out of their social context is in conflict with human nature and hence cannot form the basis for a moral principle.

The first objection is a relatively easy empirical claim to make. Zero discounting treats people equally through time – and, by implication, at a point of time too. Yet, as the advocates at Copenhagen found, politicians not only could not resolve the prisoners' dilemma problem, but also did not think they could sell even the weak proposals for a post-Kyoto framework to their voters in democracies, and

[13] N. Stern, op. cit, 35.

dictatorships were even less inclined to follow this line. The Copenhagen proposals were not remotely close to the sustainable criterion discussed above, let alone approximating zero time discounting.

A cursory inspection of preferences indicates that David Hume was right to point out that our concerns are greater for our immediate family and neighbours.[14] As we move away from our close circles, we do not display much propensity to treat the utility of people equally at a point in time. Move beyond our borders and immigration becomes a common cause for discriminating between people according to where they were born and currently live. Getting richer countries to transfer even 1% GDP for development is an uphill struggle. Indeed it is interesting that one of the core arguments in favour of emissions trading is that voters might not notice that transfers are being made by mechanisms like the Clean Development Mechanism to poorer countries.

The idea that we should weight people through time equally when we so patently do not at a point in time displays a concern for describing one possible moral ideal, rather than trying to craft an agreement now about climate change. It is an interesting intellectual exercise, but is open to the challenge that it is not itself of moral merit. By shifting the emphasis to ideal states, and the advocating policies based upon the ideal, the risk is that nothing much is achieved. The failure at Copenhagen is a good example of the moral consequences. To seek in a Humean spirit to ground moral judgements in human nature, rather than externally from human nature, points towards a broadening of our concerns, including our concern for justice, but not so far as to encompass an ideal which is unreachable given the

[14] 'We sympathise more with persons contiguous to us, than with persons remote from us: With our acquaintance, than with strangers: With our countrymen, than with foreigners… The approbation of moral qualities most certainly is not deriv'd from reason, or any comparison of ideas; but proceeds entirely from a moral taste, and from certain sentiments of pleasure of disgust, which arise upon the contemplation and view of particular qualities or characters. Now 'tis evident, that those sentiments, whence-ever they are deriv'd must vary according to the distance or contiguity of the objects; nor can I feel the same lively pleasure from the virtues of a person, who liv'd in *Greece* two thousand years ago, that I feel from the virtues of a familiar friend and acquaintance.' D. Hume, *A Treatise of Human Nature: Being an Attempt to introduce the experimental Method of Reasoning into Moral Subjects*, Volume II: Passions – Morals (A new edition, London: Thomas and Joseph Allman, 1817), 308–309.

constraints of human nature. This was very much Hume's view of the role of government and moral advancement.

Our second line of criticism is that the ideal itself may be open to challenge, given its reliance of some sort of social contract theory. This liberal rationalistic approach to ethics reached arguable its climax with Rawls' theory of justice not so much because of the two principles he derived, but from the architecture of choice upon which they are based.[15]

For Rawls, what makes people human is their rational capacity, and their conduct should be driven by the dictates of reason. Therefore all the other bits need to be stripped away. The people in Rawls' original state are behind a 'veil of ignorance', and their ignorance is profound. They do not take account of their endowments. For many this is interpreted in a rather narrow way. But 'endowments' include their human nature, their culture, their parents, their education, religion and so on – all the attributes Hume placed emphasis upon. People are not blank pieces of paper on which rational principles of justice can be written.

The alternative view does indeed owe much to Hume. For him, reason was the slave of the passions. These 'passions' are complex and historically situated, surrounded by institutions, culture and social context. They are core parts of our human nature. Moral sentiments do for Hume extend beyond self-interest – and reason has its part to play. Considerations of justice expand the domain of moral concern and develop our moral sentiments (a point his friend Adam Smith recognised too).[16]

The issue here is not whether people have concerns for others. That concern is the starting point, and the precondition for the evolution of moral sentiments. For Hume, the impressions upon which ideas are grounded have *context*. And amongst the passions are narrow and broad conceptions – of personal improvement and betterment, of concern for one's family, as well as for wider circles. People come together in common action, but their negotiating position starts with this context. Humans are defined by that context: that is what makes us what we are. Governments and institutions evolve gradually to help widen the domain of moral sentiments.

The original position of Rawls is quite alien to the Humean approach that is being advanced in this paper. People are partial – human nature and historical circumstance make them so. They are

[15] J. Rawls, *A Theory of Justice*,(Harvard, Harvard University Press, 1971).

[16] Adam Smith, 'The Theory of Moral Sentiments', 1759.

not impartial judges. Thus whilst it might be said that individuals' entitlements should be independent of the circumstances of their birth and social context, and insisted that we should treat people equally regardless of when they are born, we patently do not do this. Indeed if we were to do so, many of our actions in the specific and partial care we apply to our children and closer friends would dissipate. Why bother to create a loving and supportive home for one's children if not to give them a better chance compared with not doing so? Our domain of concern might (and should) be expanded – in part through moral education – but not to global impartiality now and for all future periods.

A further argument is that people in the original position would not in fact choose Rawls' principles. There is a vast literature on this issue, and in the climate change context it has been generalised to claim that we should maximise the welfare of the worst-off generation. Yet at the core there is a lurking assumption about human nature here too: we should be risk averse, for fear that it will be us that end up worse off. But why would we be so concerned? Risk aversion varies from person to person, but the Rawlsian version is extreme. At the generational level it is far from clear how we could identify which generation might be worse off, since over time we have little idea what technologies will be available and how the path of population might unfold. And at some future date there may be unexpected positive or negative developments. An asteroid could hit us. A disease could hit us. Or we could discover some chemical route to everlasting happiness, or the ability to directly tap into solar radiation. Previous generations had little idea of the internal combustion engine or indeed the Internet. Finally, eventually we may (and probably will) evolve into subsequent species.

Of these options, the obvious one to concentrate on is the very small probability of a very large negative event – say the asteroid or runaway climate change. At the limit there is some positive probability of extinction. In the Stern Report, this extinction risk is addressed by increasing the time discount rate from zero to 0.1%. Yet on a Rawlsian-type argument, we should devote our resources to dealing with this possible worst-off event.[17] Interestingly if we thought that the asteroid was likely to hit in the next few decades, we might well take steps. On a Humean approach, we are connected to the people who would be killed. But suppose it was just some time

[17] M. L. Weitzman, 'Why the Far-Distant Future Should Be Discounted at Its Lowest Possible Rate', *Journal Of Environmental Economics And Management*, **36** (1998), 201–208.

in the future – as there is a high probability that it will. Do we really care that some hundreds of thousands of years hence, lots of people will be killed and humans might cease to exist? Do we care what they evolve into? As an abstract question it is interesting, but as a guide to action on climate change it adds little.

4. Idealism and pragmatism

The contrast between what we have styled as the Humean and Rawlsian positions in terms of the implications for climate change policy is a stark one: the former points to gradualism, the latter to an impractical and obscure perfectionism.

The gradualist approach places a special moral weight on the starting point. History has arrived at a particular combination of institutions, beliefs and values, and a particular distribution of resources between current peoples and between current and future peoples. The starting point is not 'ideal'. No ideal outcome is in prospect.

Given this starting point, the policy options are defined in terms of incremental steps. Calls for a 'revolution' in climate change policy run into a series of objections. Revolutions by definition tear up the starting point. They are uncertain in terms of their impacts and consequences, and they involve a discontinuity with the moral sentiments of the starting point. Unintended consequences of large scale intervention, as emphasised by Hayek and Popper, point towards caution.[18,19]

This is not an argument for a conservatism: that says that the world we inhabit is Panglossian. Quite the contrary: climate change unchecked will leave many worse off, though in very different degrees. Moral sentiments are not contiguous with the status quo. Rather the case for an evolutionary pragmatism is that it fits with human nature – it is grounded in reality – and that as a consequence it is likely to work. Revolution is not a normal part of human nature – a point that Burke was keen to make in reaction to the French Revolution.[20]

[18] F. A. Hayek, 'Individualism and Economic Order', (London, Routledge and Kegan Paul, 1949).

[19] K. R. Popper, 'The Open Society and Its Enemies' (Princeton, Princeton University Press, 1945)

[20] Edmund Burke, *Reflections on the Revolution in France* [1790] (Penguin Classics, 1986)

Progress – scientific, material and moral – is a process of trial and error and of learning-by-doing. We gradually try to expand the domain of moral sentiments. Over time, we have recognised that slavery is wrong, and extended our moral sentiments beyond race. We have extended our moral sentiments to the poor close to home, with concerns about inequality increasing over time. We have extended our moral sentiments to developing countries, howbeit to a modest aspiration of 1% GDP p.a. Now the challenge is to edge forward our moral sentiments to future generations. The revolutionary goes straight to zero discounting; the gradualist lowers the rate.

5. Implications for climate change policy

So what should we do about climate change? What guidance do moral considerations give us? Stern is right to claim that we cannot design policy without taking a moral view. There is no purely *economic* case for tackling climate change. But then this is hardly new – there has been a strong distinction between positive and normative economics for a very long time, echoing Hume's distinction of 'is' and 'ought'. The question is what moral approach to take.

Stern takes the rationalistic approach – derived from utilitarianism and the maximisation of the sum of utilities through time. He might rely on Mill's diminishing marginal utility of money to motivate his equality approach, or he can draw on the principle of impartiality as part of a theory of justice. Whichever route he takes, his is a radical prescription. It would involve a revolution in the way resources are currently allocated: there would be an immediate transfer of a significant proportion of GDP from the US and Europe to developing countries. It might even be most of current GDP. There can be no reason for Stern to discriminate between different people now, and between people now and in the future. There are plenty of people worse off now than many will probably be as a result of climate change in fifty years' time. His position is a radical egalitarianism both at a point in time and over time. That is what zero time discounting means.

Translating zero discounting into climate change policy dictates a correspondingly radical de-carbonisation policy. Ultimately the task at Copenhagen was to get politicians to agree that their populations should follow these radical implications, since Stern's zero time preference assumption is a necessary condition in his analyses to justify urgent action on climate change. Without zero time discounting, his review does not lead to this conclusion. As was revealed at Copenhagen, this proved impossible. The result – the Copenhagen Accord – has been correspondingly very limited.[21]

The alternative approach is pragmatic and incremental – to focus on near term improvements and gradually to confront polluters (us) with the consequences of our actions. Public education of the consequences of global warming, helping to show not only how the moral sympathies may be attenuated towards future generations but also to show how in quite narrow domains of our sympathies, there will be negative consequences are part of the pragmatic approach. The creation of institutions helps to bolster our commitments. In this, the starting point is where we are now, and to appeal first to our self-interest as well as to our benevolence, before extending the moral appeals.

With the pragmatic approach, early emphasis falls on those options which are 'no regret' and which have little cost. Energy efficiency measures are promoted as making us better off through lower energy bills. Switching from coal to gas in electricity generation is, for example, much cheaper than building very expensive offshore wind farms. And so on.

The policy mix is then gradually extended, as the equation between cost and benefits is better understood. Time matters here too: we can do the energy efficiency and the coal to gas switches in this decade, but nuclear (if appropriate) will take longer. We do not know what technologies will be available in three decades time, and hence it makes little sense to make decisions now about future choices – though we should build up R&D, and create open institutions to ensure diverse ideas flourish. Importantly too, we do not know what the effects of climate change will be with any precision. The IPPC's range of temperature increase in this century is between 1 and 6 degrees centigrade. It may well turn out that future generations will be better off than we are now with 1–2 degrees warming – but not 6 degrees.[22,23]

[21] United Nations Framework Convention on Climate Change, *Draft decision -/CP.15 Proposal by the President: Copenhagen Accord*, (Conference of the Parties Fifteenth session, Copenhagen, 7–18 December 2009, document FCCC/CP/2009/L.7).

[22] R. Tol, 'Estimates of the Damage Costs of Climate Change. Part 1: Benchmark Estimates', *Environmental and Resource Economics*, **21** (2002), 47–73.

[23] R. Tol, 'The Economic Effects of Climate Change', *Journal of Economic Perspectives*, **23** (2009), 29–51.

Focusing on the current context is at odds with zero time discounting. Current more certain utility is worth more than future uncertain utility. Even Stern concedes that extinction gives a positive discount rate. And declining discount rates are either a reflection of a fatter tail in the probability distribution of climate change damage – the small probability of large scale damage – as time goes on (and hence arguably should be addressed in the calculations of the costs of global warming and not the discount rate), or a violation of the Humean approach to near neighbourliness.

If Stern's revolutionary approach of zero time discounting does not provide convincing moral guidance on what to do about climate change, what does? Above we have argued that the focus should be on the composition of economic growth, and on reconsidering the concept of measuring the improvements of welfare through GDP. In Stern's calculations, the decisive reason why early action on climate change is merited is his zero time preference rate. Otherwise, with a conventional time preference rate, we should do very little. The costs of action now are too great compared with the discounted benefits in the future, on the assumption that future people will all be much better off. If, as discussed in section 2 above, the US and Europe are twice as wealthy by 2050, and the Chinese and Indians are four times as wealthy, they will have so many more consumption opportunities – so much more utility – to trade off against the costs imposed upon them by global warming. Why should we make sacrifices now for those who are going to be so much better off than we are now, and for whom there will be a plethora of technologies that we can only begin to imagine? Stern's answer is that we should care about them on an equal basis and go through a moral revolution to support them.

The Stern Review does not therefore get us very far: we should only take action now if we adhere to a moral principle which does violence to human nature and in any event has virtually no chance of passing an electoral test. But fortunately the case for action now does not need Stern's discount rate. The arguments from sustainability get us there independently. We can go on with a more conventional time preference rate and still have the benefits of early action outweighing the costs.

Sustainability focuses on consumption and growth and requires us to reconsider the concept of GDP – of well-being and wealth creation. Recapping, GDP takes no account of what we are doing to our assets, and in effect treats the substitution of natural for man-made capital as at least one-to-one. (Actually, since the natural capital is not priced at all, it is worse than one-to-one). GDP does not take account of pollution and pollution costs.

It is therefore straightforward to argue that the efficiency of economies would be improved by calculating economic growth on a *net* rather than *gross* basis, accounting for asset depreciation, incorporating ecological considerations into critical depletion thresholds, and pricing in pollution. This set of steps does not directly involve distribution: we do not need to bring equity at a point in time or over time into this calculation to make the case for early action on climate change. By valuing the atmosphere and biodiversity, by calculating the depreciation and compensating for it, and by pricing the pollution (by a carbon price), very substantial changes would be dictated.

There would be consequences to current standards of living – put another way, GDP flatters us about changes in our welfare. There would be indirect distributional consequences too: by measuring the carbon emissions on a consumption basis, the burden of meeting the costs of current emissions would fall on those that cause them. Britain, for example, would not be allowed to get away with the fiction that because its production of carbon is falling, that therefore its pollution is too – because it is importing carbon intensive goods, causing the pollution elsewhere.

Such measures would not exhaust the moral arguments about intergenerational equity. Coincidental with the above sustainability-based measures, the case for an expanded moral domain can be made. But this is a long-term project, about moral progress. It involves moral education, cultural developments and the evolution of our institutions. It may not even work: human nature may not allow its full extent. The veneer of civilisation – and especially its institutions – may be thin, and indeed the history of the twentieth century dents the belief in a linear progressive path. In the climate change case, there is not enough time to evolve towards moral ideals: it will be too late.

6. Conclusions

Climate change is about inter-generational equity and it forces us to consider how the welfare of future people should be taken into account, in a context in which we are uncertain about their circumstances. The problem can be approached on the basis of an ideal moral principle – that we should be impartial between current and future people. This is the idea of zero time discounting, used to derive the Stern Review's claim about the costs and benefits of action on climate change. Alternatively it can be approached from the current context, and a more limited moral claim about our (partial) concerns for future people can be involved, widening the moral dimension on the basis of neighbourliness. Stern's starting point is Utopian, and his conclusion collapses once a positive time preference is introduced. He provides no credible basis for his conclusion on action on climate change. But the conclusion does not require his zero time preference moral principle. By looking at the impacts of climate change on economic growth (properly measured), early action may well be justified. Future people may not be so well-off once the principle of sustainability has been applied to assets, natural and man-made. It is the much more limited sustainability principle which provides the basis for both policy action and our moral responsibilities.

New College, Oxford

Depoliticized Environments: The End of Nature, Climate Change and the Post-Political Condition

ERIK SWYNGEDOUW

> "[t]he rise of the 'the rights of Nature' is a contemporary form of the opium for the people. It is an only slightly camouflaged religion .... It is a gigantic operation in the depoliticization of subjects."[1]

> " ... [w]hat if at some time in the next few years we realise, as we did in 1939, that democracy had temporarily to be suspended and we had to accept a disciplined regime that saw the UK as a legitimate but limited safe haven for civilisation. Orderly survival requires an unusual degree of human understanding and leadership and may require, as in war, the suspension of democratic government for the duration of the survival emergency."[2]

1. Welcome to the Anthropocene: celebrating the End of Nature

Nobel-price winning atmospheric chemist Paul Crutzen introduced in 2000 the concept of the Anthropocene as the name for the successor geological period to the Holocene.[3] The Holocene started about 12,000 years ago and is characterized by the relatively stable and temperate climatic and environmental conditions that were conducive to the development of human societies. Until recently, human development had relatively little impact on the dynamics of geological time. Although disagreement exists over the exact birth date of the Anthropocene, it is indisputable that the impact of human activity

[1] A. Badiou, 'Live Badiou – Interview with Alain Badiou, Paris, December 2007', *Alain Badiou – Live Theory*, O. Feltham (ed.), (London: Continuum, 2008), 139.

[2] J. Lovelock, 'The Fight to Get Aboard Lifeboat UK', The Sunday Times, 8 November 2009 http://www.timesonline.co.uk/tol/news/environment/article5682887.ece – accessed 3 August 2010.

[3] P. J. Crutzen and E. F. Stoermer, 'The 'Anthropocene', *Global Change Newsletter*, **41** (2000), 17–18.

doi:10.1017/S1358246111000300

on the geo-climatic environment became more pronounced from the industrial revolution onwards, leading to a situation in which humans are now widely considered to have an eco-geologically critical impact on the earth's bio-physical system.[4] The most obvious example is the accumulation of greenhouse gases like CO_2 and Methane (CH_4) in the atmosphere and the changes this induces in climatic dynamics. Others are the growing homogenization of biodiversity as a result of human-induced species migration, mass extinction and bio-diversity loss, the manufacturing of new (sub-)species through genetic modification, or the geodetic consequences resulting from, for example, large dam construction, mining and changing sea-levels.

We are not any longer objects of Nature, but have become subjects in what Norgaard calls the co-evolution of socio-ecological systems.[5] This raises the specter, of course, of the obligation to consider what sort of environment we wish to live in, how to produce it, and with what consequences. It calls for a new modernity that fully endorses human/non-human entanglements and takes responsibility for their nurturing.[6] We do know that the environmental catastrophe is already here, that the geo-climatic changes and other environmental transformations are already such that they are inimical to the continuation of life in some places and for some humans, and this will undoubtedly get worse as anthropogenic change accumulates.[7] The question of 'the production of Nature' – an expression that may have sounded quixotic until a few years ago – has now been put firmly on the agenda.[8] Nature as the externally conditioning frame for human life – an externalization that permitted the social sciences and humanities to condescendingly leave the matter of Nature to their natural science colleagues – has come to an end. The end of Nature and the inauguration of a socio-physical historical nature forces a profound re-consideration and re-scripting of the matter of Nature in political terms. The question is not any longer about bringing environmental issues into the domain of politics as has been the

4 D. Chakrabarty, 'The Climate of History: Four Theses', *Critical Enquiry* **35** (2009), 197–222.

5 R. B. Norgaard, *Development Betrayed: the End of Progress and a Coevolutionary Revisioning of the Future* (London: Routledge, 1994).

6 B. Latour, '"It's development, stupid!" or: How to Modernize Modernization', http://www.bruno-latour.fr/articles/article/107-NORDHAUS&SHELLENBERGER.pdf accessed 2 August 2010.

7 B. Wynne, 'Strange Wheather, Again: Climate Science as Political Art', *Theory, Culture & Society* **27** (2010), 289–305.

8 N. Smith, *Uneven Development* (Oxford: Blackwell, 1984).

case until now but rather about how to bring the political into the environment.

However, political philosopher Alain Badiou argues that the growing consensual concern with nature and the environment should be thought as a contemporary form of opium for the people. As Žižek puts it:

> '[R]eplacing the declining religion, it [ecology] takes over the old religion's fundamental function of having an unquestionable authority that can impose limits.'[9]

This seems, at first sight, not only a scandalous statement, one that conflates ecology with religion in a perverse twisting of Marx's original statement, it also flies in the face of evidence that politics matters environmentally. Yet, in this contribution, I wish to take Badiou's statement seriously and consider how exactly – in the present configuration – the elevation of environmental concerns to the status of global humanitarian cause operates as 'a gigantic operation in the de-politicization of subjects'. Ulrich Beck concurs with this:

> In the name of indisputable facts portraying a bleak future for humanity, green politics has succeeded in de-politicizing political passions to the point of leaving citizens nothing but gloomy asceticism, a terror of violating nature and an indifference towards the modernization of modernity.[10]

In this contribution, I shall explore the paradoxical situation whereby the environment is politically mobilized, yet this political concern with the environment, as presently articulated, is argued to suspend the proper political dimension. I shall explore how the elevation of the environment to a public concern is both a marker of and constituent force in the production of de-politicization.

The paper has four parts. In the first part, I problematise the question of Nature and the environment. I argue that there is no such thing as a singular Nature around which an environmental or climate policy and future can be constructed and performed. Rather, there are a multitude of natures and a multitude of existing, possible or practical socio-natural relations – and proper politicization of the environment needs to endorse this heterogeneity fully. In a second part, the emblematic case of climate change policy will be presented as *cause célèbre* of de-politicization. I argue how

[9] S. Žižek, 'Nature and its Discontents', *SubStance* **37** (2008), 53–54.

[10] U. Beck, 'Climate for Change, or How to Create a Green Modernity', *Theory, Culture & Society* **27** (2010), 263.

climate matters were brought into the domain of politics, but articulated around a particular imag(in)ing of what a 'good' climate or a 'good' environment is, while the political was systematically evacuated from the terrain of the – now Anthropocenic – environment. The third part will relate this argument to the views of political theorists who have proposed that the political constitution of contemporary western democracies is increasingly marked by the consolidation of post-political and post-democratic arrangements. In the fourth section, I discuss the climate change consensus in light of the post-political thesis. I shall conclude that the matter of the environment in general, and climate change in particular, needs to be displaced onto the terrain of the properly political.

2. The death of Nature: emergent natures

The death or the end of Nature has been announced many times.[11] The proclaimed end of Nature does not, of course, imply a de-materialization of human life, the apogee of modern 'man's' quest to severe the ties that bind him to Nature. On the contrary, humans and non-humans are ever more entangled through myriad interactions and transformative processes.[12] The death of Nature signals rather the demise of particular imaginings of Nature, of a set of symbolic inscriptions that inferred a singular Nature, at once external and internal to humans and human life.

In *Ecology without Nature*, Timothy Morton calls Nature 'a transcendental term in a material mask [that] stands at the end of a potentially infinite series of other terms that collapse into it'.[13] He distinguishes between at least three interrelated places or meanings of Nature in our symbolic universe. First, as a floating signifier, the 'content' of Nature is expressed through a range of diverse terms that all collapse in the Name of Nature: DNA, elephants, mineral

[11] See, among other, B. McKibben, *The End of Nature* (London: Random House, 1989); P. Wapner, *Living Through the End of Nature – The Future of American Environmentalism* (Cambridge, Mass.: MIT Press, 2010); A. Giddens, *Modernity and Self-identity – Self and Society in the late Modern Age* (Stanford: Stanford University Press, 1991); C. Merchant, *The Death of Nature: Women, Ecology, and the Scientific Revolution* (New York: Harper Collins, 1980).

[12] B. Latour, *We Have Never Been Modern* (Cambridge, Mass.: Harvard University Press, 1993).

[13] T. Morton, *Ecology without Nature* (Cambridge, Mass.: Harvard University Press, 2007), 14.

water, The Andes, hunger, hart-beat, markets, desire, profits, CO_2, greed, competition, ... Such metonymic lists, although offering a certain unstable meaning, are inherently slippery, and show a stubborn refusal to fixate meaning consistently and durably. Morton's argument resonates with Slavoj Žižek's statement that 'Nature does not exist!'.[14] His Lacanian perspective insists on the difference 'between [a] series of ordinary signifiers and the central element which has to remain empty in order to serve as the underlying organizing principle of the series'.[15] Nature constitutes exactly such central (empty or floating) element whose meaning can be gleaned only by relating it to other more directly recognizable signifiers. Nature becomes a symbolic tapestry, a *montage*, of meaning, held together with quilting points. For example, 'biodiversity', 'eco-cities', 'CO_2', or 'climate change' can be thought of as quilting points (or *points de capiton*) through which a certain matrix of meanings of Nature is articulated. These quilting points are also more than mere anchoring points; they refer to a beyond of meaning, a certain enjoyment that becomes structured in fantasy (in this case, the desire for an environmentally balanced and socially harmonious order).[16] In other words, there is always a remainder or excess that evades symbolization.

Second, Morton argues, Nature has 'the force of law, a norm against which deviation is measured',[17] for example when Nature is summoned to normalize heterosexuality and to think queerness as deviant and unnatural or to see competition between humans as natural and altruism as a produce of 'culture' (or vice versa), or when a particular climatic condition is normatively posited as ideal. Normative power inscribed in Nature is invoked as an organizing principle that is transcendental and universal, allegedly residing outside the remit allocated to humans and non-humans alike but that exercises an inescapable performative effect and leaves a non alienable imprint. This is a view that sees Nature as something given, as a solid foundational (or ontological) basis from which we act and that can be invoked to provide an anchor for ethical or normative judgments of ecological, social, cultural, political,

[14] S. Žižek, *Looking Awry: An Introduction to Jacques Lacan Through Popular Culture* (Cambridge, Mass.: M.I.T. Press, [1992] 2002).

[15] S. Žižek, *The Fragile Absolute* (London: Verso, 2000), 52.

[16] This particular semiological perspective draws on Slavok Žižek's reading of Jacques Lacan's psychoanalytic interpretations of the Imaginary, the Real, and the Symbolic (see S. Žižek, *The Sublime Object of Ideology* (London: Verso, 1989); J. Lacan, *The Seminar of Jacques Lacan Book III. The Psychoses 1955–1956* (New York: W.W. Norton, 1993); J. Lacan, *Ecrits* (London: Tavistock/Routledge, 1997)).

[17] T. Morton, op. cit., 14.

or economic procedures and practices. Consider for example how the vision of a stable climate is elevated to a 'public good', both by the British parliament and by the UNHCHR: '[T]he delivery of a stable climate, as an essential public good, is an immediate security, prosperity and moral imperative, not simply a long-term environmental challenge.'[18]

And, third, Nature invokes, for Morton, a plurality of fantasies and desires, like, for example, the dream of a sustainable nature, a balanced climate, the desire for love-making on a warm beach under the setting sun, the fear for the revenge of Nature if we keep pumping CO_2 into the atmosphere. Nature is invoked here as the stand-in for other, often repressed or invisible, longings and passions – the Lacanian *object petit a* around which we shape our drives and that covers up for the lack of ground on which to base our subjectivity.[19] It is the sort of fantasy displayed in calls for restoring a true (original but presumably presently lost) humane harmony by retro-fitting the world to ecological balance and in the longing for a Nature that functions as the big 'Other', the one that guides the path to redeem our predicament. Here, Nature is invoked as the 'external' terrain that offers the promise, if attended to properly, for finding a truly harmonious life,[20] but also from which threat of disaster emanates if we perturb its internal functioning.

In sum, these three uses of Nature imply simultaneously an attempt to fixate its unstable meaning while being presented as a fethishised 'Other' that reflects or, at least, functions as a symptom through which our displaced deepest fears and longings are expressed. As such, the concept of Nature becomes ideology par excellence and functions ideologically, and by that I mean that it forecloses thought, disavows the inherent slippery of the concept and ignores the multiplicities, inconsistencies, and incoherencies inscribed in its symbolization.[21] For Slavoj Žižek, any attempt to suture the meaning of

18 See http://www2.ohchr.org/english/issues/climatechange/docs/UK-annex_report2007.pdf – accessed 1 August 2010) and http://www.publications.parliament.uk/pa/cm200607/cmselect/cmenvaud/740/7070306.htm – accessed 1 August 2010 – Also cited in M. Hulme, 'Cosmopolitan Cimates: Hybridity, Foresight, and Meaning', *Theory, Culture & Society* **27** (2010), 270.

19 S. Žižek, *The Ticklish Subject – The Absent Centre of Political Ontology* (London: Verso, 1999).

20 See Y. Stavrakakis, 'Green Fantasy and the Real of Nature: Elements of a Lacanian Critique of Green Ideological Discourse', *Journal for the Psychoanalysis of Culture & Society* **2** (1997), 123–132.

21 T. Morton, op. cit., 24.

empty signifiers is a decidedly political gesture. The disavowal or the refusal to recognize the political character of such gestures, the attempts to universalize and suture the situated and positioned meanings inscribed metonymically in Nature lead to perverse forms of de-politicization, to rendering Nature politically mute and socially neutral.[22] The disavowal of the empty core of Nature by colonizing its meaning, by filling out the void, staining it with inserted meanings that are subsequently generalized and homogenized, is the gesture *par excellence* of de-politicization, of placing Nature outside the political, that is outside the field of public dispute, contestation, and disagreement. In addition, such symbolizations of Nature disavow the Real of natures, the heterogeneous, unpredictable, occasionally catastrophic, acting out of socio-ecological processes that mark the Anthropocene. It is these un-symbolized natures that haunt in their excessive acting: droughts, hurricanes, tsunamis, oil-spills, recombinant DNA, floods, globalizing diseases, disintegrating polar ice are a few of the more evocative markers of such socio-natural processes.

Bruno Latour, albeit from a rather different perspective, equally proposes to abandon the concept of Nature and suggests instead considering the world as filled with socio-natural quasi-objects. For Latour, there is neither Nature nor Society (or Culture) outside the cultural and discursive practices that produced this binary formulation.[23] For him, the imbroglios of human and non-human things that proliferate in the world consist of continuously multiplying nature-culture hybrids that stand between the poles of nature and culture.[24] Think of, for example, greenhouse gases, Dolly the cloned sheep, dams, oil-rigs, or electromagnetic waves. They are simultaneously social/cultural and natural/physical, and their coherence, i.e. there relative spatial and temporal sustainability, is predicated upon assembled networks of human and non-human relations.[25] Nature is always already social.[26] This perspective, too, rejects retaining the concept of Nature and suggests in its stead to consider the infinite heterogeneity of the procedures of assembling

22 E. Swyngedouw, 'Impossible/Undesirable Sustainability and the Post-Political Condition', *The Sustainable Development Paradox*, J. R. Krueger and D. Gibbs (eds.), (New York: Guilford, 2007), 13–40.

23 B. Latour, op cit. (1993).

24 B. Latour, *Reassembling the Social: An Introduction to Actor-Network-Theory* (Oxford: Oxford University Press, 2005).

25 E. Swyngedouw, 'Circulations and Metabolisms: (Hybrid) Natures and (Cyborg) Cities', *Science as Culture* **15** (2006), 105–121.

26 V. Jankovic, *Reading the Skies: A Cultural History of English Wheather* (Chicago: University of Chicago Press, 2000).

– dissembling – reassembling the rhizomatic networks through which things, bodies, natures and cultures become enmeshed and through which relatively stable quasi-objects come into purview.[27] This gesture also attempts to re-politicize the 'environment', to let quasi-objects enter the public assembly of political concerns.

Eminent natural scientists echo these critical social theory perspectives. Harvard biologists Levins and Lewontin, for example, argue too that Nature has been filled in by scientists with a particular set of universalizing meanings that ultimately de-politicize Nature and facilitate particular mobilizations of such 'scientifically' constructed Nature.[28] In contrast, they insist that the biological world is inherently relationally constituted through contingent, historically produced, infinitely variable forms in which each part, human or non-human, organic or non-organic, is intrinsically bound up with the wider relations that make up the whole.[29] Levins and Lewontin abhor a simplistic, reductionist, teleological and, ultimately, homogenizing view of Nature. They concur with the view that a singular Nature does not exist, that there is no trans-historical and trans-geographical transcendental natural state of things, of conditions or of relations, but rather are there a range of different historical natures, relations, and environments that are subject to continuous, occasionally dramatic or catastrophic, and rarely, if ever, fully predictable changes and transformations. They eschew such expressions as 'it is in the Nature of things' to explain one or another ecological or human behaviour or condition. Both individuals and their environments are co-produced and

[27] N. Castree, 'Environmental Issues: Relational Ontologies and Hybrid Politics', *Progress in Human* Geography **27** (2003), 203–211; B. Braun, 'Environmental Issues: Global Natures in the Space of Assemblage', *Progress in Human Geography* **30** (2006), 644–654.

[28] R. Levins and R. Lewontin, *The Dialectical Biologist* (Cambridge, MA.: Harvard University Press, 1985); R. Lewontin and R. Levins, *Biology under the Influence - Dialectical Essays on Ecology, Agriculture, and Health* (New York, NY: Monthly Review Press, 2007).

[29] Of course, the geo-philosophical thought of Giles Deleuze and Felix Guattari articulates in important ways with complexity theory and has spawned an exciting, albeit occasionally bewildering, literature that takes relationality, indeterminacy and the radical heterogeneities of natures seriously (see, among others, G. Deleuze and F. Guattari, *What is Philosophy?* (New York: Columbia University Press, 1994); V. Conley, *Ecopolitics: The Environment in Poststructural Thought* (London: Routledge, 1996); B. Herzogenrath (ed.), *An [Un]likely Alliance: Thinking Environment(s) with Deleuze/Guattari* (Newcastle upon Tyne: Cambridge Scholars Publishing, 2008).

co-evolve in historically contingent, highly diversified, locally specific and often not fully accountable manners.[30] For Levinas and Lewontin, therefore, no universalizing or foundational claim can be made about what Nature is, what it should be or where it should go. This is also the view shared by the late evolutionary biologist Stephen Jay Gould who saw evolution not as a gradual process, but one that is truncated, punctuated, occasionally catastrophic and revolutionary but, above all, utterly contingent.[31] There is no safety in Nature – Nature is unpredictable, erratic, moving spasmodically and blind. There is no final guarantee in Nature on which to base our politics or the social, on which to mirror or dreams, hopes or aspirations.

In sum, and in particular as a result of the growing global awareness of 'the environmental crisis', the inadequacy of our symbolic representations of Nature becomes more acute as the Real of Nature, in the form of a wide variety of ecological threats (global warming, new diseases, biodiversity loss, resource depletion, pollution) invades and unsettles our received understandings of Nature, forcing a transformation of the signifying chains that attempt to provide 'content' for Nature, while at the same time exposing the impossibility of capturing fully the Real of natures.[32] The point of the above argument is that the natures we see and work with are necessarily radically imagined, scripted, and symbolically charged as Nature. These inscriptions are always inadequate, they leave a gap, an excess or remainder, and maintain a certain distance from the co-produced natures that are there, which are complex, chaotic, often unpredictable, radically contingent, historically and geographically variable, risky, patterned in endlessly complex ways, ordered along 'strange' attractors.[33] In other words, there is no Nature out there that needs or requires salvation in name of either Nature itself or a generic Humanity. There is nothing foundational in Nature that needs, demands, or requires sustaining. The debate and controversies over Nature and what do with it, in contrast, signal rather our political inability to engage in directly political and social argument and strategies about re-arranging the socio-ecological co-ordinates of everyday life, the production of new socio-natural configurations, and the arrangements of socio-metabolic organization (something

[30] See also D. Harvey, *Justice, Nature, and the Geography of Difference* (Oxford Blackwell, 1996).

[31] S. J. Gould, *The Panda's Thumb* (New York: W.W. Norton, 1980).

[32] S. Žižek, *In Defense of Lost Causes* (London: Verso, 2008).

[33] See, for example, I. Prigogine and I. Stengers *Order out of Chaos: Man's New Dialogue with Nature* (London: HarperCollins, 1985).

usually called capitalism) that we inhabit. In the next section, I shall exemplify and deepen further this analysis by looking at climate change policies and arguments as de-politicizing gestures, predicated upon a growing concern for a Nature that seems to veer off-balance.

3. The Climate as Object Cause of Desire

> "If we do nothing, the consequences for every person on this earth will be severe and unprecedented – with vast numbers of environmental refugees, social instability and decimated economies: far worse than anything which we are seeing today."[34]

Irrespective of the particular views of Nature held by different individuals and social groups, consensus has emerged over the seriousness of the environmental condition and the precariousness of our socio-ecological predicament.[35] The successive IPCC reports and Al Gore's evangelical *An Inconvenient Truth* landed both with the Nobel Peace price, surely one of the most telling illustrations of how climate matters are elevated to the status of global humanitarian cause.[36] There is a virtually unchallenged consensus over the need to be more 'environmentally' sustainable if disaster is to be avoided; a climatic sustainability that centres around reducing and stabilizing the CO_2 content in the atmosphere.[37] In this consensual setting, environmental problems are generally staged as universally threatening to the survival of humankind and sustained by what Mike Davis called 'ecologies of fear'[38] on the one hand and a series of decidedly populist gestures on the other. The discursive matrix through which the contemporary meaning of the environmental condition is

34 From Speech of HRH Prince Charles, March 2009. http://www.princeofwales.gov.uk/newsandgallery/news/hrh_warns_of_the_urgent_need_to_protect_the_environment_at_a_1876977673.html – accessed 5 August 2010.

35 E. Swyngedouw, 'The Antinomies of the Post-Political City. In Search of a Democratic Politics of Environmental Production', *International Journal of Urban and Regional Research* **33** (2009), 601–620.

36 See also A. Giddens, *The Politics of Climate Change* (Cambridge: Polity Press, 2009).

37 M. Boykoff, D. Frame and S. Randalls, 'Stabilize this! How the Discourse of 'Climate Stabilization' became and remains entrenched in climate science-policy-practice interactions', *Journal of the American Association of Geographers* forthcoming.

38 M. Davis, *Ecology of Fear – Los Angeles and the Imagination of Disaster* (New York: Vintage Books, 1999).

woven is one quilted by the invocation of fear and danger, and the spectre of ecological annihilation or at least seriously distressed socio-ecological conditions for many people in the near future. 'Fear' is indeed the crucial trope through which many of the current environmental and other biopolitical narratives are woven.[39] This cultivation of 'ecologies of fear', in turn, is sustained by a particular set of phantasmagorical, often apocalyptic, imaginations.[40] The apocalyptic imaginary of a world with endemic resource shortages, ravaged by hurricanes whose intensity is amplified by climate change, pictures of scorched land as the geo-pluvial regime and the spatial variability of droughts and floods shifts, icebergs that disintegrate around the poles and cause sea levels to rise, alarming reductions in bio-diversity, the devastations raked by wildfires, tsunamis, spreading diseases like SARS, Avian Flu, or HIV. These imaginaries of a Nature out of synch, destabilised, threatening, and out of control is paralleled by equally disturbing images of a society that continues piling up waste, pumping CO_2 into the atmosphere, deforesting the earth, etc... We seem to have an unquenchable fascination with such dystopian imaginaries. Our ecological predicament is sutured by a series of performative gestures signalling an overwhelming, mind-boggling danger, one that threatens to undermine the very co-ordinates of our every day lives and routines and may shake up the foundations of all we take for granted. Yet, despite the fact we know very well that the ecological catastrophe is already here (rather than a disavowed promise of disaster to come – the apocalyptic pledge that few really believe in), we fail to take nature really seriously, to think and act really as subjects inscribed in the very dynamics of natural processes.

The attractions of such an apocalyptic imaginary are related to a series of characteristics. At the symbolic level, apocalyptic imaginaries are extraordinarily powerful in disavowing or displacing social conflict and antagonisms. As such, apocalyptic imaginations foreclose a proper political framing. Or in other words, the presentation of climate change as a global humanitarian cause produces a thoroughly depoliticized imaginary, one that does not revolve around choosing one trajectory rather than another, one that is not articulated with specific political programs or socio-ecological

[39] See A. Badiou, The Meaning of Sarkozy (Verso: London, 2008).

[40] C. Katz, 'Under the Falling Sky: Apocalyptic Environmentalism and the Production of Nature', *Marxism in the Postmodern Age*, A. Callari, S. Cullenberg and C. Biewener (eds), (New York: The Guilford Press, 1995), 276–282.

projects. It is this sort of mobilizations without political issue that led Alain Badiou to state that 'ecology is the new opium for the masses', whereby the nurturing of the promise of a more benign retrofitted climate exhausts the horizon of our social and political aspirations and imaginations. We have to make sure that radical techno-managerial and behavioral transformations, organized within the horizons of a liberal-capitalist order that is beyond dispute, are initiated to retrofit the climate. The proposed transformations often take a distinct dystopian turn when the Malthusian specter of overpopulation is fused with concerns with the climate, whereby, perversely, newborns are indentified as the main culprits of galloping climate change and resource depletion, a view supported by luminaries like Sir David Attenborough (OM CH CVO CBE), Dr Jane Goodall (DBE), Dr James Lovelock (CBE), and Sir Crispin Tickell (GCMG KCVO), among others.[41] In other words, the techno-managerial eco-consensus maintains, we have to change radically, but within the contours of the existing state of the situation – 'the partition of the sensible' in Rancière's words[42] – so that nothing really has to change!

The negativity of climatic disintegration finds its positive injunction around a fetishist invocation of CO_2 as the 'thing' around which our environmental dreams, aspirations as well as policies crystallise. The '*point de capiton*' for the climate change problematic is CO_2, the *objet petit a* that simultaneously expresses our climate fears and around which the desire for change, for a better socio-climatic world is woven,[43] but one that simultaneously disavows

[41] See www.optimumpopulation.org – accessed 2 August 2010; see also G. Baeten, '"Less than 100 months to save the planet": the Politics of Environmental Apocalypse', paper delivered at IBG-RGS Annual Conference, (Manchester: 26–28 August 2009).

[42] J. Rancière, *Disagreement* (Minneapolis: University of Minnesota Press, 1998).

[43] '*Object a* is not what we desire, what we are after, but rather that which sets our desire in motion, the formal frame that confers consistency on our desire. Desire is of course metonymical, it shifts from one object to another; through all its displacements, however, desire nonetheless retains a minimum of formal consistency, a set of fantasmatic features which, when encountered in a positive object, insures that we will come to desire this object. *Object a*, as the cause of desire, is nothing but this formal frame of consistency.' S. Žižek, Plague of Fantasies (New York: Verso, 1997), 39. See also Y. Stavrakakis, 'On the Emergence of Green Ideology: The Dislocation factor in Green Politics', *Discourse Theory and Political Analysis – Indentities, Hegemonies and Social Change*, D. Howarth, A. J.

radical change in the socio-political co-ordinates that shape the Anthropocene. The fetishist disavowal of the multiple and complex relations through which environmental changes unfold finds its completion in the double reductionism to this singular socio-chemical component (CO_2). The reification of complex processes to a thing-like object-cause in the form of a socio-chemical compound around which our environmental desire crystallises is indeed further inscribed with a particular social meaning and function through its enrolment as commodity in the processes of capital circulation and market exchange.[44] The procedure of pricing CO_2 reduces the extraordinary socio-spatial heterogeneities and complexities of 'natural' CO_2's to a universal singular, obscuring – in Marx's view of commodity fetishism – that a commodity is 'a very strange thing, abounding in metaphysical subtleties and theological niceties'.[45] Commodification renders strictly homologous the pumping of a ton of CO_2 into the atmosphere by a coal-fired power plant in, say, the United Kingdom on the one hand and sinking one ton of CO_2 through planting trees by, say, a local Brazilian community on the other. While the socio- and political-ecological framings of these two processes are radically different and incommensurable, monetizing CO_2 renders them fully interchangeable and commensurable.

The commodification of CO_2 – primarily via the Kyoto protocol and various off-setting schemes – has triggered a rapidly growing derivatives market of futures and options.[46] On the European climate exchange, for example, trade in CO_2 futures and options grew from zero in 2005 to pass the 3 billion tons mark in June 2010; 585,296 contracts were traded during that month, with prices fluctuating from over 30 Euro to less than 10 Euro per ton over this time period.[47] CO_2's inscription as a commodity (and financialised asset) is dependent on its insertion in a complex governance regime

---

Norval and Y. Stavrakakis (eds), (Manchester: Manchester University Press, 2000), 100–118.

[44] D. M. Liverman, 'Conventions of climate change: constructions of danger and the dispossession of the atmosphere', *Journal of Historical Geography* **35** (2009), 279–296.; A. G. Bumpus and D. Liverman, 'Accumulation by Decarbonization and the Governance of Carbon Offsets', *Economic Geography* **84** (2008), 127–155.

[45] K. Marx, *Capital: Critique of Political Economy v. 1* (London: Penguin Classics, 2004), 162.

[46] L. Lohmann, 'Uncertainty Markets and Carbon Markets: Variations on Polanyian Themes', *New Political Economy* **15** (2010), 225–254.

[47] See www.ecx.eu – accessed 2 August 2010.

organized around a set of managerial and institutional technologies that revolve around reflexive risk-calculation, self-assessment, interest-negotiation and intermediation, accountancy rules and accountancy based disciplining, detailed quantification and benchmarking of performance. This regime is politically choreographed and instituted by the Kyoto protocol (only marginally amended by the Copenhagen debacle) and related, extraordinarily complex, institutional configurations. The consensual scripting of climate change imaginaries, arguments and policies reflect a particular process of de-politicization, one that is defined by Slavoj Žižek and others as post-political and becomes instituted in what Colin Crouch or Jacques Rancière term 'post-democracy'.

4. Post-Political and Post-Democratic Environments

Slavoj Žižek and Chantal Mouffe define the post-political as a political formation that actually forecloses the political.[48] Post-politics reject ideological divisions and the explicit universalization of particular political demands. Post-politics reduces the political terrain to the sphere of consensual governing and policy-making, centered on the technical, managerial and consensual administration (policing) of environmental, social, economic or other domains, and they remain of course fully within the realm of the possible, of existing social relations. 'The ultimate sign of post-politics in all Western countries', Žižek argues, 'is the growth of a managerial approach to government: government is reconceived as a managerial function, deprived of its proper political dimension'.[49] The consensual times we are currently living in have thus eliminated a genuine political space of disagreement. Under a post-political condition, '[e]verything is politicized, can be discussed, but only in a non-committal way and as a non-conflict. Absolute and irreversible choices are kept away; politics becomes something one can do without making

[48] S. Žižek, 'Carl Schmitt in the Age of Post-Politics', *The Challenge of Carl Schmitt*, C. Mouffe (ed.), (London: Verso, 1999), 18–37; S. Žižek, 'The Lesson of Rancière', *The Politics of Aesthetics*, J. Rancière (ed.), (London: Continuum, 2006), 69–79; C. Mouffe, *On The Political* (London: Routledge, 2005).

[49] S. Žižek, *Revolution at the Gates – Žižek on Lenin – The 1917 Writings* (London: Verso, 2002), 303.

decisions that divide and separate'.[50] Difficulties and problems, such as re-ordering the climate or re-shaping the environment that are generally staged and accepted as problematic need to be dealt with through compromise, managerial and technical arrangement, and the production of consensus. The key feature of consensus is 'the annulment of dissensus … the 'end of politics''.[51]

Climate governance and the policing of environmental concerns are among the key arenas through which this post-political consensus becomes constructed, when 'politics proper is progressively replaced by expert social administration'.[52] The post-political environmental consensus, therefore, is one that is radically reactionary, one that forestalls the articulation of divergent, conflicting, and alternative trajectories of future environmental possibilities and assemblages. There is no contestation over the givens of the situation, over the partition of the sensible; there is only debate over the technologies of management, the timing of their implementation, the arrangements of policing, and the interests of those whose stake is already acknowledged, whose voice is recognized as legitimate. In this post-political era, adversarial politics (of the left/right variety or of radically divergent struggles over imagining and naming different socio-environmental futures for example) are considered hopelessly out of date. Although disagreement and debate are of course still possible, they operate within an overall model of elite consensus and agreement,[53] subordinated to a managerial-technocratic regime.[54] Disagreement is allowed, but only with respect to the choice of technologies, the mix of organizational fixes, the detail of the managerial adjustments, and the urgency of their timing and implementation, not with respect to the socio-political framing of present and future natures.

In this sense, environmental and other politics are reduced to the sphere of the police, to the domain of governing and polic(y)ing through allegedly participatory deliberative procedures, within a given hierarchical distribution of places and functions. Consensual policy-making in which the stakeholders (i.e. those with recognized

[50] B. Diken and C. Laustsen, '7/11, 9/11, and Post-Politics', (2004), 15.

[51] J. Rancière, 'Ten Theses on Politics', *Theory & Event* **5**, §32. See E. Swyngedouw, op. cit. (2009) for further details.

[52] S. Žižek, 'Against Human Rights', *New Left Review* **34** (2005), 117.

[53] C. Crouch, *Post-Democracy* (Cambridge: Polity Press, 2004).

[54] See also D. Jörke, 'Auf dem Weg zur Postdemokratie', *Leviathan* 33 (2005), 482–491.; I. Blühdorn, 'Billich will Ich - Post-demkratische Wende und Simulative Demokratie', *Forschungsjournal NSB* **19** (2006), 72–83.

speech) are known in advance and where disruption or dissent is reduced to debates over the institutional modalities of governing, the accountancy calculus of risk, and the technologies of expert administration or management, announces the end of politics, annuls dissent from the consultative spaces of policy making and evacuates the proper political from the public sphere.

5. Consensualising Climate Change

The climate change argument is one of the domains through which this post-political consensual framework is forged; one that disavows dissensus and prevents agonistic disagreement over real alternative socio-ecological futures. The climate change conundrum is not only portrayed as global, but is constituted as a universal humanitarian threat. We are all potential victims. 'THE' Environment and 'THE' people, Humanity as a whole in a material and philosophical manner, are invoked and called into being. However, the 'people' here are not constituted as heterogeneous political subjects, but as universal victims, suffering from processes beyond their control. As such, the argument cuts across the idiosyncrasies of often antagonistic human and non-human 'natures' and their specific 'acting outs', silences ideological and other constitutive social differences and disavow democratic conflicts about different possible socio-ecological configurations by distilling a common threat to both Nature and Humanity.[55]

The nature–society dichotomy and the causal power of Nature to derail civilizations are re-enforced. It is a process that Neil Smith refers to as 'nature washing':

> Nature-washing is a process by which social transformations of nature are well enough acknowledged, but in which that socially changed nature becomes a new super determinant of our social fate. It might well be society's fault for changing nature, but it is the consequent power of that nature that brings on the apocalypse. The causal power of nature is not compromised but would seem to be augmented by social injections into that nature.[56]

While the part-anthropogenic process of the accumulation of greenhouse gases is readily acknowledged, the related ecological problems

[55] See M. Hulme, 'Geographical Work at the Boundaries of Climate Change', *Transactions of the Institute of British Geographers* **33** (2008), 5–11.

[56] N. Smith, 'Afterword to the Third Edition', *Uneven Development*, N. Smith (Athens, Georgia: Georgia University Press, 2008), 245.

are externalized. CO_2 becomes the fethishised stand-in for the totality of the climate change calamities and, therefore, it suffices to reverse atmospheric CO_2 built-up to a negotiated idealized point in history, to return to climatic status quo ex-ante. An extraordinary techno-managerial apparatus is under way, ranging from new eco-technologies[57] of a variety of kinds to unruly complex managerial and institutional configurations, with a view to producing a socio-ecological fix, to make sure nothing really changes fundamentally in the socio-ecological structuring of the Anthropocene. Stabilizing the climate seems to be a condition for life as we know it to continue.

Consensual discourse 'displaces social antagonism and constructs the enemy ... the enemy is externalized or reified into a positive ontological entity [excessive CO_2] (even if this entity is spectral) whose annihilation would restore balance and justice'.[58] The enemy is conceived as an 'Intruder' who has *corrupted* the system. CO_2 stands here as the classic example of a fetishised and externalised foe that requires dealing with. Problems, therefore, are not the result of the 'system', of unevenly distributed power relations, of the networks of control and influence, of rampant injustices, or of a fatal flaw inscribed in the system, but are blamed on an outsider.[59] That is why the solution can be found in dealing with the 'pathological' phenomenon, the resolution for which resides in the system itself. The 'enemy' remains socially empty or vacuous, and homogenised; it is a mere thing, not socially embodied, named, and counted. While a proper politics would endorse the view that CO_2-as-crisis stands as the pathological symptom of the normal, one that expresses the excesses inscribed in the very normal functioning of the system, the dominant policy architecture around climate change insists that this state is excessive to the system, while prophylactic qualities are assigned to the mobilization of the very inner dynamics and logic of the system that produced the problem in the first place (privatization, commodification and market exchange of, often fictitious, CO_2).

The climate consensus is conjured in the 'Name of the People', but supported by an assumedly neutral scientific technocracy, and

[57] Some of these eco-climatic techno-solutions are of truly Herculean dimensions – see Royal Society, *Geoengineering the Climate: Science, Governance and Uncertainty* (London: The Royal Society, 2009). See also B. Szerszynski, 'Reading and Writing the Weather: Climate Technics and the Moment of Responsibility', *Theory, Culture & Society* **27** (2010), 9–30.

[58] S. Žižek, 'Against the Populist Temptation', *Critical Inquiry* **32** (2006), 555.

[59] Ibid., 555.

advocates a direct relationship between people and political participation. It is assumed that this will lead to a good, if not optimal, solution. The architecture of consensual governing takes the form of stakeholder participation or forms of participatory governance that operates beyond-the-state and permits a form of self-management, self-organization, and controlled self-disciplining,[60] under the aegis of a non-disputed liberal-capitalist order. Such consensual tactics do not identify a privileged subject of change (like the proletariat for Marxists, women for feminists, or the 'creative class' for competitive capitalism), but instead invoke a common condition or predicament, the need for common humanity-wide action, multi-scalar collaboration and co-operation. There are no internal social tensions or internal generative conflicts. Yet, it is precisely this constitutive split of the people, the recognition of radically differentiated and often opposing social, political, or ecological desires, that calls the proper democratic political into being.

The ecological problem does not invite a transformation of the existing socio-ecological order but calls on the elites to undertake action such that nothing really has to change, so that life can basically go on as before. In this sense, the climate consensus is inherently reactionary, an ideological support structure for securing the socio-political status quo. It is inherently non-political and non-partisan. A Gramscian 'passive revolution' has taken place over the past few years, whereby the elites have not only acknowledged the climate conundrum and, thereby, answered the call of the 'people' to take the climate seriously, but are moving rapidly to convince the world that indeed, capitalism cannot only solve the climate riddle, but that it can actually make a new climate by unmaking the one it has co-produced over the past few hundred years.

Post-political climate governance does not solve problems; they are moved around. Consider, for example, the current argument over how the nuclear option is again portrayed as a possible and realistic option to secure a sustainable energy future and as an alternative to deal both with CO_2 emissions and peakoil. The redemption of our CO_2 quagmire is found in replacing the socio-ecologically excessive presence of CO_2 with another socio-natural imbroglio, U235/238,

[60] See M. Dean, *Governmentality – Power and Rule in Modern Society* (London: Sage, 1999); E. Swyngedouw, 'Governance Innovation and the Citizen: The Janus Face of Governance-beyond-the-state', *Urban Studies* **42** (2005), 1–16.; T. Lemke, 'The Birth of Bio-Politics' – Michel Foucault's Lectures at the College de France on Neo-Liberal Governmentality', *Economy & Society* **30** (1999), 190–207.

and the inevitable production of all manner of co-produced socio-natural transuranic elements. The nuclear 'fix' is now increasingly (and will undoubtedly be implemented) staged as one of the possible remedies to save both climate and capital. It hardly arouses passions for a better and ecologically sound society.[61]

Most problematically, no proper names are assigned to a post-political consensual politics. Post-political populism is associated with a politics of not naming in the sense of giving a definite or proper name to its domain or field of action. Only vague concepts like climate change policy, biodiversity policy or a vacuous discourse of sustainability replaces the proper names of politics. These proper names, according to Jacques Rancière[62] are what constitutes a genuine democracy, that is a space where the unnamed, the uncounted, and, consequently, un-symbolised become named and counted. Climate change has no positively embodied political name or signifier; it does not call a political subject into being or, rather, there is not political subject inaugurating its name. In contrast to other signifiers that signal a positively embodied content with respect to the future (like socialism, communism, liberalism), an ecologically and climatologically different future world is only captured in its negativity; a pure negativity without promises of redemption, without a positive injunction that 'transcends'/sublimates negativity and without proper subject. Yet, the gaze on tomorrow permits recasting social, political, and other pressing issues today as future conditions that can be retro-actively re-scripted as a techno-managerial issue. Poverty, ecological problems of all kinds, socio-ecological inequities will eventually be sorted out by dealing with CO_2 today. As demands are expressed (reduce CO_2) that remain particular, post-politics forecloses universalization as a positive socio-environmental project. In other words, the environmental problem does not posit a positive and named socio-environmental situation, an embodied vision, a desire that awaits realization, a passion to be realized.

[61] This paper was written before the Fukushima nuclear disaster. Despite this, the U.S. and the U.K. continue to explore the nuclear option as a viable energy alternative. In contrast, Germany has decided to phase out nuclear energy completely.

[62] J. Rancière, *La Mésentente - Politique et Philosophie* (Paris: Editions Galilée, 1995); see also A. Badiou, 'Politics: A Non-Expressive Dialectics', Is The Politics of Truth still Thinkable?, A conference organized by Slavoj Zizek and Costas Douzinas, Birkbeck Institute for the Humanities, Birkbeck College, London, 25–26 November 2005.

6. Conclusion: From Environmentalizing Politics to Politicizing the Environment

Taking the environmental and climatic catastrophe seriously requires exploding the infernal process of de-politicization marked by the dominance of empty signifiers like Nature, and urges us to re-think the political again. The claim made above to abandon Nature in no way suggests ignoring, let alone forgetting, the Real of natures or, more precisely, the diverse, multiple, whimsical, contingent and often unpredictable socio-ecological relations of which we are part. Rather, there is an urgent need to question legitimizing all manner of socio-environmental politics, policies and interventions in the name of a thoroughly imagined and symbolised Nature or Sustainability, a procedure that necessarily forecloses a properly political frame through which such imaginaries become constituted and hegemonised, one that disavows the constitutive split of the people by erasing the spaces of democratic agnostic encounter. The above re-conceptualisation urges us to accept the extraordinary variability of natures, insists on the need to make 'a wager' on natures, forces to chose politically between this rather than that nature, invites us to plunge in the relatively unknown, to expect the unexpected, to accept that not all there is can be known, and, most importantly, fully to endorse the violent moment that is inscribed in any concrete socio-environmental intervention.

Indeed, the ultimate aim of political intervention is to change the given socio-environmental ordering in a certain manner. Like any intervention, this is a violent act, erases at least partly what is there in order to erect something new and different. Consider, for example, the extraordinary effect the eradication of the HIV virus would have on sustaining livelihoods (or should we preserve/protect the virus in the name of biodiversity?). Proper political interventions are irredeemably violent engagements that re-choreograph socio-natural relations and assemblages, both distant and nearby; that always split the consensus and produce in-egalitarian outcomes. Engaging with natures, intervening in socio-natural orders, of course, constitutes a political act *par excellence*, one that can be legitimised only in political terms, and not – as is customarily done – through an externalised legitimation that resides in a fantasy of Nature. Any political act is one that re-orders socio-ecological co-ordinates and patterns, reconfigures uneven socio-ecological relations, often with unforeseen or unforeseeable, consequences. Such interventions signal a totalitarian moment, the temporary suspension of the democratic, understood as the presumed equality of all and everyone qua speaking beings in a space that permits and nurtures dissensus. The dialectic between the democratic as a political given and the totalitarian moment of policy intervention as the suspension of the democratic needs to be radically endorsed. While the democratic political, founded on a presumption of equality, insists on difference, disagreement, radical openness, and exploring multiple possible futures, concrete environmental intervention is necessarily about closure, definitive choice, a singular intervention and, thus, certain exclusion and silencing. The democratic political process dwells, therefore, in two spheres simultaneously. Jacques Rancière[63] defines these spheres respectively as 'the political' and 'the police' (the policy order). The (democratic) political is the space for the enunciation and affirmation of difference, for the cultivation of dissensus and disagreement, for asserting the presumption of equality of all and everyone in the face of the inegalitarian function of the polic(y)e order. Any policy intervention, when becoming concretely geographical or ecological, is of necessity a violent act of foreclosure of the democratic political (at least temporarily), of taking one option rather than another, of producing one sort of environment, of assembling certain socio-natural relations, of foregrounding some natures rather than others, of hegemonizing a particular metonymic chain rather than another. And the legitimation of such options cannot be based on corralling Nature into legitimizing service. The production of socio-environmental arrangements implies fundamentally political questions, and has to be addressed and legitimized in political terms. Politicizing environments democratically, then, becomes an issue of enhancing the democratic political content of socio-environmental construction by means of identifying the strategies through which a more equitable distribution of social power and a more egalitarian mode of producing natures can be achieved. This requires reclaiming proper democracy and proper democratic public spaces (as spaces for the enunciation of agonistic dispute) as a foundation for and condition of possibility for more egalitarian socio-ecological arrangements, the naming of positively embodied ega-libertarian socio-ecological futures that are immediately realisable. In other words, egalitarian ecologies are about demanding the impossible and realising the improbable, and this is exactly the challenge the Anthropocene poses. In sum, the politicization of the environment is predicated upon the recognition of

[63] J. Rancière, op. cit. (1995); For a review, see O. Marchart, *Post-Foundational Political Thought – Political Difference in Nancy, Lefort, Badiou and Laclau* (Edinburgh: University Press, 2007).

the indeterminacy of natures, the constitutive split of the people, the unconditional democratic demand of political equality, and the real possibility for the inauguration of different possible public socio-ecological futures that express the democratic presumptions of freedom and equality.

Geography, School of Environment and Development University of Manchester

Index of Names

Index of Names